RADICAL TRANSFORMATION

THE UNEXPECTED INTERPLAY OF CONSCIOUSNESS AND REALITY

Imants Barušs

imprint-academic.com

Published in the UK by
Imprint Academic Ltd., PO Box 200, Exeter EX5 5YX, UK

Distributed in the USA by
Ingram Book Company,
One Ingram Blvd., La Vergne, TN 37086, USA

ISBN 9781788360418 paperback

A CIP catalogue record for this book is available from the
British Library and US Library of Congress

Previous Books by Imants Barušs

*The Personal Nature of Notions of Consciousness: A Theoretical and Empirical
Examination of the Role of the Personal in the Understanding of Consciousness*

Authentic Knowing: The Convergence of Science and Spiritual Aspiration

Alterations of Consciousness: An Empirical Analysis for Social Scientists

Science as a Spiritual Practice

*The Impossible Happens: A Scientist's Personal Discovery of the Extraordinary
Nature of Reality*

Transcendent Mind: Rethinking the Science of Consciousness
(with Julia Mossbridge)

There is not much time.[1]

Contents

Acknowledgments

I thank the following reviewers for reading the manuscript at various stages of preparation and providing me with comments: Monika Mandoki, Stephen Braude, Emily Cochrane, Antonio Calcagno, Gerry McKeon, Daniel Masri, William Bengston, Eugene Carpenter, Brenda Sanders, Ron Leonard, Brookelynn Rogers, Deric Gorman, Donald Rhynas, Curtis Michael Lee, Gayle Kimball, Bill Gladstone, Rob Horvath, and Dianne Trussell. None of the readers is responsible for any errors or omissions that might remain in the book, nor do they necessarily agree with any of what I say. I thank Shannon Foskett for research assistance, providing critical feedback, and assisting with editing and the production of the book. I am grateful to King's University College at Western University for research grants that have facilitated my writing. I thank Graham Horswell and the personnel at Imprint Academic for their unreserved support for my writing over the years. And I want to say how much it means to me to have had the encouragement of so many of my students, colleagues, and readers of my books who have expressed their appreciation for my work. Thank you!

Prologue

The unleashed power of the atom has changed everything save our modes of thinking and we thus drift toward unparalleled catastrophe.[2]

The academic landscape supporting the study of consciousness is shifting. It is moving away from materialist versions of reality toward some yet-to-be-articulated post-materialist interpretation. In a book co-authored with Julia Mossbridge, *Transcendent Mind: Rethinking the Science of Consciousness*,[3] we have described this shift, bringing readers from one side of the crevasse to the other. In particular, we have reviewed empirical evidence that some version of consciousness is not a by-product of brain activity, that it has nonlocal properties including the ability to perceive and act at a distance without apparent physical mediation, and that human consciousness appears to survive the death of the physical body. Those are the fundamental characteristics of a post-materialist notion of consciousness. I will review them briefly here as part of Chapter 1, "Consciousness Unplugged." Beyond them, this book takes up several substantive issues that arise in the new academic landscape.

The nonlocality of consciousness raises questions about boundaries. How does nature know where to draw them? In Chapter 2, "Meaning Beyond the Human," I look at some experiments with non-contact healing, anomalous quantum processes, and poltergeist activity to bring this question into focus before suggesting the existence of "meaning fields" as a solution to this problem. We will also see the extent to which direct mental influence can affect physical manifestation. In Chapter 3, "Anomalous Transformations of Physical Manifestation," I look at examples of dramatic physical changes associated with direct mental influence and conclude that it appears that physical manifestation is considerably more malleable than we usually think that it is. At the time of my writing this book, humanity faces substantial crises, among them a viral pandemic, degradation of the environment, and the threat of nuclear war. These sharpen our focus. Are there ways in which our expanded knowledge of consciousness can be used for the resolution of these crises? Can we engage in "subtle activism," whereby mental activity, such as meditation, directly moves our planet toward greater well-being? That subject matter is taken up in Chapter 4, "Planetary Transformation." And finally, increasing numbers of people are finding themselves in temporary or permanent expanded states of consciousness characterized by attenuated mental chatter and enhanced feelings of intimate connection to reality. In Chapter 5, "Radical Self-Transformation," we will have a look at such self-development and consider its significance for the crises that we face today.

When I say that the study of consciousness is shifting, that mind could exist without the brain, and that human consciousness could survive the death of the physical body, I am not merely gesturing toward some vaguely imagined human potential, I am talking about concrete anomalous events that manifestly occur for people. Those people include scientists and academics who usually remain silent about such experiences so as not to incur the disapproval of their peers. And those people include myself, so I will use examples from my own experience in order to engage with the material in this book. Each person has a *boggle threshold* for how much craziness she can accept before shaking her head and rolling her eyeballs in disbelief.[4] I am fully aware of that, but at some point, we need to get past the introductory material and start moving the discussion about consciousness forward onto more substantive territory, irrespective of how crazy that landscape might initially seem to be to us. So, to boldly set the tone for this book, let me start with a personal experience that appears, on the surface, to be an interaction with a deceased scientist. And, yes, I am my own harshest critic, so I, myself, am not sure what to make of this. And the reader will no doubt make her own judgments about it.

Richard Feynman?

One evening I was driving by myself to a hot yoga class when I smelled cigarette smoke in my car for about a minute. Not active cigarette smoke, but rather the smell of a heavy smoker sitting beside me. And, in recalling the event, it does not seem to me that the smell was physically present in the car so much as it was directly present to my awareness. I do not smoke, nor had a smoker recently been in my car, nor do I just smell smoke in my car as a matter of course. However, I had been reading some of Richard Feynman's writing, so that he had been on my mind, and I wondered whether Richard, a deceased physicist who had at one time been a smoker,[5] was "showing up" in my car. The following day, driving by myself home from school, once again, for a minute or so, I had the distinct impression of smelling a heavy smoker together with me in the car.

Is it possible that the deceased Richard Feynman was actually together in the car with me? This might seem manifestly impossible, but there is a growing body of literature about *after-death communication* (ADC), the ostensible communication of the living with the deceased.[6] In a 1974–75 survey, 31% of a representative sample of 902 people living in Iceland responded in the affirmative to the question: "Have you ever been aware of the presence of a deceased person?"[7] Aggregation with a second survey in 1980–86 led to the identification of 449 people who claimed to have had such experiences. Of those 67% had experienced visual impressions, 28% auditory, 13% tactual, and 5% olfactory, with 11% claiming to have only had a "vivid sense of presence."[8] In other words, in some cases people had claimed to have perceived distinctive smells that had been associated with the deceased. On the one hand, such experiences could be misperceptions, created by longing for the deceased, and so on. However, there is little evidence that all ADC phenomena are misperceptions. On the other hand, these could be actual visits from the deceased. There is insufficient evidence to reach such a strong conclusion but, on balance, it does tip in favour of survival, so that these types of experiences could be expressions of discarnate activity.[9]

I contacted Angie Aristone, a medium with whom I had done some work for about a decade, to come over to my place to see if we could "talk to Richard." We had done this sort of thing before. As readers might already know, a *medium* is a person who appears to have the ability to communicate with the deceased. In a number of experimental studies, it has been shown that good mediums can obtain correct information through anomalous means.[10] I met with Angie on Wednesday morning, December 10, 2014 and asked her if Richard Feynman were around. She had not known that I would be asking about him. I took handwritten notes of our interaction.

The answer appeared to be "yes." Angie received a considerable amount of information, ostensibly from Richard. Although Angie had been accurate numerous times in the past, and I expected the same level of accuracy in this case, I did not know how much of this specific information was true. After checking, it turned out that Angie had given correct information about Richard's appearance, accent, and various other details. There were two things that stood out for me. One was the cause of death, which the ostensible Richard had given as kidney failure, even though it has been commonly reported that he died of cancer.[11] I have "kidneys, slow passing" written in my notes. Apparently, Richard suffered for about a decade from cancer which crushed one of his kidneys, then died when his remaining kidney failed, and he refused further treatment.[12] The other thing that I found interesting was that Angie saw Richard taking off his glasses. In my notes I have "on again/off again." Richard Feynman was present at the first ever nuclear explosion in 1945 at the Trinity Test Site in the New Mexico desert where he famously claimed to have been the only one watching without wearing dark welder's glasses.[13] That may be a whimsical correspondence to the glasses going on and off.

But it was something else that the ostensible Richard had said during my session with Angie that stayed with me. I have written in my notes: "you guys are barely hanging on | on the brink of destruction." This was a grim message. Certainly not a new one, from conventional or anomalous sources. And one that I had spent considerable effort trying to understand throughout my adult life, even though I had never formally researched it or written about it. As I thought about it this time, what came to mind was that humanity is precariously teetering between more-or-less holding it together and losing complete control. There are planetary problems in all spheres of life: the quality of the ecosystem on which our biological well-being depends, financial liquidity, political stability, religious tolerance, interpersonal harmony, and so on, are all stressed. It seemed clear to me that simultaneous further degradation of even just a few of these spheres of activity could lead to an infrastructure collapse. That, in turn, could loosen up the security of the nuclear weapons caches around the world to the point where they could be used by various demagogues to trigger a nuclear war of sufficient proportion to end human life and much of the rest of life on earth as well. I do not know if that was Richard's intended message, or if, indeed, there was a Richard behind the message, but it did occur to me that, perhaps, if it were to have been Richard, that he may have felt some responsibility for helping out now given that he had been instrumental for inventing the nuclear bomb in the first place.[14]

We do not need an ostensible deceased physicist to tell us that we are in serious trouble. That alarm has been sounded by various scientists and analysts over the last several decades. When I was a high school student in the 1960s in Toronto, I attended a talk given at York University about global warming. The speaker explained how carbon dioxide and other greenhouse gasses trapped heat in the atmosphere leading to extreme weather fluctuations and a gradual heating of the surface of the planet. At the end of his lecture, there was stunned silence in the auditorium. I only remember one of the questions asked of the speaker: "What can we do about it?" — to which he replied that no one will bother to do anything about it until it is too late. A more contemporary voice is that of Peter Ward: "There is no doubt that planet Earth is radically changing through global warming. Those resisting this conclusion are doing so for political, economic, or deficit-of-intelligence reasons, not as a result of scientific facts."[15] And climate change is just one of the infrastructure breakdowns with which we are faced.

The second half of my apocalyptic scenario — the nuclear threat — is just as frightening. There had already been nervous moments when only five nations had achieved nuclear weapons capability during the Cold War. I still recall the drills in which I participated in grade school. When the air raid sirens went off, we had to walk to the back of the classroom and stand against the walls of the cloakroom to learn to prepare for a nuclear blast. Now we are up to nine nations and a total of about 16,300 warheads,[16] with others in the process of developing such capability.[17] There are simply too many opportunities for proliferation, not just by nation states, but rogue organizations whose members would really like to blow up some of those nuclear weapons. "There is no secret here, and there is also no defense. The nuclear age is upon us, and it cannot be undone."[18] It is not unreasonable to conclude that it is just a matter of time before the leaking containment net is breached and someone sets off a nuclear device. "In Western capitals today there are quiet people, serious people, who, while recognizing the low probability of such an attack, nonetheless worry that the successful use of just a single atomic bomb could bring the established order to its knees—or lay it out flat."[19]

We are likely to need all of the cognitive and material resources at our disposal in order to effectively address these global threats. And that includes whatever knowledge we can glean from the effort to understand consciousness from a postmaterialist perspective. So, the purpose of this book is to look unflinchingly at data from the cutting edge of consciousness research and to apply that to the serious situation that we face today on our planet.

Chapter 1

Consciousness Unplugged

One (perhaps literally) redeeming feature of sociological per-spective is that relativizing analysis, in being pushed to its final consequence, bends back upon itself. The relativizers are relativized, the debunkers are debunked — indeed, relativization itself is somehow liquidated. What follows is not, as some of the early sociologists of knowledge feared, a total paralysis of thought. Rather, it is a new freedom and flexibility in asking questions of truth.[20]

What do we see if we direct our attention to that which is emerging? Perhaps we need to start with a quick look back at the territory that we are leaving. In order to show the reader where the study of consciousness has gone beyond the usual boundaries set by conventional ideas about it, I will take the following path. I will start by describing the core of the two main materialist con-ceptions of consciousness — computationalism and neuroscientism — and point out their fatal flaws. Then I note that the effort to understand consciousness has been largely based on information about consciousness in the ordinary waking state. I give a fairly long list of alterations of consciousness that also need to be taken into account. And as we start to look at the experiences that make up that list, we notice the occurrence of anomalous phenomena that cannot easily be explained by materialist interpretations of reality. In particular, there is now sufficient evidence from near-death experiences, experiences that sometimes occur around the time of a person's death, to suggest that consciousness can exist independently of the brain. Now we need a new theory, and I propose that we use a flicker theory, whereby we conceptualize physical manifestation as turning on and off, moment by moment. I end the chapter by discussing self-development. In the past, the investigation of consciousness was largely "from the outside," that is to say, using third-person approaches. Because of the sub-jective nature of consciousness, its future study necessarily needs to proceed also "from the inside," using a mixture of first- and third-person methodologies. But then, the apparatus of observa-tion is a person's own mind; an adequately prepared mind. And those ideas will take us to the end of this chapter.

The Failure of Computationalism

In 1983, I had completed an MSc in mathematics and switched to psychology for my PhD with the intention of acquiring expertise in the study of consciousness. My primary interest in mathematics had been in mathematical logic,[21] and mathematical logic had formed the basis for an emerging way of thinking about con-sciousness called *computationalism*,[22] so that I had inadvertently ideally prepared myself for my next area of study. Let me explain the idea behind computationalism. Well, there are actually many different ways of thinking about computationalism and its relationships to other ideologies, such as functionalism.[23] I do not want to get distracted here, so let me just stay close to the essence, namely, that the computation of computationalism is based on formal logic.

One of the ways that we can set up logic is to start with a collection of symbols, which is to say, markings on paper that can be distinguished from one another. Then we create rules for writing these symbols in strings that we call *well-formed formulae*.

This gives us a *formal language*. Then we create rules, called a *predicate calculus*, for ordering these well-formed formulae into sequences that allow us to start with one set of well-formed formulae, which we can call *premises*, at one end and end with a well-formed formula at the other end, which we can call a *theorem*.[24] Progression from the beginning of the sequence to the end of the sequence can be instantiated using a *universal Turing machine*, which we can just think of as a computer that mechanically executes a set of instructions for a sequence of inputs to produce a deterministic output.[25] There is more—a lot more—but just this much is already enough for the point I want to make.

Now suppose that we use this logical construction as a metaphor for the relationship between the brain and the mind. We posit that cognitive events are just sequences of well-formed formulae running on the wetware of the brain. And some of those well-formed formulae, those that cross a particular threshold of consciousness (whatever that might mean), are just the contents of our subjective experience.[26] It is as simple as that.

Or is it? Notice that, for this analogy to hold, there actually needs to be a formal language in the brain. This inner formal language has sometimes been dubbed *mentalese*,[27] or sometimes also the *language of thought*.[28] That formal language is going to be needed to be used for identifying the symbols that are going to be the representations of what it is that we are calculating. So we have an assignment problem. How are representations assigned? But we can ask an even more obvious question: "Does mentalese exist?" The answer is "No!" There is no evidence that such a language exists, nor, in my experience in talking to them, do computationalists ever hope to find it. Their response, again, in my experience, has been to say that there are no other options for a theory of consciousness, so we need to proceed anyway, even if the enterprise is fatally doomed at the outset. That is, of course, an illogical position.

In addition to the lack of evidence that mentalese exists, there is the problem that the brain is far too sloppy in its functioning[29] to instantiate its use. The sequence of well-formed formulae leading from a set of premises to a theorem is an exact sequence. Given all the biochemical activity going on in the brain, it is not at all clear how any exact sequence could be executed with any reliability. Let me spell this out in more detail. In predicate calculus we get from the premises to the theorem that we are trying to prove by a sequence of logical steps. There is only one path, and each symbol of each step of that path has to be written correctly, or the proof does not carry through. A properly programmed computer is a closed system that can execute such a program. It does so by assigning specific settings of transistorized circuits to the symbols in the language and then mechanically instantiating the rules of inference to move from one set of symbols to the next.[30] But now suppose that while the computer is executing the program, you pour some coffee into it, so that you get some arcing and maybe some steam comes off. If you interfere with any of the circuits, then the chain of execution is broken, and you will not be able to prove the theorem. You could get around this problem by creating a sophisticated cybernetic system designed to manage local system failures. But the brain is an open system with the equivalent of coffee constantly pouring every-where into it. So, not only do you have the problem of how symbols in a nonexistent mentalese are instantiated in the brain, but you also have so much interference that you could never com-plete a mechanical sequence of actions to bring that nonexistent symbol sequence to a conclusion. For computationalism to work, the language of thought must perfectly match the manner in which the brain actually instantiates the symbols and there cannot be any interruptions to the calculating process. Neither of these is realistic.

Nor are the missing language and sloppiness of the brain the only problems. As one of the originators of the paradigm has said: "I would have thought that the last forty or fifty years have demonstrated pretty clearly that there are aspects of higher mental processes into which the current armamentarium of computational models, theories, and experimental techniques offers vanishingly little insight."[31] Then what is the point of pursuing this line of investigation?

Maybe we just need to try harder. If we look at the neurons in the brain, we can think of each neuron as either being "on" or "off" and use networks of neurons in place of the transistorized circuits for making calculations.[32] This notion has developed into *connectionism*, which is computation that more closely mimics the activity of neural networks.[33] But it turns out that nothing is gained by doing that, given that connectionist models are Turing computable,[34] so that they are formally equivalent to the computational models that we have already discussed.[35] Furthermore, the neurons in the brain are neither just "on" or "off," nor are they the only relevant cells in the brain. In particular, various glial cells, the support cells, also play a cybernetic role.[36] We still have the problem of the sloppy brain. And these connectionist models are not really models of brain activity anyway, so that we are left with an explanatory gap between the brain and these computational processes.[37] And it is even less clear where to stick symbols into all of this, if anywhere.

The Failure of Neuroscientism

So, let us get rid of the computational layer and just keep the "wetware," which is to say, the "hardware" on which the programs are supposed to be running. In other words, we get rid of representation, symbols, logic, all of that, and just keep the physiological functioning of the body. In this way, we pass from computationalism to neuroscientism, looking directly at the brain for explanations of the mind. This takes us back to where we were in the first place before the advent of computationalism. In this conceptualization, we have a dynamic system that moves from one state to another as a result of biochemical processes. The problem is that, in and of itself, such a system has nothing to do with subjective experience. It can run perfectly well "in the dark" without the "light of consciousness." This is known as *conscious inessentialism*.[38] In fact, consciousness becomes a nuisance that has to be finessed into the system somehow. At least with computational modelling, although deeply problematical, there was a supposed parallel between well-formed formulae and subjective experience. But if we throw out the well-formed formulae, we have thrown out the analogue of subjective experience. How do we get subjective experience back?

Let me make this more precise. When we talk about "consciousness" we usually want to refer to events that occur subjectively for a person within the domain of her experience.[39] The word *qualia* is sometimes used to refer to the quality of what it feels like to experience specific events.[40] Suppose that I see black text on a white page. In addition to the sensory process of seeing black text on a white page and the cognitive process of interpreting the text, there is also an accompanying distinct impression of what it is like to be seeing black text on a white page. That impression, of which we are usually not explicitly aware, would be a *quale*. More generally, I have started using the expression *existential qualia* to refer to the felt sense that anything at all is occurring. In other words, a person can introspectively check for herself if it feels as though anything is happening. The answer, for many people, is that "Yes, it feels as though something is going on." So, let us use the word *consciousness* to refer to "subjective events suffused with existential qualia that occur privately for a person."[41] Here, the words "subjective" and "privately" refer to the fact that this definition applies "from the inside" for a person for herself, and does not restrict those events as to whether they apparently originate from sensory perceptions or not. It is this notion of consciousness that needs to be explained in a theory of consciousness.

Now we have a problem, the so-called *hard problem of consciousness*:[42] how does consciousness arise from the activity of the brain? Or, more specifically, how do existential qualia arise from the activity of neurons? One solution is to just categorically assert that that must be the case:

> On my view mental phenomena are biologically based: they are both caused by the operations of the brain and realized in the structure of the brain. On this view, consciousness … [is] as much a part of human biology as digestion or the circulation of the blood. It is an *objective* fact about the world that it contains certain systems, viz., brains, with *subjective* mental states, and it is a *physical* fact about such systems that they have *mental* features.[43]

The usual way to talk about this is to say that consciousness is an emergent property of the brain. An *emergent property* of a physical system is a property of a system that is not immediately apparent by simply examining its constituent parts. The overused example is that of the wetness of water. What we mean by wetness is just the activity of water molecules interacting with one another.

Here is the problem with emergentism. The whole point of invoking physical processes such as brain events to explain consciousness is precisely so as to eliminate any reference to subjective events. So now we want something from which we have stripped any tinge of subjectivity to produce subjectivity for us.[44] What? Note that the analogy with water is just an instance of the hard problem. Wetness is a quale and it is not at all clear how water molecules can produce a quale. If we are not talking about wetness as a quale but just the collective properties of water molecules, then the emergentist statement is just that the collective properties of water molecules arise from the collective action of water molecules. But then the analogy breaks down. All we can say is that the activity of the brain is just the collective activity of its constituent biological parts. But there are no qualia in this equation. To reinsert the qualia, we would need to say that qualia are made up of physical bits of qualia that we find when we look at brain events. But no one has ever found physical bits of qualia anywhere. That is precisely the hard problem.[45] As neuroscientist Christof Koch has decisively expressed it: "Subjectivity is too radically different from anything physical for it to be an emergent phenomenon."[46]

If not emergentism, then what other candidates do we have? We can continue to insist that there must be some way in which events that have nothing to do with subjective experience actually do create subjective experience and that someday an explanation will be forthcoming. Such a position is known as *promissory materialism*.[47] But it is difficult to regard that as anything other than an effort to salvage materialism well beyond its expiration date as a useful theory of consciousness.

Thus far we have engaged in the negative program of demonstrating the inadequacy of computation and neuroscience to account for consciousness. So, is consciousness, then, a funda-mental feature of reality that cannot be reduced to any physical process? How about a positive program? Is there any direct empirical evidence for the ontologically fundamental nature of consciousness? Is there any evidence that consciousness can function independently of the brain? The answer is yes. In order to see that, we need to look at evidence from altered states of consciousness.

Alterations of Consciousness

There is an epistemological point that needs to be made here. Philosophers, scientists, and scholars of various sorts frequently use their own experiences in the ordinary waking state as their measure of reality. For example, on the basis of his own experi-ence, William James found that consciousness is just the breath moving from the glottis to the nostrils.[48] Daniel Dennett's cog-nitivist theory of consciousness fit "all the dear features" that he discovered in his "inner life."[49] And so on. First-person methodol-ogies are important in the study of consciousness, beginning with their application to one's own experience. However, a problem occurs when one's own experience is taken to be the limit of what is possible. This is an instance of the *availability heuristic*. Our understanding of reality is limited by the data that have been available to us. In particular, in this case, our understanding of reality is limited by the experiences that we have had and have not had. The antidote is to seek out and examine the experiences of others through field studies and, where possible, laboratory studies, using a combination of first-person and third-person methodologies.[50]

Another problem with the strategy of relying on one's own experiences is that the experiences that are usually deemed to be relevant to an understanding of consciousness are those that have occurred in the ordinary waking state. This necessarily leads to a distorted theory of consciousness. The antidote for this is to seek out and examine phenomena relevant to consciousness that occur during alterations of consciousness. I use the expression *alterations of consciousness* as a general term to refer to overall shifts of psychological functioning and reserve the expression *altered states of consciousness* to refer to shifts of psychological functioning that are clearly maintained as stable states. For example, mind wandering is an alteration of consciousness that is usually regarded as a normal aspect of the ordinary waking state whereas sleep is an altered state of consciousness that has a distinctive stable physiology and phenomenology associated with it.[51] As another example, we can experience feelings of well-being as an aspect of our ordinary waking state. However, in the fifth chapter, "Radical Self-Transformation," we will consider persistent states of exceptional well-being with altered psychological functioning as altered states of consciousness.

The following is a partial list of alterations of consciousness that need to be considered in any acceptable theory of consciousness. Except where noted by additional citations, these alterations have been described in the book *Alterations of Consciousness*.[52]

1. *The ordinary waking state, daydreaming, mind wandering, absorption, mindfulness*. Within the ordinary waking state, we tend to meander between some degree of focused, deliberate thinking and more diffused forms of ideation and emotions, with a considerable number of spontaneous images, self-talk, and feelings arising throughout.

2. *Sensory restriction*. Previously known as *sensory deprivation* and also called *restricted environmental stimulation technique*, sensory restriction refers to the attenuation of sensory input, or its uniform presentation, such as in so-called *Ganzfeld experiments*.

3. *Sleep, parasomnias*. Sleep is a biologically induced altered state of consciousness; parasomnias are sleep disorders such as sleep terrors and sleepwalking, during which highly complex behaviours can occur.

4. *Hypnagogic and hypnopompic states, sleep paralysis*. Hypnagogic and hypnopompic states occur upon falling asleep and waking up, respectively, sometimes accompanied by sleep paralysis, during which vivid imagery, in any sense modality, frequently occurs; and which can be liminal states in that nonconscious material sometimes surfaces into awareness.

5. *Dreaming, nightmares, lucid dreaming, precognitive dreaming, shared dreaming*. Dreaming can occur any time during sleep, including rapid eye movement (REM) sleep and non-REM sleep when brain metabolism is lower than it is during the waking state; nightmares are dysphoric dreams; lucid dreams are dreams in which one knows that one is dreaming; precognitive dreams are dreams in which one dreams about events that occur in the future; shared dreams can include dreams in which two or more people dream the same content and dreams in which people apparently meet together in their dreams.[53]

6. *Hypnotic trance, fantasy proneness, trance, dissociated states, possession, mediumship*. Hypnotic trance is whatever state it is that occurs when a person is hypnotized, which will depend on whether a person is compliant, fantasy prone, or

dissociative; trance, more generally, is a state in which behaviour consistent with self-awareness and self-determination occurs in the absence of any actual self-awareness or self-determination; dissociated states are states in which there are disconnections between various aspects of a person's psyche and can include *dissociative identity disorder* whereby different alternate personalities appear to sequentially use the body; possession is a state in which a person appears to have been "taken over" by some entity external to that person's psyche; and mediumship is the apparent communication of information or "energy" from a source that is not the ordinary waking state.

7. *Out-of-body experiences.* Out-of-body experiences are characterized by a somaesthetic sense of being outside of one's own body.

8. *Alien abduction experiences.* Alien abduction experiences are experiences in which a person has a complex of symptoms such as missing time, extreme terror, bodily scars such as "scoop marks" on the skin, and so on that have led that person to believe that she has been abducted by aliens.

9. *Drug-induced states.* Drugs, such as anaesthetics and psychedelics (such as d-lysergic acid diethylamide, psilocybin, mescaline, dimethyltryptamine, harmine, harmaline, tetrahydroharmine, and ketamine), can induce a variety of experiences in alterations of consciousness.

10. *Transcendent states.* States of flow, mystical states, pure consciousness, nondual states, states of no-self, and so on can include feelings of exceptional well-being, a sense of unity with all that exists, awakening to the fact of one's own existence, joy, the disappearance of the subject–object duality, and the disappearance of the sense of self.

11. *Death, impending death, terminal lucidity, near-death experiences, shared near-death experiences, and shared death experiences.* Death is an altered state of consciousness of oblivion or the continuation of consciousness in some manner; impending death can

bring with it hallucinations and anomalous experiences such as terminal lucidity, whereby a person who has been cognitively unresponsive for some time functions normally for a few minutes;[54] near-death experiences (NDEs) are experiences that occur around the time that a person is close to death; and shared near-death and shared death experiences are similar to shared dreams in that a person who is not close to death appears to have been drawn into a near-death experience or the dying process of someone who is having those experiences.[55]

12. *Pre-birth, previous-lifetime, future lifetime, between-lives experiences.* Either spontaneously or through some form of induction such as hypnosis or guided imagery, people apparently recall or re-experience events that appear to have occurred during a time when they were not alive.

13. Pathological states such as derealization, depersonalization, depression, psychosis, anxiety, the ordinary waking state, and so on. Consciousness is frequently altered in psychopathological syndromes; for instance, during derealization disorder feelings of reality are missing; and in depersonalization disorder a person loses her sense of self (accompanied by dysphoric feelings).

A few comments about this list. First, note that I have included the ordinary waking state both at the beginning and at the end of the list. I included it at the beginning of the list in order to strip it of its privileged status and reduce it to "just another alteration of consciousness." I included it at the end of the list in the collection of pathological states to be provocative, and to draw attention to the fact that the ordinary waking state, far from being optimal, as we usually suppose that it is, could be a psychotic state in which we have gotten things really badly wrong. For instance, to think that there is an objective reality "out there" independent of our perception of it could be a persistent delusion from which we need to awaken.[56]

Second, it is not clear why any theory of consciousness should be taken seriously that does not make an effort to address all of the 13 phenomena on this list. To simply disregard them or label the ones that we do not like as "psychopathology" or to deem irrelevant anything that is actual "psychopathology" is not useful. A theory of consciousness needs to take into account all of the available data and not just the data that confirm one's cherished interpretation of reality.

Third, in this list, I am blurring the distinction between phenomena that are widely acknowledged as occurring, such as sleep, and anomalous phenomena such as shared dreaming, whose occurrence could be disputed. However, I have only included in this list phenomena for which I have good evidence that they occur *as phenomena* for some people. In other words, there is good evidence that these experiences do occur. How they are ultimately explained is another matter—for example, as misperception, fraud, hallucination, delusion, veridical perception, mental communication, absorption in shared mind, or whatever. For instance, how about shared dreaming? Shared dreaming appears in the dream literature.[57] In addition, several of my students have spontaneously told me about their apparent shared dream experiences for which the most reasonable explanation was that these experiences were what they appeared to have been. And I have had shared dreams myself. None of this proves the existence of shared dreaming as shared dreaming, but, in my experience, the phenomenon is sufficiently robust to be placed on a list of phenomena that could occur during alterations of consciousness for which an explanation is required. Furthermore, for many of the entries of apparent anomalous phenomena in the list, there is actually good evidence that the most reasonable explanation is that they really are anomalous. Let us look at anomalies more closely.

Anomalous Phenomena

A variety of anomalous phenomena associated with consciousness occur. However, there has sometimes been considerable resistance to accepting the evidence for their occurrence. Lance Storm has described the sort of repression that exists:

> We must now recognize what appears to be a growing conspiracy (not just in universities) where the aims are: (a) to argue and demonstrate, by any means necessary (e.g., omissions and half-truths in scientific papers) and, by way of institutional policy, to ban or deny psi research and its subsequent publications, in order to convince naïve academics and a non-thinking public that there is, and can be, no such thing as psi, and therefore (b) show that paranormal belief and alleged experience can never be healthy or normal, but must be pathological or delusional. Through ostracization and peer pressure, and occasional success in aims (a) and (b) which work in harmony, this sweeping and prejudicial agenda is reinforced.[58]

Such corruption of the scientific enterprise by some of its participants sometimes makes it difficult for those of us who look at anomalies as part of our research to do our work. Science is an empirical investigation of whatever one is interested in learning about, as well as logical reasoning from the results of any studies. This includes the open investigation of anomalies.[59] The actual evidence for the occurrence and characteristics of different anomalous phenomena associated with consciousness varies so it is important to pay attention to the type and quality of evidence. And then make judgments about what appears to be happening. So, having said that, what do we know?

In general, consciousness has both spatial and temporal nonlocal properties. I think of this, from the perspective of a given individual, as having an "input" and an "output" side. The input side is characterized by the ability to directly know something that is happening somewhere else or at some other time without sensory mediation. I usually use the expression *remote viewing* for such input. The output side is characterized by the ability to directly mentally affect physical manifestation without the exertion of any "mechanical" force. This can also be time displaced. I usually call this *remote influencing* even if what it is that is being influenced is physically nearby. The picture that emerges is that of a universe that is massively mentally inter-connected across space and time.[60]

What becomes clear from examining the evidence is that a few people are able to demonstrate these phenomena in experimental situations, whereas most are not able to do so. Studies seeking to demonstrate their existence using convenience samples of who-ever shows up run the risk of failing to get statistically significant results. A more reasonable strategy is to identify, as much as possible, those who can manifest particular phenomena and then pre-screen them before proceeding with a formal experiment, in order to increase the likelihood of demonstrating their existence.

In addition to living in a mentally interconnected universe, as just described, there is good empirical evidence for the *survival hypothesis*, the hypothesis that consciousness survives the death of the physical body. There have been multiple streams of relevant research (going back at least to 1882 with the founding of the Society for Psychical Research) that converge on support for the notion. But this is difficult material to digest and evaluate. To see the complexity involved, it is fairly easy to experimentally demonstrate in rigorous studies that good mediums get correct information.[61] It is maddeningly difficult to attribute the source of that information to discarnate entities.[62] Nonetheless, I agree with others who have thoroughly examined the history of survival research[63] that the evidence tips in favour of survival. Further-more, it is important to note a secondary observation, that it is not just that consciousness survives in a diffuse form, but that a person's individuality remains intact, including her psychological characteristics, memories, and dispositions.[64] This raises questions, of course, about the nature of mind and personality, and the similarities and differences between their incarnate and discarnate versions. Pursing such questions would take us beyond the scope of our discussion here. So let us just come back to our original question of whether there is any evidence to suggest that consciousness can exist independently of the brain.

Consciousness Unplugged

In evaluating the available data, it seems to me that the most direct evidence for the independent existence of the mind comes from cases in which a person was able to correctly identify features of her environment during a near-death experience at a time when there was insufficient brain activity to support the sort of mentation that would be required for perceptual processing. A number of such cases exist, some of which have good documentation.[65] The following is a famous case.

In a prospective study of 101 cardiac arrest patients, nine reported having had near-death experiences. Of those nine, two reported auditory and visual details of their resuscitation, one of whom was available for a follow-up interview.

> He accurately described people, sounds, and activities from his resuscitation. … His medical records corroborated his accounts and specifically supported his descriptions and the use of an automated external defibrillator (AED). Based on current AED algorithms, this likely corresponded with up to 3 min of conscious awareness during [cardiac arrest] and CPR.[66]

During the time that he was being resuscitated, the patient described hearing an automated voice saying "shock the patient, shock the patient," then looking down from an upper corner of the room and seeing himself as well as a nurse and "another man who had a bald head" wearing "blue scrubs" and a "blue hat." The patient claimed that he recognized the bald-headed man the following day when he came to see the patient.[67]

Aside from the presence of specific information that was unique to that patient, the argument has been made that patients are simply describing what they think occurs during resuscitation procedures based on information from observations of the medical equipment around them and depictions of resuscitation in the popular media. There have been several studies done with cardiac arrest patients comparing the accuracy of descriptions of their resuscitation procedures given by those who claimed to have seen them during their near-death experiences and "control" patients who had had similar exposure to resuscitation equipment and, in some cases, media portrayals of resuscitation, but had not made any claims of having seen their own resuscitations. While there have been some methodological problems with some of these studies,[68] it is reasonable to conclude that those who claimed to have seen their resuscitation procedures described the events that had occurred correctly, without major errors, whereas most of the "control" patients said they had no idea what had been done or made major errors.[69]

The argument has also been made that there is sufficient residual activity in the brain to explain the phenomenology of near-death experiences. As a biological process, death consists of a sequence of events that take place over time. For instance, following circulatory arrest, there is "immediate failure of the sodium/potassium pump; accumulation of calcium ions intracellularly," and so on.[70] Then a loss of oxygen and the onset of unconsciousness after 10 to 15 seconds.[71] Usually within about 20 seconds of cardiac arrest there would be insufficient neuronal activity to detect with an electroencephalogram.[72] In other words, ordinary neuronal functioning stops within a minute of circulatory arrest. However, even without neuronal activity, there are cellular processes that continue to take place in various parts of the brain, so that it is not as though the brain has completely stopped functioning.[73] The conventional argument is that whatever remaining processes are still occurring are those that are responsible for a near-death experience.[74]

There are two problems with the residual biological processes hypothesis of veridical perception during near-death experiences. The first is that it does not account for the fact that a patient is frequently not physically located in a position so as to be able to perceive the relevant events using the physical senses, even if those senses were to be operative.[75]

The second problem is that it is contrary to our knowledge of brain functioning to propose that a severely compromised brain is the source of ordinary perceptual experiences. We can argue about exactly how disabled a brain has become as a result of a lack of oxygen after 1 minute, or 3 minutes, or 20 minutes, but the point is that it is not functioning in the way that it would need to be functioning according to our neuroscientific knowledge about the brain in order to produce the kinds of perceptual experiences that survivors describe as having occurred. A compromised brain, as a result of concussion, or fever, or degeneration, or whatever, exhibits confusion, delirium, and dementia, not normal cognitive functioning. In fact, what is striking is that, in many cases, experiencers have reported having had exceptional mental clarity during their near-death experiences. For instance, in one study, 45% indicated that their thinking had been "clearer than usual" and 29% indicated that it had been "more logical than usual."[76] If such metacognitive reports are accurate, then how do clarity and logic arise in a dysfunctional brain when that brain's efficient functioning is precisely what is required for the occurrence of clarity and logic?

A third objection to taking these accounts of veridical perception seriously is the claim that there has not been a single definitive case in which all alternative possible hypotheses could be completely ruled out. As one science journalist pointed out, in a collection of about 100 such reports "there was not a single clincher — an absolutely inarguable case of someone seeing something that only a disembodied spirit could have seen."[77] There are three things to keep in mind with such an objection. The first is that there needs to actually be evidence that alternative hypotheses are, in fact, reasonable, rather than just positing wildly imaginative ways in which someone could have correctly seen something while she was incapable of doing so. The second is that there only needs to be a single case of veridical perception while the brain was (reasonably) silent in order to falsify the hypothesis that the brain is necessary for the occurrence of conscious experience. That means that every one of the apparent instances of veridical perception needs to be properly explained in physiological terms. And that is a tall order. The third is that deciding what is or is not a "clincher" is a loose heuristic, which will be applied differently by different people. I just finished teaching a single-semester, third year, undergraduate psychology course about death as an altered state of consciousness in which, among other things, my students and I carefully examined a number of these veridical perception cases, and many of my students *did* find them to be "clinchers."

Taken as a whole, what I have argued is that materialist accounts cannot capture consciousness and that there are some data to suggest that consciousness exists without a physical nervous system. Thus, the argument here is that consciousness is not a by-product of the brain but, rather, that *consciousness is a primary element of the universe with the brain functioning as a filter for its expression.* Consciousness has become unplugged. The cat is out of the (materialist) bag and I think that it will be difficult to try to wrangle it back into the bag. This is the starting point for the cutting edge of consciousness research. So, I will start the discussion by describing a theory that is consistent with this contention and that has anchor points into the work of a couple of physicists—David Bohm's notion of an implicate order and Julian Barbour's theory of time.

A Flicker Theory

We experience space and time as continuous, but there is good reason to think that it actually flickers on and off, moment to moment, at a subliminal level. Let me start by telling a personal story about where I might have gotten the idea that the universe flickers. In a chemistry course in high school, I was astonished to learn about electron orbitals surrounding the nuclei of atoms. Up until that point, I had had the misconception that electrons were little particles that go around a stationary nucleus of an atom in the same way that the planets of the solar system go around the sun. As above, so below. Not so. Electron orbitals define the spatial volume within which electrons can be found with a certain probability when someone looks for them. Some of them are spheres centred on the nucleus, but others are in the shape of dumbbells, some with doughnuts hanging from the ends of them out in space. There are no flight paths! There is no actual motion through space from one position to the next. If an electron is found in a particular place at one time, this says nothing about where it will be found the next time someone looks. Electrons just appear at different places determined by the probability of occurrence in those places.

Much later, I was trying to apply the notion of "observation" in quantum mechanics developed in the context of an experimental apparatus to the notion of "observation" in everyday life. In quantum mechanics, by the Kochen-Specker Theorem, the values of "observables," such as position and momentum, do not exist until we choose which observables we are going to measure, or they change depending upon which combinations we choose.[78] In other words, the observational process in an experiment shapes what we find. How does this observational process play out in everyday life?

There is another theorem of quantum mechanics, called "a watched pot never boils theorem," which states that a continuously observed system does not change.[79] But we live our lives as a dynamic stream of differing experiences. Something has to give, and thus far quantum mechanics has always been vindicated. So, what has to give is the appearance of continuity. Thus, I proposed that the universe is not continuous but, rather, that it turns itself on and off. In other words, we live in a *flicker universe*.[80] This is consistent with the electron in the orbital. It is here, then it is there, then it is over there, and so on. And in between? Nowhere. It does not exist.

Here is where we can bring in some ideas from our list of altered states of consciousness. Item 10 refers to transcendent states of consciousness. During his experience of "endarkenment" John Wren-Lewis found that "... what I perceive with my eyes and other senses is a whole world that seems to be coming fresh-minted into existence *moment by moment*."[81] For Wren-Lewis, the universe is not continuously existing, but rather consists of pulses of existence. This is a single first-person observation, so we need to treat it as such, but it is compatible with some ideas about time in physics as we shall see in the next section.

If the universe disappears, then where does it go? In thinking about this, I brought in David Bohm's notion of an *implicate order* to address that question. Bohm has used the analogy of an insoluble droplet of ink placed in a viscous fluid which is then stirred. As the stirring proceeds, the droplet of ink is stretched out into a fine thread to the point that the fluid appears to be grey. If the stirring is stopped and precisely reversed, the ink droplet will be reconstituted as though nothing had happened. The implicate order is represented by the single droplet of ink placed at a particular location in the fluid. The explicate order is the stretched-out droplet of ink giving a grey appearance to the fluid.[82] This is the idea. For Bohm, what we experience as mental and physical events are explications of the same implicate order. "The explicate order of matter in general is also in essence the sensuous explicate order that is presented in consciousness in ordinary experience."[83]

We usually experience a duality between subjective and objective events. But these can be regarded as two different expressions of the same nondual inner domain. And now there is a "somewhere" to which the universe can disappear between manifestations, namely the *implicate order*. Viewed from a subjective aspect, this *deep reality* can be called *deep consciousness*, and viewed from an objective aspect it can be called *prephysical substrate*. However, at the deep level, they are the same.[84]

So, the universe "emerges from" and "returns to" the deep reality. Now we bring back the idea that the values of observables are not determined until such time as we "look." But then, why is there any coherence to manifestation at all? How does our "looking" create a stable world moment-by-moment? The answer, I have proposed, is that there are conditioned patterns of expectations that give manifestation its expected appearance; that can guide the structure and dynamic sequences of events to occur as they do. They are part of the implicate order that determines what the explication looks like for any particular manifestation.[85] We will examine these patterns in more detail in Chapter 2, "Meaning Beyond the Human." But now we really need to look at the nature of time more carefully in order to understand the temporal aspect of the flickering.

Temporality

The flicker theory was enriched to become the *flicker-filter theory* when Julia Mossbridge and I looked at the nature of time in Chapter 3, "Rethinking Time," in our book *Transcendent Mind*.[86] One of the things that we did was to separate time into two streams, *apparent time* and *deep time*, in order to reflect the richness of the manifestations of time discussed in the multidisciplinary literature about it. Each of those has both subjective and objective aspects. Thus, *subjective apparent time* is time as it is experienced by a person in the ordinary waking state of consciousness. *Objective apparent time* is time as measured by a clock on a wall or, more precisely, by an atomic clock. *Subjective deep time* is time as it is experienced in some transcendent states of consciousness, namely, usually, as *timelessness*. And, finally, *objective deep time* is whatever orders sequences of events in apparent time.

Also, we noticed that apparent time is frequently regarded as illusory, both in its objective and subjective aspects. Objectively, time has frequently been *spatialized* in physics, so that all instances of time are available simultaneously in a *block universe* and, in that sense, disappears as time.[87] Subjectively, time does not appear to be the well-ordered linear sequence that we frequently assume it to be. For instance, in some cases during near-death experiences, life reviews of a person's entire life can be phenomenologically indistinguishable for that person from actual lived experience yet take place apparently within minutes of apparent objective time while that person is close to death.[88]

In order to make sense of this "disappearance" of time, Mossbridge and I considered physicist Julian Barbour's idea that all that exist are self-sufficient *nows* that occur in a sequence as determined by a density function.[89] The way we conceptualized it, these *nows* are not punctate, but entail the occurrence of indeterminate duration. Furthermore, each *now* has its own past and future, but neither the past nor the future attached to a *now* has any existence apart from that *now*. This is a critical feature of the *nows*. The past and future of a *now* are fictional scenarios that do not necessarily have anything to do with the content of other *nows*. The fact that there is actually a sequence, rather than just a "simulcast" of all *nows* at once, suggests the existence of a "deep time" along which these *nows* are ordered. Thus, the past attached to a given *now* could include information from *nows* that were prior along deep time. This sort of view is consistent with the phenomenology of time in the ordinary waking state.

Again, we can bring in some insights from our list of altered states of consciousness. From Item 9, about drug-induced states, we note that in some psychedelic states there appears to be an experience of a continuously regenerating present:

> The present is self-sufficient, but it is not a static present. It is a dancing present—the unfolding of a pattern which has no specific destination in the future but is simply its own point. It

leaves and arrives simultaneously, and the seed is as much the goal as the flower.[90]

And, again, Item 10, which refers to transcendent states of consciousness. For the American philosopher and mystic Franklin Wolff, there exists a "'life-current' constantly moving but, at the same time, so turning upon itself that there is no progress from past to future."[91] In other words, there are arguments "from the outside" as well as experiences "from the inside" that are consistent with the notion that only present *nows* exist. That there is no other apparent time.[92]

The *filter* aspect of the theory is taken from the notion that the brain acts as a "reducing valve" for a greater mind.[93] Thus, apparent time is a feature of brain-mediated consciousness whereas deep consciousness lies on the expanded mind side of the filter. Ordinary physical manifestation is on the filtered side, whereas the prephysical substrate is unfiltered. There is support for a model such as this from experiences in alterations of consciousness in which deep consciousness has occurred directly for someone. These would be alterations in which the reducing valve of the brain had been compromised in such a way as to "release" consciousness. Such experiences lead us to the final topic for this chapter, that of self-development.

Self-Development

In 1986, Robert Moore and I conducted a survey about the notions of consciousness and beliefs about reality of those who could potentially write about consciousness in the academic literature. Upon analysing the data from 334 completed questionnaires, we found that beliefs ranged from materialist beliefs through conservatively transcendent to extraordinarily transcendent beliefs. In effect, respondents could either tend toward materialism whereby all of reality is regarded as being fundamentally physical in nature or they could tend toward a transcendent position whereby all of reality is regarded as being fundamentally mental in nature. Not surprisingly, ideas about consciousness corresponded with beliefs about reality.[94] In fact, the two were so intimately intertwined that we simply regarded them together as *beliefs about consciousness and reality*.[95]

What is relevant here is that those tending toward the extraordinarily transcendent position tended to believe that a process of self-development is necessary in order to understand consciousness. To begin with, they were likely to agree with Item Q8 that "The inner experiential world is vaster, richer and contains more profound meanings than most people think." And to endorse "Q67. A process of psychological change is necessary in order to fully experience human consciousness." And also affirm "Q25. In order to fully understand human consciousness, a process of psychological change is necessary which may be achieved through meditation or a spiritual way of life."[96] On the other hand, a survey of 212 actual consciousness researchers at the Toward a Science of Consciousness 1996 'Tucson II' academic conference revealed that those tending toward materialism were less likely to have even examined their own fundamental beliefs about reality.[97] The point is that, for some consciousness researchers, *the investigator becomes the apparatus of investigation.*

Given that the study of consciousness is about the study of experiences in subjective states of consciousness, at some point subjective investigation becomes indispensable if research concerning consciousness is to advance. There needs to be a development of the apparatus of observation. Such development has a number of aspects.

Perhaps the first necessary aspect of self-development is to become free of the expectations of others to conform to particular ideologies, such as materialism or idealism, and to learn to think critically and to examine the relevant empirical evidence on the basis of its merits. This is a crucial notion that comes up again in Chapter 4, "Planetary Transformation," as a contributing factor to global crises. In this context, the point is that an investigator needs to learn to offset the psychological biases that distort reasoning.

For instance, we have a *confirmation bias* whereby we tend to seek out data that support what we already believe and avoid and discount data that conflict with our beliefs. As already mentioned, we also have an *availability heuristic,* so that we tend to take the limits of our own experience as the limits of reality. And we tend to exhibit *bias blindness* so that we are unaware of our biases![98] In other words, as aspiring scientists, we begin from a compromised position and need to seek out and correct psychological tendencies that interfere with our ability to practice science authentically. Clearly, this would be experienced as a process, in the same way that a scientist seeks to improve her mathematical expertise, critical thinking skills, and writing ability. Self-development is a necessary addition to that list if a scientist is to practice science authentically.[99]

A second aspect self-development is that of learning how to observe one's own mind, namely, learning to *introspect.* That ability has had a tortured history in Western culture precisely because such observation entails the apparatus of investigation investigating itself.[100] Nonetheless, there are numerous approaches that could be used for acquiring skill in self-examination. One way of proceeding is to deliberately disidentify from the contents of one's thinking and consider thinking as thinking that is going on within the scope of one's own experi-ence. What is the nature of these thoughts? From whence do they arise? Where do they go? What are they doing in my head? How are feelings and behaviours tied to these thoughts? And so on. Entire systems of self-examination have been developed, such as that of Dzogchen, a type of Tibetan Buddhist practice,[101] that could potentially be harnessed for this purpose.[102] We will return to these issues in Chapter 5, "Radical Self-Transformation," when we consider strategies for creating psychological changes.

One of the questionnaire items from the beliefs about con-sciousness and reality survey that was associated with the extra-ordinarily transcendent position was Item Q41: "There are modes of understanding latent within a person which are superior to rational thought."[103] A third aspect of self-development is concerned with the development of such putative latent abilities. Logical empiricism is the necessary ground for scientific investigation but what if there were ways in which a researcher's knowledge could be supplemented? Such as what? Could researchers be trained in remote viewing? Precognitive dreaming? Mediumship? The acquisition of knowledge in transcendent states? Cutting through to deep consciousness to make observations (whatever that would involve) of the prephysical substrate? And so on.[104] These are some of the ways in which an investigator, herself, could be regarded as the apparatus of investigation.

So, this is where the study of consciousness is found today, if we follow it to its edge. We have realized that it is imperative that we take into account data from alterations of consciousness in any theory of consciousness. We have seen that consciousness has nonlocal properties and appears to be able to exist independently of a nervous system. We have a flicker theory that we can use and further develop as we move forward. And it is clear that any adequate investigation of consciousness is going to entail at least some self-transformation of the investigator. With this background, we are ready to look at some specific issues that arise in this expanded context. The first of those is a question about meaning. Does meaning exist beyond the human? We will seek to answer that question by examining three quite different experiments.

Chapter 2

Meaning Beyond the Human

Forests think. ... Wait. How can I even make this claim that forests think? Shouldn't we only ask how people think forests think? I'm not doing this. Here, instead, is my provocation. I want to show that the fact that we can make the claim that forests think is in a strange way a product of the fact that forests think. These two things – the claim itself and the claim that we can make the claim – are related: It is because thought extends beyond the human that we can think beyond the human.[105]

We have seen in Chapter 1, "Consciousness Unplugged," that consciousness is no longer bounded by brains but extends across space and time, so that both remote viewing and remote influencing occur. And consciousness appears, at least at times, to be independent of the brain. And there is evidence for the survival of consciousness after the death of the body. In fact, I reached the conclusion that consciousness is an elementary aspect of reality. And, from my definition of consciousness, that is a statement that the occurrence of subjective experience extends beyond the physical body.

In the 1986 consciousness survey conducted by Robert Moore and myself, discussed at the end of Chapter 1, we found that 78% of 334 respondents agreed with Item Q31 "Consciousness gives meaning to reality," whereas 15% disagreed.[106] For those with conservatively transcendent beliefs, meaning is important, as evidenced, for instance, by endorsement of Item B1 "I think about the ultimate meaning of life."[107] And it is consciousness that provides that meaning. Given the dependence of meaning on consciousness, and given that consciousness extends beyond the body, does meaning follow consciousness and extend beyond the body? Does meaning extend beyond the human?

Meaning does appear to extend beyond the human for some consciousness researchers. In Chapter 1, we noted that Christof Koch rejected the notion that consciousness is an emergent property. He has also said that he thinks that meaning exists in the universe:

> It's just that I often feel—I don't know—I find it very difficult to talk about. I can't really describe it. I just feel the universe is filled with meaning. I see it everywhere and I realize it's a psychological mindset. I fully realize other people don't have this. I have it. It's very difficult to explain where it comes from. I just have this firm belief and the experience of numinosity. It's difficult to put into words.[108]

It is worth noting here that Koch is relying on an epistemology that goes beyond empirical observation and rational reasoning as we usually think of those. In that sense, he is utilizing a latent mode of understanding that could be used for the exploration of consciousness. Of course, his impressions could simply be mistaken. But they are not unique. The widespread assumption that "mind is limited to humans and perhaps the 'higher animals'"[109] has been challenged and there has been increasing interest in extending the attributes of mind to non-sentient aspects of the physical universe.[110]

I want to talk about meaning beyond the human. And I want to enter that discussion by describing three different experiments in which there is a *boundary problem*, in the sense that it is not clear how the boundaries of the phenomena are established since they seem to depend upon the meanings of those phenomena. The first of these experiments are the non-contact healing studies with mice by William Bengston. In what follows, I trace the nuances of the reactions of the mice to the healing efforts.[111] In particular, I was struck by the fact that *some of the control mice remitted from cancer along with most of the experimental mice.* This led me to think about the idea that boundaries had somehow been established on the basis of what it meant to be in Bengston's experiments. Unable to find a "mechanistic" establishment of boundaries, it seemed to me that there could be a semantic one. The second series of experiments are the quantum eraser[112] and delayed quantum eraser experiments[113] in subatomic physics, in which a subatomic apparatus switches between two different settings without any apparent mechanical causal action between the settings. These experiments seem to face some of the same boundary problems as Bengston's experiments. Third, I describe the "Philip experiment" in which a group of people interested in anomalous phenomena created an imaginary ghost they named Philip, who then apparently interacted with them by answering their yes-or-no questions with table-raps in a manner that was consistent with their expectations. However, when the group had not predetermined the answer to a particular question, the "ghost" produced hesitant raps or scratching sounds. How is this boundary between rapping and scratching established?

The answer to the boundary problem, I propose, is the existence of *meaning fields*, which are found in reality beyond the human but interact with humans, and which have the capacity for denotative meaning and the ability to structure events within physical manifestation. I conceptualize these meaning fields as acting through, more or less, the same mechanisms through which human beings act when they are remote viewing and remote influencing. I show how such fields could explain the three series of anomalous experiments. Then I consider the possibility of connotative meaning, existential meaning, and what I will call "inherent meaning," as also existing separately from the ordinary human psyche. Throughout, I argue that it is reasonable to posit the existence of such meaning fields as a reasoning heuristic and as possibly being ontologically existent. I end with a list of their possible characteristics.

Healing Mice with Breast Cancer

We begin by looking at some of the problems posed by anomalous phenomena found by William Bengston, a sociologist who has carried out a number of studies of non-contact healing with mice. One series of four experiments involved a total of 33 mice with transplanted breast cancer. These mice typically have a 100% fatality rate within 14 to 27 days. Bengston's method was to treat the mice by placing his hands on their cages for one hour a day for one month, while using a mental technique that he has called *cycling*. Cycling consists of imagining each of the entries in a list, one after the other, from the top of the list to the bottom. The items in this previously created list are objects or situations that the person doing the cycling finds desirable. They can also include an image of celebrating a successful healing outcome. When a person gets to the bottom of the list, she goes through it again. Over time, this process becomes quicker and quicker, as well as becoming automated, so that it does not require any cognitive effort on the part of the person engaged in it.[114] What happened? The tumours became blackened, ulcerated, imploded, and then closed. Of the 33 mice, 29 were healed. That is to say, the cure rate was 88%.[115]

We shall take up the phenomenon of the actual healing in the next chapter, when we discuss various anomalous transformations of physical manifestation. What we are interested in in this chapter is how boundaries are created in reality. And to do that we consider the fact that many of the control mice, who are not supposed to be affected by experimental actions, also went into remission just as did the experimental mice. In the design of the study, there were control mice that were in the proximity of Bengston and control mice that were off-site. In the series of studies discussed here, 69% (18 of 26) of the control mice that were on-site were healed, whereas 0% (none of 8) of the control mice that were off-site were healed.[116] How is it that many of the on-site control mice remitted?

One obvious explanation is that the strain of cancer used in these experiments only sporadically kills mice. That is not true. The H2712 strain of mouse mammary adenocarcinoma tumour fragments which contain the mouse mammary tumour virus was injected into mice with host strain C3J/HeJ and strain of origin C3H/HeHu. That combination makes spontaneous tumour remissions "highly unlikely."[117]

Is it possible that the pattern of remissions of the control mice can be explained by differences in physical proximity? To answer that question, we should note that Bengston has used this method for healing at a distance. In other words, the technique appears to work even though the healer is, in some cases, hundreds of kilometres from the animal or person being healed.[118] This is not to say that in-person healing necessarily works through the same mechanism as distance healing, but it calls into question mere proximity as an explanation for the remission of the on-site control mice.

In order to answer that question, we need to look at the details of the four experiments. In Experiment 1, five mice were treated by Bengston using his technique. All five remitted. Six control mice were kept in a separate laboratory. Two of the control mice died on schedule. At that point Bengston looked at the four remaining mice in the control lab and saw that they were in the "last stages of the disease."[119] Several days afterwards, those control mice started to show the pattern of healing of the experimental mice, and all four remitted.

For Experiment 2, the healers were two faculty members, one of whom was skeptical, and two skeptical students who thought that this was an experiment about student gullibility. Over a six-week period, Bengston trained the volunteer healers. Each healer was given a cage with two mice. One of the mice died of natural causes two days into the treatment, so there were seven experimental mice. All seven experimental mice remitted. Six control mice were located in an "adjacent laboratory in the same building."[120] After two control mice had died, in spite of warnings not to do so, the skeptical faculty member looked in on the remaining four control mice each day. All four of the remaining on-site control mice remitted. This is the same result as that of Experiment 1.

In Experiment 3 there were five volunteer student healers. Two, a sociology major and a child study major, were selected by Bengston. Three were selected by an "extremely skeptical chairperson of the biology department." Each volunteer received "one mouse to treat in the laboratory and one mouse to treat at home."[121] All of the mice taken home by students remitted. "But in the laboratory, *all three of the experimental mice treated by the biology majors died within the expected time frame.* Only the sociology and child study majors were able to remit their mouse in the laboratory."[122] There were six control mice "in an adjacent laboratory in the same building."[123] After three of the control mice had died, the biology students started looking in on these mice. All three of these remaining on-site control mice remitted. Four mice were sent to another city that was unknown to Bengston or the volunteer student healers. All four of those off-site control mice died.

There were six volunteer student healers in Experiment 4, three of whom had previously participated as healers. The three new student healers were not biology majors. Each healer was given two mice. However, unknown to Bengston, one of the mice was not injected with cancer so that there were only 11 viable mice. Of those, 10 were in various stages of remission when they were sacrificed on day 38 for the purpose of carrying out histological analysis. One mouse died at day 30. There were eight on-site control mice and four off-site control mice. "Seven of eight on-site control mice, which were regularly looked in on by the student volunteers, remitted."[124] All of the off-site control mice died.

We have more evidence against a mere proximity effect. The difference is not being on-site or off-site, because the on-site mice are also in the process of dying until someone looks at them. Then they remit. Of course, while looking, whoever was doing the looking was physically closer to the mice than when that person was simply in an adjacent room, but she was not deliberately engaged in healing during the time of "looking." For the mere proximity effect to be the explanation, the healing would need to have been the result of having applied the technique in the adjacent room. But then it should have affected all of the mice equally. Also, in Experiment 3, the biology students' laboratory mice died, yet the mice in their cages were less than a foot away from the cages of the non-biology students' mice, all of which remitted.[125] If mere proximity were all that were to be required for healing to occur, then the biology students' mice would have remitted as a result of the healing applied to the non-biology students' mice. In other words, mice that were physically further from the healing remitted, whereas those that were physically closer to the healing died.

So, we have a boundary problem. How is the boundary drawn between the mice that are healed and those that died? What determines at which mouse the healing ends and is not extended to other mice in the world who could use some healing, such as other mice in the same experiment or mice in other researchers' experiments that are in physical proximity to the healers? What I suggest is the existence of *meaning fields* that understand what it means to be in the experiment and that understand the nuances of the mental states of the human participants in the experiment. But before doing so, I want to consider two other sets of anomalies in which similar problems arise.

Two-Slit Experiments

I am going to describe a series of two-slit experiments in sub-atomic physics. While the results of these experiments were predicted by quantum mechanics, they are anomalous from the point of view of our everyday understanding of reality because the events appear to follow what an observer can know about the system under observation rather than some independent mechanical process. We will begin with a simple two-slit experiment, then move to quantum eraser and delayed-choice quantum eraser experiments, and, finally, end with a remote influencing version of these experiments. Readers who do not wish to follow the details of these experiments can just skip down to the Philip experiment.

The fundamental set-up is as follows. We have photons, which are the particles that make up light, being sent one-by-one from a source of some sort toward a barrier with two closely spaced slits in it that are wide enough to allow for the passage of the photons. On the other side of the barrier is a detector that can register the impact of each of the photons after it has passed through the barrier. What we would expect is that the photons would land on the detector across from the slits. However, what is found when the experiment is carried out is that the photons land in light and dark bands. Upon examination, these bands correspond to the places at which the photons would land were the impact of the photons on the measuring device to be determined by a probability density function that can be calculated by imagining that a wave had come through the two slits and interfered with itself. In other words, we do not know what happens to a photon when it encounters the two-slit apparatus, except that it lands on the detecting device in locations that are consistent with the probabilities determined by a wave interference pattern.

Given that all particles have a *matter wave* associated with them, such interference is not limited to light but could also be demonstrated by other particles, some of which are quite large.

For instance, interference has been found with the organic molecules $C_{168}H_{94}F_{152}O_8N_4S_4$, made up of 430 atoms and having a mass of 5,310 AMU.[126] We note that *quantum interference is not confined to the subatomic realm, but intrudes into the "classical" domain as well*, given the massive size of these organic molecules, so that, for these molecules, we are not properly in the realm of the subatomic anymore.

What is at the root of this strange behaviour? Why the interference pattern? This has to do with uncertainty in quantum mechanics. If there were some way in which we could tell through which of the two slits a photon emerged, then we would find that, indeed, it did come through one or the other of the two slits, and the interference pattern would be lost. We could set this up experimentally by placing *special detectors* behind each of the slits so that we could tell through which of the slits a photon emerged. When that is done, the interference pattern does, indeed, disappear.[127]

There is a "delayed-choice" version of this experiment. We place our special detectors behind the two slits but wait until a photon has passed through the two slits before making a decision whether or not to turn the detectors on. We know how quickly the photon travels, so we know when it will have cleared the slits and wait until then before making a decision whether or not to turn on our special detectors. When we do that, we find that when the special detectors are on, we can tell through which of the slits a photon emerged, and we lose the interference pattern. When the special detectors are off, we cannot tell through which of the two slits a photon emerged, and we get an interference pattern.

There are two explanations for the delayed-choice effect. One is *retrocausation*, that future events can reach causally into the past. The other is that a photon is in a state of *superposition* so that three physical realities are present simultaneously until a measurement is made: the reality that the photon went through one of the slits; the reality that the photon went through the other of the slits; the reality of whatever it is that a photon does that results in an interference pattern. One of those three realities is somehow chosen when the photon encounters a measuring device such as one of the detectors.

Perhaps these results have nothing to do with what we can know or not know about photons passing through slits. Perhaps our special detectors are simply messing up the interference pattern. So, the idea is to get rid of them but to reproduce the effect to show that it truly is anomalous. This has been demonstrated with *quantum eraser experiments*.

Quantum Eraser Experiments

Quantum mechanics predicts that, under some conditions, when pairs of particles are created, their properties will remain correlated as they fly off in different directions. This is called *entanglement*. Furthermore, those properties are not determined at the time they fly off in separate directions[128] but, consistent with the Kochen-Specker theorem, are determined at the time a measurement is made to look for them. In particular, if we measure the value of an observable for one of the particles, we immediately know what the value of that observable is for the other of the two particles without having to measure it. This is what is meant by *nonlocality* in quantum mechanics. And it is this nonlocality that Albert Einstein famously rejected when he said that "no reasonable definition of reality could be expected to permit this."[129] The idea here is that these nonlocal properties of photons are going to be used in such a way as to replace the special detectors in the two-slit experiment.

We start with a 351.1 nm photon from an argon laser which is pumped into a beta-barium borate crystal thereby generating two 702.2 nm photons which go off at the speed of light in separate directions that we will call p and s (and refer to the photons on those paths as p and s photons, respectively). The properties of these photons are correlated. In particular, if the planar electrical field of one of them is polarized in the x direction, then we know that the other one is polarized in the y direction. Now, photon s goes down a path through a two-slit device and impacts the detector D_s. As expected, we get an interference pattern.

Here is how we determine through which of the two slits a photon emerged. We could theoretically measure the polarization of photon p, using detector D_p, to determine if it is polarized in the x direction or the y direction. Because the photons are *entangled*, we would immediately know the polarization of photon s. Now, we use that information to "mark" the s photon as it goes through the two slits so that we can tell through which of the two slits it emerged. Here is how we do that.

We place *quarter wave plates* (QWPs) in front of each of the slits so that the linearly polarized light is converted into circularly polarized light. So, suppose that the s photon is polarized in the y direction. Then QWP1 in front of slit 1 will change the photon's polarization to a right-handed polarization and QWP2 in front of slit 2 will change the photon's polarization to a left-handed polarization. If photon s is polarized in the x direction, then the circular polarization would be reversed. Now, if we were to measure the polarization of the light at D_s we could tell through which of the two slits the photon had emerged. That is to say, if we measured that photon p was polarized in the x direction and we measured a right-handed polarization at D_s, then we would know that photon s emerged from slit 1, and if we measured a left-handed polarization at D_s, then we would know that photon s emerged from slit 2. And, indeed, when we do the experiment we lose the interference pattern.

Now, we are not going to do anything to the s beam but use the fact that the photons are entangled to remove the polarization information from the s photon. We do this by placing a polarizer in front of the detector D_p which has the effect of removing the x and y orientations of the p photon and replacing them with a mixture of x and y. Hence, we no longer know the polarization of photon p and hence of photon s. *This is the quantum eraser!* The result is that we get back the interference pattern. We can move the polarizer and detector D_p back so as to increase the length of path p so that photon s has been detected before photon p encounters the polarizer cancelling out the information. That also works. The interference pattern is restored! That is the delayed-choice version of the quantum eraser.[130]

We notice that path s has not changed. There are no special detectors now behind the slits to see through which of the slits a photon emerges; just the detectors used for capturing the photons to determine their location. The only thing that has changed is our ability to tell through which of two slits a photon emerged. And the interference pattern is back, consistent with the notion that if we cannot tell through which of the two slits a photon emerged, then it will do whatever it does that creates the interference pattern. There are no conventional explanations for this phenomenon. Somehow the photons in path s know how to behave based on what eventually happens to photons in path p so as to preserve the "rules" of quantum mechanics.

But the situation is actually even stranger than this. According to quantum physicist Anton Zeilinger, "the world is not as real as we think. My personal opinion is that the world is even weirder than what quantum physics tells us."[131] So let us go a bit past conventional quantum physics.

Imagining the Two-Slit Experiments

Suppose now that instead of actually finding a physical way, however clever, to determine through which of the two slits a photon emerged, we instead just *imagine* looking at the two slits? While this could be construed as a weak form of observation,[132] we are actually in the domain of remote influencing experiments. Can we affect this particular device with our minds? I will describe three experiments that have tested this notion.

In these experiments, there was an optical system consisting of a photon gun, a barrier with two slits in it, and appropriate detectors. Participants in these experiments, who were physically isolated from the optical system, were asked to do one of two things. In the "attention-toward" condition, participants were told to "concentrate" and "focus their attention on the two slits located inside the optical system." In the "attention-away" condition, participants were told to "relax" and to remove their attention from the apparatus. In the attention-toward condition, participants listened to a "droning tone" that got louder as the interference pattern got weaker and softer as the interference pattern got stronger. The droning tone was set to a "uniformly low volume"[133] for the "attention-away" condition. In other words, auditory feedback during the attention-toward condition allowed participants to know when they were being successful at influencing the optical system in the intended direction.

Comparing the attention-toward patterns with the attention-away patterns registered by the detectors revealed large differences with a z value of $z = -6.81$. The probability of occurrence of such a large z value is less than 1 in 208 billion. During an additional control condition, without participants present, the machine ran without differences between designated attention-toward and attention-away conditions. In other words, having participants pay attention to the two-slit apparatus in their imaginations in the experimental condition was enough to attenuate the interference pattern.[134]

There is one last twist to these two-slit phenomena. In a further experiment by the same research group, by mistake, the auditory feedback to participants got reversed by the computer code controlling it, so that the tone got louder when the interference pattern got stronger and softer when the interference pattern got weaker. At the time of the experiment, the experimenters did not know that the feedback had been reversed. *The results followed the intentions of the participants.* This time interference patterns were stronger in the attention-toward condition and weaker in the attention-away condition with $z = 3.41$ ($p = .000645$, $N = 1,676$ sessions).[135] In other words, the expectations of the participants in the experiment overrode those of the experimenters.

What can we learn from these two-slit experiments? Whenever we could decipher, through whatever means, through which of two slits a particle emerges, then a particle will emerge through one or the other of the two slits. When we cannot tell through which of the two slits a particle emerges, then the particle will do whatever it does and land on the detecting screen in a manner that is consistent with an interference pattern. This occurs even if the decision to obtain or not obtain which-path information is delayed until after the particle has been detected.[136] And it occurs even if there is no physical apparatus present in the path of the particle to determine through which of two slits a particle emerged. We can also attenuate the interference pattern in a two-slit device just by paying attention to that device in our minds. These phenomena seem to be following rules about what we can know and, more generally, what we think will happen, that cannot be explained through some physical mechanism. Let us consider our third example.

The Philip Experiment

In the 1970s, the Toronto Society for Psychical Research created a fictional ghost they named "Philip." They drew a portrait of how they imagined Philip to appear and concocted an autobiography of an Englishman living in the mid-1600s. Then they sat around a "plastic-topped card table, with folding wooden legs, strengthened at the corners by metal stays," with their hands placed on top of the table, and created a light-hearted atmosphere by chatting, telling jokes, singing songs, and reciting poetry.[137] After some three or four weeks of this, the table began to move around. It would tilt, sometimes perching precariously on just two legs, and slide around the carpeted floor, sometimes with the group members trying to keep up with it. These phenomena occurred in good light and have been filmed. These table-movements could not be reproduced by the participants trying to move the table in the way that it moved spontaneously.[138]

Sometimes a rapping sound was also heard coming from the table. The members of the group set up a code so that a single rap meant "yes" and two raps meant "no."[139] When participants asked questions of "Philip" they received loud answers consistent with the fictional story they had created. If they asked a question about something that had not been unanimously decided, then there would be a delay before hearing a rap. If a question could not be answered with "yes" or "no" then they would hear scratching sounds.[140] In other words, the phenomena manifested in a manner that was consistent with the expected behaviour of Philip. Although the context is quite different in this experiment from that of the quantum eraser experiments, there is the same *dependence of the phenomena on knowledge.* Yes-or-no questions are recognized as such and answered correctly, unless the answer has not been unanimously decided.

Boundary Problems

Let us investigate these phenomena a little more deeply, first by considering William Bengston's own interpretation of events. In trying to rationalize the pattern of remission among the control mice, Bengston proposed a "hypothesis of resonant bonds." The idea is that the control mice in the experiments are "entangled" with the experimental mice receiving the treatment so that whatever happens to the experimental mice happens to the control mice. According to Bengston and Margaret Moga, "consciousness itself, including that of the experimenter, can delimit the boundaries of experimental subjects, effectively defining those who are 'in' and those who are 'out.' Those who are 'in' form something akin to a larger 'collective,' analogous to those formed by colonies of insects, flocks of birds, and schools of fish."[141]

In Experiment 1, according to Bengston, the experimenter created a resonant bond upon feeling empathy for the control mice, "so that future treatments to the experimental mice also inadvertently included treatments to the remaining controls." In other words, "resonant bonding" is created by the experimenter's thoughts. In Experiment 3, biology students could successfully induce remission in their "home" mice and the control mice, but not the mice they treated in the laboratory. To account for this, Bengston used information from the biology students' logs, which showed that they felt embarrassed and vulnerable to ridicule by their peers, to propose that such dysphoric emotions served to decouple their experimental mice from any group effects that could have been produced by the other students. We should also note that the dysphoria not only broke the resonant bonds, but also interfered directly with the biology students' abilities to heal their mice.[142]

What about the control mice sent off-site? Why did they die? Why were they not bonded? Bengston has speculated that maybe distance does matter, perhaps by creating stressors caused by the shipping that broke whatever bonds were present. Or, what I think might be more likely, the physical shipping off-site created psychological distance in the minds of the experimenters that decoupled them from the experimental mice. But Bengston has also suggested that no one who knew the healing techniques had come in contact with the off-site control mice, thereby perhaps depriving them of an opportunity to become bonded. However, "in other informal experiments there have been second control groups not known to the volunteer healer, and those mice followed the same patterns as control groups who were known to exist." In other words, in some experiments, mice unknown to the healer, which were designated as control mice by someone else, also remitted.[143]

It was when Bengston told me, during one of our conversations, about the control mouse surreptitiously placed by students within his physical proximity that I was struck by the oddity of what had happened. I started trying to understand what these data were telling us. Bengston had not known about the extra control mouse, so there was no opportunity for him to bond with her through any ordinary means. So how did the mouse end up remitting? And if she remitted without his even knowing about her, why did mice sent off-site also not remit? Why do not all mice in anyone's experiments, unrelated to non-contact healing, also not remit? I conceptualized this as a boundary problem. What is the process by which it is decided which mice heal and which mice die? Or, to express this another way, what parameters determine which mice experience the treatment and which mice do not?

A similar situation arises in subatomic physics. Lee Smolin has said that "when an atom does recognize another atom as having a similar history, it copies its properties. ... There's no need for the two atoms to be close to each other for one to copy the other's properties; they just both have to exist somewhere in the universe."[144] This raises some provocative questions: What does it mean for an atom to "recognize" another atom's properties? How is "similarity" established? What does it mean for an atom to "copy" the properties of another atom? For that matter, how does a hydrogen atom know the states of all of the other hydrogen atoms in the universe? And why do atoms get to be psychic, but not humans? And so on. In particular, we have a boundary problem. How does a hydrogen atom know to reach out to *all* of the other hydrogen atoms in the universe and not just some in its physical proximity? How is it that a single hydrogen atom somewhere in the universe does not get "missed" when some other hydrogen atom is reaching out?

In the two-slit experiment, the boundary has been clearly drawn. We can determine, in principle, through which of two slits a particle passed, or we do not have a way of telling. The boundary is knowing or not knowing. If we cannot tell, then we get an interference pattern; if we can tell, then we lose the interference pattern. *But how does a system know whether or not we can tell?* Particularly in the case of a delayed-choice quantum eraser experiment when there is no mechanical connection between the polarizers and the two-slit device? When participants affect the interference pattern by their thinking, we not only have the which-path problem, but also a problem of extent. How is it that participants are only affecting the two-slit system that they are supposed to be affecting? Why are they not affecting other two-slit systems that have nothing to do with the experiment in which they find themselves? And why are they limited to two-slit devices? Why are they not also affecting, for example, the brains of the experimenters, or the brains of people living on the other side of the planet? What establishes the boundary of their influence? These are not frivolous questions, as we shall see in Chapter 4, "Planetary Transformation."

In the Philip experiment, there is a clearly defined boundary between "yes" and "no" for questions that have previously been decided. The table raps gave the correct answers. From where did the table raps emanate? And how did that source know the answers? How was that source able to recognize the difference between a "yes-or-no" question and one that was not? How did it know to rap the card table and not something else in some other room? And why rapping and scratching instead of, say, melodious tones or sweet fragrances?

Morphic Fields

In a nonlocal universe, there needs to be a way of keeping track of where things end and, having established where they end, of determining what goes on which side of the boundary. There is a candidate for such structuring that seems to be on the right track, namely Rupert Sheldrake's *morphic fields*, which apply to all self-organizing systems. Morphic fields impose "patterns on otherwise random events in the systems under their influence" and are "shaped by morphic resonance from all similar past systems" so that they "contain a cumulative collective memory."[145] *Morphic resonance* refers to the entanglement of self-organizing systems with similar systems that have existed in the past in such a way that what has happened previously guides subsequent behaviour. For example:

When an orb-web spider starts spinning its web, it follows the habits of countless ancestors, resonating with them directly across space and time. The more people who learn a new skill, such as snowboarding, the easier will it be for others to learn it because of morphic resonance from previous snowboarders.[146]

So, we have morphic fields that structure the behaviour of self-organizing systems.

Can the theory of morphic fields explain the data that we are considering here? No. There are several problems. The first is that, for all that they are "fields," morphic fields are still "mechanical," in the sense that they operate through automatic processes. In a critique of Sheldrake's theory, Stephen Braude has pointed out two substantial problems that arise from the mechanistic nature of the theory. The first is a parsing problem. As Braude has said elsewhere:

We can't attribute a structure to nature (or history)—that is, slice it into elements (or events)—apart from a background of activities within which certain things (rather than others) matter to us. Without the perspective which those activities provide, nothing about nature or history intrinsically stands out from anything else. ... But then meaningful relations ... presuppose a perspective, a contingent background of activities, needs, and interests, from which certain things (rather than others) matter to us and stand out as relevant.[147]

In other words, nature cannot identify snowboarding as snow-boarding; that is something that human beings do. The second problem is that of establishing similarity. How does a self-organizing system come under the influence of its appropriate morphic field? How is the entanglement of morphic resonance formed? The problem is that there are no absolute guidelines for what constitutes similarity, so there is no effective mechanism of associating self-organizing systems with their morphic fields.[148]

Even without these two problems, the theory of morphic resonance cannot account for the selective remission of experimental and control mice in Bengston's experiments.[149] In particular, it appears as though membership in a particular group is not established by the mice through morphic resonance with other mice directly, but by the intentions and behaviours of humans who are handling the mice, who appear to allow for resonant bonding to occur between experimental and control mice and, possibly, between the healers and the experimental and control mice.[150]

Braude has also pointed out the need to "rule out the rival hypothesis of experimenter expectancy effects"[151] in Sheldrake's experiments. There is considerable evidence in the remote influencing literature that experimenters' conscious or nonconscious attitudes can affect the outcomes of experiments. This can take place through one or both of two mechanisms: psychological and anomalous. For example, psychological influence could be exerted on participants in a study through "subtle cues that create demand characteristics" thereby changing performance.[152] But there can also be anomalous effects by experimenters on the outcomes of experiments. The idea is that anyone who comes in contact with the study, as it is ongoing or in the future, even by just reading about it in an academic journal, could be contributing to the outcome.[153] Again, there are boundary problems. How are experimenter effects confined to the appropriate studies? Braude's criticism is consonant with the problems that we have identified here.

Meaning Fields

I want to gather together some of the ideas that we have considered. First, from William Bengston's experiment, the notion that the healed mice all somehow belong to the same collective. And from the theory of morphic fields we can use the idea of a field to define that collective. Second, from the quantum eraser experiments, we see that reality reliably acts in a way that is consistent with what can be known, even when there are no mechanical ways of accounting for that action. This suggests that reality has some way of tracking knowledge. Third, from the Philip experiment, we see clearly that fictional ideas created by human beings can be taken up by reality and fed back as poltergeist activity that is consistent with those ideas. Putting all of this together, I propose that there exist *meaning fields* in reality, which have the capacity for denotative meaning, which interact with human meanings, and which structure events within physical manifestation.

Let us unpack this. I think of meaning fields as formal fields, such as quantum fields, so that they are defined at each point in space and apparent time. They are necessarily nested and interrelated as different meaning fields can apply to the same phenomena. As fields they can be regarded as a reasoning heuristic whose ontological status remains unknown. Or, they can be taken as actually existent, perhaps as actual existent "beings," in which case nature could have some of the properties of mind. Even without positing actual existence to meaning fields, the use of meaning fields as a reasoning heuristic already strongly suggests that nature could be mindful. By "nature" I simply mean reality as it occurs in the *nows*, including both subjective events and physical manifestation. The word "nature" has connotations of reality beyond the strictly human, so I find it convenient to use in this context.

I am going to rely on a tuning metaphor for associating meaning fields with particular phenomena. In other words, events are tuned to a particular meaning field. Such tuning requires that nature be able to parse reality. How can that be done? From the three examples that I have given, human parsing has already occurred, so we can simply suppose that nature has the ability to use our parsing. Similarly, for these three examples, humans have already determined what it is that is being affected, so that the meaning fields have already been tuned to these phenomena. But not all events, apparently, result from human invention, so I want to posit that nature has a self-sufficient capacity to parse without the need for human parsing. Later in the discussion, I will offer some ideas as to how this could occur. Nature can also use our representations, even those that are symbolic or idiosyncratic. Let me explain how I extrapolate the likely presence of this occurrence from dream research.

The expression *dream architect* is sometimes used to designate whatever implicit psychological processes create the multisensory content of dreams. Sometimes people dream at various times during the night, so there are mechanisms that generate whatever it is that occurs in dreams. There is only a loose connection between actual events that have occurred in a person's life and what appears in her dreams.[154] So whatever the psychological processes are that modify actual events and fabricate additional ones as dream contents can be called the "dream architect." But the dream architect does not concoct material unilaterally. There is an interplay between ourselves as conscious agents and the productions of our dream architects. In particular, dream architects can take cues from us about what to present and how to do it. The following is one example of that.

As a doctoral student, I became disillusioned with the process of academic publication. It seemed to me that frequently papers of high quality (well-written, with interesting ideas in them) would be rejected for publication, whereas papers of low quality (poorly written, with nothing of substance in them) would end up getting published. I came to regard academic publishing as a lottery in which the quality of one's work was irrelevant. The point here is not whether my attitude was supported by facts or not, but that my dream architect picked up this whimsical notion to give me information in my dreams about the publication of my papers and books. For instance, I was trying to find a publisher for one of my books, when I had a dream of buying a winning lottery ticket with an expiration date of October 17. I interpreted this dream as a precognitive dream about the book in which the date on the ticket represented the date on which I would receive an offer to publish the book. And, indeed, a year and a month later, on October 17, that is what happened.[155]

There are several comments that I want to make about this example. First, by itself, this dream does not prove anything. Systematic studies of precognitive dreaming have resulted in demonstrating its existence[156] but that does not mean that this was necessarily a precognitive dream. Given my history of precognitive dreaming, it is likely. However, it is also possible that the correct date resulted not from precognition but from the experimenter effect. In other words, having had a date show up in my dreams, I managed to nonconsciously finagle reality into complying with that date through remote influencing. But let us continue as though the dream were precognitive.

Second, the dream architect is using the lottery imagery to convey information about the publication of a book, indicating that the psyche has the ability to use idiosyncratic symbols that are meaningful to a specific individual.

Third, the dream architect appears to have access to information that is outside the psyche itself, in that the occurrence of the events referenced in the dream are interactions with another person that lie in the future. In a nonlocal universe, our psyches are leaky, so that they are already interacting with events that are external to themselves. My extrapolation is that meaning is embodied not only in the psyche but also in nature beyond the human during these interactions. In the same way that the dream architect plays along with a person by presenting her with dreams using imagery that she understands, so nature plays along with people through meaning fields that use the denotative meanings that we understand.

Fourth, if the psychodynamics of dream imagery carries over to meaning fields, then, on the basis of this example, they are not just arrays of information, but embody the capacity for understanding. There is a degree of intelligence manifested by the whimsical representation of the publication process as a lottery based on my irreverent attitude. But such understanding implies access to associations between publication and lotteries that imply the capacity for connotative meaning. So, let us say that, in addition to denotative meaning, meaning fields have the capacity for a wider range of significance beyond discrete representations.

How is any of this supposed to make sense? Meaning fields do not have sensory organs with which to sense anything, so how would they be able to perceive what a person is thinking? And how would they be able to know anything? Or to affect anything? The answer to these questions lies in understanding that human beings already have the capacity for remote viewing and remote influencing. Furthermore, the brain is optional, in that, sometimes, human beings appear to be able to engage in these activities when their brains are compromised. In fact, these are probably not primarily brain activities anyway.[157] So, the contention here is that meaning fields have the same capabilities that are implied in remote viewing and remote influencing.

To illustrate the type of knowledge that could be obtained through remote viewing without sensory organs, I want to bring in some research about near-death experiences of the blind. A man who "had been blind from birth maintained that he could clearly see billions of books in a library" during his near-death experience.[158] Of course, his brain had never been developed for processing visual information, so how was he able to "see?" And how could he identify books as books given that he had never seen what a book looked like? Kenneth Ring and Sharon Cooper, the authors of the study, used the expression *transcendental aware-ness* to refer to the type of seeing that occurs during near-death experiences, which appears to be part seeing and part just knowing.[159] The contention here is that meaning fields have at least the same capability for transcendental awareness as a blind person.

Let me go through the three examples now in reverse order to illustrate how meaning fields would apply to them. In the Philip experiment, creating a fictional ghost leads to the creation of a meaning field that contains the information about Philip. But because the members of the Toronto Society for Psychical Research are interested in producing a manifestation of Philip, they are also tuned to the meaning fields that govern poltergeist activity. So, the table moves and Philip "speaks" through raps and scratches, giving correct answers to yes-or-no questions.

The participants in the Philip experiment discussed the concept of *thought-forms*, nonphysical entities that can ostensibly be created by thoughts. They also discussed an extension of the notion of thought-forms, that of *tulpas* — entities, usually in human form, that are presumably created by thoughts and that can be seen objectively by others. The idea is that usually thought-forms are generated inadvertently, simply through the process of thinking. But they can also be created deliberately[160] such as in the case of Philip. Philip can be regarded as a *tulpa* created by the participants in the experiment who then interacted with them.[161] In other words, one of the ways that the participants in the experiment conceptualized what was happening was that they were interacting with an objective entity. This would be consistent with the notion of Philip being a meaning field.

For the two-slit experiments, we can conceptualize a meaning field that holds the rule that which-path knowledge would destroy the interference pattern so that a two-slit device performs as expected. We note that information from the future can determine what happens earlier. How did this rule arise? Well, quantum mechanics was a theory invented by human beings, so the rule could have arisen with the advent of the theory. It is not clear in this case whether the rule could have already been in place prior to its development, since it is a rule about human knowledge. If it did, then this would be an example of a self-sufficient meaning field.

In the case of just imagining the two slits in the two-slit experiment, the behaviour of the two-slit device follows the feedback given to participants both when reducing interference, even though there is no known physical interaction with the system, consistent with the rule (decreasing interference) and experimenter effects (decreasing interference); as well as when increasing interference, contrary to the rule (decreasing interference) and contrary to experimenter effects (decreasing interference). It should be noted that the effect size in these experiments is only about 0.001% of the potential variability, so that the rule is, for the most part, preserved.[162] This result reveals a possible parameter for the expression of meaning fields, namely that meaning fields associated with psychokinetic influence can modify the meaning fields associated with quantum mechanical rules, probably depending upon additional parameters concerning the strength of the psychokinetic effect. In summary, then, whereas in the Philip experiment the Philip meaning field was created by the participants and worked consistently for them, in the imagined two-slit experiment, the participants were only able to modify slightly the meaning field for the which-path rule that already existed prior to their efforts.

There is a meaning field for William Bengston's experiments that determines the boundaries of which mice are healed and which are not. But here there is a more complex interplay of the fields with the attitudes and intentions of the various human beings who are involved in these experiments. When Bengston heals the experimental mice, on-site control mice frequently remit if they are somehow part of the experiment. The biology students were nervous about healing mice in the biology laboratory, so they damped the healing effect in the lab. The meaning fields patterned an outcome based on some weighting of the different parameters affecting the experiment. Such weighting need not be computational but could involve a form of judgment with or without computation.[163]

Transcendent Meaning

Thus far we have considered meaning fields starting from three specific series of experiments and tried to rationalize meaning fields as a way of explaining the anomalous results of those experiments. I have tried to motivate their existence from the empirical data, from the bottom up. Let me reverse the order now and consider meaning fields from the top down, which is to say, from the point of view of theory.

The foundational element of a materialist theory is the stuff of the universe from which everything is made. Usually we think of this stuff as being inertial, with considerable pushing and pulling being required to change anything. Remote influencing is a nightmare for the materialist. How can an ephemeral epiphenomenon such as the mind push and pull real stuff? It does not make any sense, so it is easier to reject the whole notion that remote influencing can occur in the first place. In contrast, by the flicker theory, the stuff of the universe is ephemeral. It appears and disappears, over and over again. So now we have the opposite problem. Instead of wondering how anything can change, we can wonder how anything can possibly stay the same. When a *now* emerges from the prephysical substrate, why should it have any of the contents of a *now* that occurred previously in deep time?

Let me propose that the answer is meaning fields. Or rather, given that meaning fields are defined on space and apparent time, which are within physical manifestation, we want the implicate version of meaning fields. So, let us just call those *implicate meanings*. It is the implicate meanings that hold the structure in the prephysical substrate for the shape that each *now* takes. This allows us to explain the stability of physical manifestation from *now* to *now* but to also explain its overall *instability*. For instance, the physical constants, such as the fine structure constant, one of the constants in quantum electrodynamics, are supposed to stay the same, yet there is evidence that they have changed over the course of time.[164] If physical manifestation is essentially just a sequence of momentary appearances, then the so-called "physical constants" can wobble around as much as they like. And, in fact, this theory allows for the appearance of the subatomic particle zoo that has sprung up over the last century. But this notion of

implicate meanings also gives a way of explaining radical transformations, where there are dramatic changes over short periods
of time; namely, by proposing that one implicate meaning has
been substituted for another. We will see examples of these types
of phenomena in Chapter 3, "Anomalous Transformations of
Physical Manifestation."

From a subjective point of view, the prephysical substrate is
the deep consciousness that can be accessed in a transcendent
state of consciousness. It is a nondual state in which the
intentional subject–object structure of the mind is no longer
operative. It is important to note that deep consciousness is not an
aspect of human consciousness in the ordinary waking state, but
that consciousness in the ordinary waking state is a filtered
version of deep consciousness. Furthermore, human beings are
not necessarily the only beings whose consciousness originates
from the deep consciousness. It is not clear who or what those
are,[165] but we could use the analogy with dark matter and dark
energy[166] to conceptualize the idea that there could be other
beings out there of whom we know little.

For Franklin Wolff, there is a faculty of knowledge, which he
called *introception*, that he said becomes activated upon
transitioning to a nondual state. Introception is not introspection,
which is usually conceptualized as having a subject–object
structure, although, as we shall see in Chapter 5, "Radical Self-
Transformation," it is not at all clear what introspection entails.
Introception, according to Wolff, is direct knowledge through
identification with that which is known without a subject–object
structure.

Franklin Wolff has also made a distinction between "meaning"
in the denotative sense of pointing to a referent and "meaning" in
the sense in which a concept can enrobe an "inner Significance."[167]
For Wolff, that inner significance can be known directly through
introception. In fact, for Wolff, we can abstract meaning from a
concept to the point where "thought ... deals with a disembodied
Meaning."[168] For Wolff, there are transcendent states of

consciousness that we can enter in which new ways of knowing become available to us. In those states, meaning is no longer tied to concepts, which belong to the realm of duality, but has now become disembodied. Upon embodiment, such disembodied meaning can be conceptualized as that which suffuses concepts with inherent significance. So, let us say that another meaning of "meaning" is that of *inherent meaning*, the presence of inherent significance within cognition.

Do implicate meanings have inherent significance? If they do, then their explication as meaning fields could carry their inherent significance with them. In other words, if implicate meanings are suffused with inherent significance, then explication could result in meaning fields with inherent meaning. As a consequence, meaning fields could have self-sufficient parsing that would allow them to structure physical manifestation. In that case, alongside Eduardo Kohn in the epigraph to this chapter, we could propose that humans understand meanings because nature understands meanings.

We have considered denotative meaning, connotative meaning, and inherent meaning. There is one more meaning that I would like to consider, namely *existential meaning*. We began this chapter with a quotation from Christof Koch in which he has expressed his intuition that "the universe is filled with meaning."[169] This is a different sense of "meaning" — existential meaning, perhaps, or purposiveness. Does nature beyond the human embody existential meaning? Possibly. If meaning fields have denotative and connotative meaning, then perhaps the understanding associated with such fields is suffused with qualia. If such qualia extend to existential qualia, then the issue of existential meaning could arise in nature beyond the human. And it would make sense to posit the possibility of the presence of existential meaning for meaning fields.

What is the relationship between denotative, connotative, inherent, and existential meaning? For a particular person, denotative and connotative meanings are usually simply an aspect of the ordinary waking state whereby an implicit understanding of concepts is used in order to negotiate one's way through reality. Inherent meaning lends significance to our understanding of reality. And personal existential meaning can be present in varying degrees. For those tending toward a conservatively transcendent position, it is consciousness itself that gives meaning to reality. So, for some people, the existence of existential qualia endows existence with existential meaning. For nature beyond the human, we have established, at least functionally, that meaning fields embody denotative and connotative meanings. Possibly also inherent meaning. And possibly meaning fields experience existential qualia and hence also embody existential meaning.

Characteristics of Meaning Fields

We started this chapter with the results of three different series of experiments that call attention to a boundary problem that exists in a nonlocal universe. Through inductive reasoning, I proposed that the boundary problem could be solved by positing the existence of meaning fields. The following is a summary of the characteristics of the proposed meaning fields.

1. *Fields.* Meaning fields are fields defined at each point in space and apparent time and potentially apply to whatever is in that space at that time.
2. *Capacity for nonlocal interactions.* Meaning fields acquire knowledge and affect reality with at least the same ability as human beings do through remote viewing and remote influencing.
3. *Denotative meaning.* Meaning fields have the capacity for denotative meaning, which is to say that meaning fields are able to distinguish between specific events on the basis of the meanings of those events.
4. *Interaction with human meanings.* Meaning fields can interact directly with human meanings so that the effects of different

human beings on a meaning field are weighted in some manner that could involve meaning fields making judgments.

5. *Structure events.* Meaning fields structure the form that events take.

6. *Interrelatedness.* Meaning fields are interrelated both in that they can overlap as well as be nested.

7. *Ontologically undetermined.* Meaning fields can be regarded as a reasoning heuristic for describing whatever processes occur in reality that subsume their function, or they can be regarded as actually existent in some nonphysical domain.

8. *Tuning metaphor.* Events can be tuned to different meaning fields that can guide their structure. Where humans are involved, the initial match-up is made using human meanings.

9. *Temporal displacement.* The content of meaning fields can be modified by apparent events from the apparent past or the apparent future.

10. *Connotative meaning.* Meaning fields have the capacity for connotative meaning, which is to say that they have the capacity for holding rich sets of associations to denotative meanings, and which further allows them to parse events.

11. *Implicate meanings.* The implicate version of meaning fields in the prephysical substrate are implicate meanings.

12. *Inherent meaning.* It is possible that implicate meanings have inherent significance, which implies that the explication of implicate meanings as meaning fields could suffuse meaning fields with inherent significance with an additional capacity for parsing that allows them to act within physical manifestation.

13. *Existential meaning.* It is possible that meaning fields embody existential qualia and existential meaning.

This is a brief summary of the characteristics of meaning fields. I have published an even briefer synopsis elsewhere.[170] I have also gone on to incorporate the theory of meaning fields into a mathematical model of the flicker theory, which also has been published elsewhere.[171]

The theory of meaning fields raises as many questions as it answers. For instance, what exactly are the parameters that determine the strength of a meaning field? How exactly is tuning between meaning fields accomplished by humans? How does non-human tuning occur? And so on. At least we have a heuristic for moving forward. But perhaps we have a lot more, in that nature could be richly endowed with meaning, as we shall consider again in Chapter 5, "Radical Self-Transformation."

I want to return now to the obvious anomaly with which we began this chapter — that of mice remitting from cancer in non-contact healing experiments. We can regard these as anomalous transformations, in that these events do not follow a conventionally predicted pattern. But such remission is just the tip of an iceberg. In the next chapter, I bring to the surface a disparate array of such transformations that will strengthen the evidence for the existence of meaning fields and the utility of the flicker theory as an explanatory scheme.

Chapter 3

Anomalous Transformations of Physical Manifestation

We are all agreed ... that your theory is crazy. The question which divides us is whether it is crazy enough to have a chance of being correct. My own feeling is that it is not crazy enough.[172]

Physical reality does not always behave the way we assume that it should. Rather, what happens seems to be tied to what happens in our minds. In particular, remote influencing sometimes occurs. We have already seen several examples of this. In Chapter 2, "Meaning Beyond the Human," we saw that mice were healed through non-contact healing, a two-slit optical device was deflected in the direction of intention, and a card table moved around. I proposed the notion of meaning fields to assist us in conceptualizing the boundaries of such phenomena and, in some cases, to help us to understand them. But, in general, the mechanisms for the occurrence of these phenomena remain unknown. The purpose of this chapter is to look at more examples of anomalous transformations, to look at some possible explanations for them, including the theory of meaning fields and the flicker theory, and then to discuss a particular system of deliberately creating effects. The examples I have chosen have been well documented and are unlikely to be the result of lying, cheating, or mental illness. I am deliberately pushing the edge of consciousness research outward as far as possible in order to see what such phenomena can reveal about the nature of reality.

I use the expression *anomalous transformation* for events that appear to break with our usual notions of the way in which reality works. If the transformations are abrupt, or particularly dramatic, I use the expression *radical transformation*. Conventional labelling is confusing and overlapping but here are some of the terms that have been used for these types of phenomena. Some of these events could be labelled as poltergeist or psychokinetic phenomena. *Poltergeist phenomena* are physical phenomena such as the spontaneous movement of objects, appearance and disappearance of objects, the occurrence of unexplained noises, or somatic effects such as scratches on the skin that are sometimes associated with discarnate entities.[173] *Psychokinetic phenomena* can be defined as "the causal influence of an organism on a region *r* of the physical world, without any currently recognized physical interaction between the organism's body and *r*."[174] For instance, the example of influencing the two-slit optical device could be labelled as psychokinesis, in particular *micro-psychokinesis* (micro-pk), since subatomic processes are ostensibly being affected. *Macro-psychokinesis* (macro-pk) refers to effects that are "large enough, or strong enough, to be apparent to the physical senses,"[175] although the distinction between micro-pk and macro-pk is somewhat arbitrary.[176] Let me start by reviewing a historical case of levitation; then some laboratory experiments of macro-pk; some examples of dematerialization; then materialization of biological organisms; and, finally, a field study of large-scale macro-pk. I consider all of these under the rubric of "anomalous transformation" with the understanding that the mechanisms underlying them could turn out to be quite different.

Macro-PK

We already considered partial levitation in the context of the Philip experiment in Chapter 2, "Meaning Beyond the Human." Here I want to start by considering a historical case of apparent full levitation that has been described and analysed by philosopher Michael Grosso, who has been lauded for his careful scholarship.[177] St. Joseph of Copertino was a Catholic monk living from 1603 to 1663 for whom various anomalous phenomena would ostensibly occur on a regular basis, including levitation. (Given the quality of documentation for this case, I will suspend the use of descriptors of tentativeness, such as "ostensibly," "apparently," and so on, with the understanding that any eyewitness description that anyone gives could be erroneous.) As reported by those who attended mass, St. Joseph would frequently levitate three or four times during a single mass on a daily basis. He was witnessed to have reached a height of 30 metres and remained aloft for up to 30 minutes. For instance, in one case, he landed on the branch of an olive tree from which he had to be rescued by a priest with a ladder. These levitations appeared to cause shame and embarrassment for St. Joseph and, as a result of the public spectacles that they caused, cost him the right to celebrate mass in public. Eyewitness evidence of levitation by St. Joseph was publicly recorded over 70 times in Grotella, Italy. Witnesses have also described his levitations in "Assisi, Rome, Naples, Perugia, Osimo, Fossombrone, and Pietrarubbia."[178] There is also relevant testimony from the time that St. Joseph was brought before the inquisition for lack of humility.

Preceding his levitations, St. Joseph's subjective state was one of absorption in "some heavenly scene, state, or personage"[179] leading to "a taste of the true glory of paradise" during his "ecstacies."[180] For witnesses, St. Joseph appeared with "eyes upturned, body insensible to witnesses poking, burning, stinging, or pushing various parts of his body. ... Joseph's body appeared *as if it were dead* — cold, stiff, unresponsive."[181] It was as though ordinary reality had been suspended for a while. "The space around Joseph during ecstasy seemed to freeze or bracket ordinary physical constraints like gravity, combustion, pain, atmospheric effects, mechanical damage, and so on."[182] The symbolism of St. Joseph's maxim, "Raise my soul, raise it high!" was literally played out in physical manifestation.[183] And because of the religious and cultural views of 1600s Italy, such behaviour did not create the concern that it would create in our contemporary Western culture. Even at the inquisition, the fact of St. Joseph's levitations was not questioned, just whether they "were signs of divine or diabolic influence."[184] What is going on here?

One way to think about what is happening is to think of this as though there were the superposition of a dream-like reality onto the ordinary waking state. St. Joseph was behaving as though he were in a dream while those observing him were in an ordinary waking state:

> he floats in the air, not a ruffle in his clothing, his feet resting in tapering flames, people jabbing his ribs as a fly crawls on his glazed eye, his arms outstretched in bliss; meanwhile outside the bubble waking people are moving about confusedly, understandably startled by what they see.[185]

Of course, the idea that a bubble of dream events has become inserted into the ordinary waking state is just an alternative description, rather than an explanation, of these phenomena.

The example with St. Joseph is a historical case study, so let us now consider a laboratory example of macro-pk. In a laboratory, from a distance of 5 or 6 feet, Suzanne Padfield apparently had the ability to move a light mobile hanging inside a glass bottle mounted on a vibration-free platform. She was able to demonstrate this successfully about 70% of the time usually once a week over the course of nine years before multiple observers. Either she or an experimenter would state the direction and degrees of rotation before she tried to move the mobile. These results were replicated at Stanford Research Institute where she could only see the apparatus on a closed-circuit television monitor in a room separate from herself. With regard to her subjective experience, Padfield has stated, "I must emphasize here that I feel myself to be a part of these processes and these events and not in any way separate from them. I am a part of the events, of the sequences, not merely observing them."[186]

Similarly, in an experiment at the Institute for Parapsychology in Durham, North Carolina, Felicia Parise was able to deflect a compass needle. The compass had been placed in a magnetic field detector, which was "connected to an audio oscillator" and placed on top of a "carefully sealed packet of unexposed photographic film" on a chair in front of Felicia. Over the course of two minutes, there was a change in "the sound frequency of the magnetic field detector, which finally shattered completely as the compass needle reached its maximum deflection of 15 degrees." Even after Felicia had stopped concentrating on it, "the needle remained 15 degrees off north ... [and] was totally unresponsive to either a knife blade or a bar magnet placed directly over its surface." When the compass was moved about four feet from the chair, it returned to true north and was "normally affected by the knife blade." When it was moved back to the chair, it deflected again through 15 degrees and could not be influenced by the knife or the magnet. "The needle gradually returned to north, over a period of almost half an hour, and was then normally responsive to the knife blade." The film on the chair "was found to be almost totally exposed."[187]

In these two laboratory examples we have objects that appear to have been moved as a result of the intentions of people who appear to have the ability to create the necessary movement. In the case of Felicia, not only was the compass affected, but also a magnetic field detector and photographic film. It is interesting to note that there was a region of space in which the effects created by Felicia persisted, just as there seemed to be a region of space, including his clothing, that seemed to be suspended from the conventional laws of physics during St. Joseph's levitations. Let me consider yet more dramatic forms of transformation.

Dematerialization and Materialization

There was a range of phenomena that occurred in the course of the Scole experiment, in which there was ostensible communication with discarnate entities. In particular, there appeared to be an instance of dematerialization. The Scole experiment is a complex case which has created considerable debate about what did or did not happen, as do all of these cases, but we will just focus on one particular event for which there is good eyewitness testimony from reliable observers.

A number of sessions were held in a cellar room in a house in Scole, England, from 1993 to 1998, by two mediums, who would go into a full trance, and two other people, who managed the activities that took place. Three investigators from the Society for Psychical Research—Montague Keen, Arthur Ellison, and David Fontana—joined them for 36 sessions from October 2, 1995 to August 16, 1997, although not all three were necessarily present for all of those sessions. The investigators experienced a range of unusual phenomena, such as lights, sounds, touches, images on film, and so on. These events occurred in the "dark," and infrared filming was not allowed. However, the room was sometimes illuminated by points of light that zipped around the room and sometimes apparently through the investigators' bodies as judged by the occurrence of "internal sensations."[188]

During a session on November 9, 1996, a light settled on a crystal that was "about four inches long," irradiating the crystal, which then levitated and "descended into a Pyrex semi-translucent bowl" where the investigators could see it.[189] The following is Montague Keen's account of what happened next:

> Then Arthur Ellison, sitting on my right, was invited to pick it up. He picked it up and satisfied himself that it was there, and it was glowing, and he put it down again. He was asked right

away to pick it up again. He picked it up, or he tried to, and
his fingers closed right over it. In other words, he could see,
and we could see, the essence of it, but not the reality of it. It
had been dematerialized. Then he was asked to pick it up
again and it rematerialized in his hand. Now, this dumb-
founded him. This is what Arthur Ellison, after years and
years of investigation, finally convinced him that this was real,
because it couldn't have been faked in any way. And he had
his head right over the top of the bowl in order to ensure that
no hand or no instrument could interfere with it. Then the
experiment was repeated, because I wanted to do the same
thing, I could hardly believe it. And exactly the same thing
happened with me. And then on my left was David Fontana,
and Professor Fontana insisted on having his go, too, and it
was repeated a second time.[190]

That is to say, in each case, at one point the crystal could be seen,
but apparently had no tactile substance.

The following is a possible case of apparent dematerialization
of biological material. Anita Moorjani was dying of lymphoma, a
type of cancer. She used an oxygen tank in order to breathe; she
had to remain upright so as not to drown in her own bodily
fluids; there were skin lesions covering her body; she rarely slept;
she could not absorb any nutrients through her digestive system
so that she lost weight and acquired a skeletal appearance; her
muscles failed; and she could not walk. Finally, she went into a
coma and her husband was told that there was nothing further
that could be done to save her.[191]

During this time of extremis, Anita was having a near-death
experience in which she felt that she had awakened into an
expanded consciousness that was at the root of her physical
expression. Furthermore, she was convinced that if she came back
to life, her body would be healed. "I understood that my body is
only a reflection of my internal state. If my inner self were aware
of its greatness and connection with All-that-is, my body would

soon reflect that and heal rapidly."[192] And, indeed, there was a 70% reduction in the size of her tumours over the next several days. This puzzled Peter Ko (a physician who subsequently investigated her case using hospital records) given that her internal organs would have been incapable of processing that many cancer cells, given their deteriorated state.[193] What happened? Did the cancer cells "just" dematerialize? "Just" disappear?

The opposite can also occur. We can have the materialization of living organic material. Perhaps the most striking cases are those ostensibly produced by Thomaz Green Morton Souza Coutinho who, at one time, lived in Brazil. Apparently Thomaz hatched baby chicks from infertile chicken eggs. The first of four such instances occurred in 1982, witnessed by several people including a judge, a physician, a psychiatrist, and an American journalist. We have seven black and white photographs of the sequence of events as well as a written account. Gary Richman, the American journalist, investigated Thomaz by living and travelling with him for over eight months, interviewing 200 people, 90% of whom had personally witnessed phenomena produced by Thomaz, and "scrutinized the surroundings for alternative causal mechanisms." No evidence of trickery was ever found.[194]

On the first occasion in 1982, Thomaz asked to have 15 eggs brought to him from the market. Once he received them, he appeared to enter an altered state of consciousness with eyes open but unfocused. He picked up and stared at each egg, then held it before his forehead, then put it back down. Following that, he cracked each and emptied it into a flat bowl. His chest became "puffed" and his face became "taut and crimson" as he hyperventilated and stretched his arms out with "palms down over the eggs." Within five minutes, the "fetal forms of baby chicks could be identified."[195] At seven minutes, "the internal organs of the embryos could be seen through thin membranes." At nine minutes could be heard the cheeping of baby chicks. Altogether nine of the 15 eggs hatched, four survived for more than three days, and a couple of the chicks from the four demonstrations continued to live in the yard until they were eaten for dinner.[196]

Thomaz was ostensibly able to produce a wide range of phenomena. Let me give an example that is in keeping with the levitation theme with which we opened this chapter. On March 17, 1979, Thomaz asked his friend Zanata "to find a lime and place it on a small table." Then Zanata was asked to "take a coin out of his pocket and place it next to the lime." With closed eyes and outstretched arms, Thomaz began vibrating. The "ten centavo coin began to levitate" rising several centimetres from the tabletop and then imploding into the lime without leaving any trace of its insertion.

> The astonishment and perplexity of the four observers were predictable. Finding no marks of any kind on the surface of the lime, Zanata sliced the fruit in half. Embedded in the center was the ten centavo piece, as if an invisible sword of consciousness had silently sectioned away another cherished version of reality.[197]

In Anita Moorjani's case, we have the egress of cancer cells from a human body, without leaving any apparent trace, whereas in this ostensible case of insertion, we have the ingress of a coin into the centre of a fruit without leaving any visible trace.

We can contrast these changes in biological systems to William Bengston's non-contact healing studies from Chapter 2, "Meaning Beyond the Human." In Bengston's experiments, the mice's immune systems seemed to be enhanced through some unknown mechanism, triggering the remission of the tumours. Here there are more dramatic changes, in that organic material seems to simply disappear. The chicken hatching episode is particularly puzzling, given that there is not just the rapid appearance of appropriate cells, but their appearance in the proper temporal and structural sequence so as to allow for the normal expression of life. We could say that a meaning field for the ordinary development of chickens has been accessed but accessed in such a way that its temporal dimension has been contracted. And, as in the case of St. Joseph, that altered reality has been interjected into the ordinary waking state in such a way that the events belonging to it are sensorially available to those who are in its vicinity.

Large-Scale Macro-PK

Let us conclude this list of examples by considering the large-scale macro-pk phenomena associated with Ted Owens, who lived from 1920 to 1987. Ted Owens called himself the "PK Man" and could apparently create large-scale macro-pk phenomena on demand, such as lightning strikes, weather changes, and erratic behaviour of sports teams. He was investigated by a number of psychologists, physicists, and others, but most notably by psychologist Jeffrey Mishlove,[198] who wrote a book about him. According to Mishlove, as of 1976, Owens would announce all of his predictions to Mishlove in advance of his "demonstrations."[199] Mishlove's "personal assessment" has been that "about a third to two-thirds of Owens' statements seem to have been more or less supported by the facts,"[200] with odds against chance of that occurring possibly being "less than one in a billion."[201]

For instance, on June 1, 1977 Owens had warned the police chief of Cape Charles, Virginia, that he was going to bring a hurricane to the area. On June 6, it was sunny out mid-afternoon when it suddenly got dark and a storm unexpectedly hit the Virginia Coast.

> Boats were sunk in the Chesapeake Bay, radar screens were blanked out, TV broadcasts were interrupted, and even airplanes parked on airstrips were blown over. Hailstones the size of golf balls pelted the ground, while ninety-eight-mile-per-hour winds whirled over the Bay and ripped into Virginia. The storm, which struck without warning, was so severe that it left five dead in its wake.[202]

According to Mishlove, the police chief "confirmed this event and verified the content and timing of Owens' advance warning."[203]

Is this actually macro-pk or just precognition on the part of Owens? Is Owens just taking credit for something that he knew precognitively would occur anyway? That is possible. However, some evaluations of Owens' "demonstrations" fall on the side of macro-pk. Why? Here is one reason. Ted Owens believed that he was in contact with "space intelligences (SIs)" who he claimed were behind the effects that he created. In particular, upon spontaneous requests from others, Owens was able to "produce" UFO sightings, including a videotaped sighting with hundreds of witnesses that had been requested by Jeffrey Mishlove.[204] Because of such specific responses to others' requests, macro-pk appears to be the more suitable explanation for at least some of the cases.

But the reader has probably already detected that, if Ted Owens is in any way responsible for any of these phenomena, then they have a dark side to them. The following is an example of that darkness, although it is unlikely that Owens was responsible for what happened. According to Mishlove, Owens phoned him one evening in late December 1985 to tell him, "in an angry tone of voice," that he "must warn the U.S. government to cancel the next space shuttle flight." Ostensibly Owens told him that "'The SIs really mean business. They will destroy the shuttle. It's up to you to prevent it.'"[205] Mishlove has written that "A month later, on January 28, 1986, I was shaken to my bones when the Challenger disaster occurred. The space shuttle exploded, killing all seven crew members."[206]

So, with Ted Owens we apparently have a person who is capable, not just of moving a light mobile, or deflecting a compass needle, but manipulating the weather, creating UFO sightings, and possibly causing a rocket to explode. Another interpretation of the hurricane and the shuttle explosion, but not the requested UFO sighting, would be to say that Owens had become pre-cognitively aware of the devastation that was about to occur in those cases and that his claim that they were the result of psychokinetic activity on the part of himself or aliens was just a back-story that he used when warning others.

Dimensions of Anomalous Transformations

So, what do we have? We have some small-scale mental "pushing and pulling," with the healing, two-slit experiment, and light mobile. We have levitation and anomalous movements of a table and a person. And we have materialization and dematerialization of a crystal, cancer cells, and baby chicks. And we have some apparent large-scale "pushing and pulling" of the weather and explosions. So, what are we to make of these? These phenomena might not have that much to do with one another, beyond the fact that we do not have good explanations for them. But it is interesting to consider them in the same context. So let us start by gathering together some of the information from this list of examples to identify a few of the dimensions of these anomalous transformations.

1. *Types of anomalous transformations.* Anomalous transformations can include levitation, movement of physical objects, change in behaviour of magnetic field detectors, exposure of photographic film, dematerialization and rematerialization of physical objects, dematerialization of biological mass, materialization of living processes, weather changes, UFO sightings, and explosions.

2. *Complexity.* The events that appear to be affected can be apparently simple, such as moving a light mobile, or complex, as in the case of healing a physical body, hatching baby chicks, or bringing on a storm.

3. *Altered states.* In our examples, anomalous transformation is associated with a person whose consciousness is altered to some degree: Suzanne Padfield as well as the participants in the two-slit experiment were perhaps just in a state of absorption, William Bengston engaged in mental cycling, St. Joseph appeared to have been in some sort of religiously-inspired

trance, the mediums in the Scole experiment were in a deep trance during which they ostensibly channelled discarnate entities, and Anita Moorjani had a near-death experience.

4. *Meddling by discarnate entities.* Sometimes the anomalous transformation is attributed to forces outside of oneself, as in the case of Bengston; St. Joseph; the Scole experiment; Thomaz; Moorjani; and Owens.

5. *Ethical valence.* The anomalous transformations range from ethically benevolent (such as Bengston's and Moorjani's healing) to neutral (such as the dematerialization of a crystal) to malevolent (such as Owens' storms and explosions).

We shall consider some of these dimensions in more detail below as we try to explain what is happening and discuss in the "Epilogue" the ethical questions raised in Item 5.

Explanations of Anomalous Transformations

How are we to explain these phenomena? The simplest reaction would be to deny that anything unusual happened; that these must all be cases of misperception, fraud, mental illness, and so on. Is there evidence that that is the best explanation? Not for the examples that I have chosen. In fact, the evidence points in the opposite direction, that something truly anomalous occurred in each case.

The next course of action could be to acknowledge that something odd occurred, but then forget about it and get on with life as usual. And, indeed, the walls of censorship around the academy are so thick that these sorts of phenomena are filtered out well before anyone has to take them seriously.[207] One of the problems with such a course of action is that we miss an opportunity to learn from anomalies.

An obvious observation is that, in each of the examples, there appears to have been a person who is involved in some sort of mind–matter interaction with physical manifestation. And there has usually been an alteration of consciousness that is experienced by that person. Such alterations can be nominal, such as the cycling practiced by healers in William Bengston's experiments, or they can be dramatic, as in the case of St. Joseph's absorption in his religious visions. In the Philip experiment, participants cultivated an atmosphere of frivolity, whereas in the Scole experiment, two mediums were in "deep trance" throughout the sessions. On a superficial level, the ordinary waking state appears to support the "ordinary" functioning of nature, whereas alterations of consciousness away from the ordinary waking state allow the "ordinary" functioning of nature to break down, thereby creating space for anomalous events to occur.

If we have gotten this far in accepting these phenomena, then an obvious explanation for them is to suggest that there is another force in nature, previously undiscovered, that some people are able to harness to create these effects. For instance, as the physicist William Crookes remarked upon observing the levitations of the British medium D.D. Home: "These experiments appear conclusively to establish the existence of a new force, in some unknown manner connected with the human organization, which for convenience may be called the Psychic Force."[208] This could apply, for instance, as an explanation for Felicia Parise's ability to move the compass needle. Not only did the compass needle move, but the magnetic field detector and photographic film were also affected, suggesting that there had been some sort of physical effect created in the vicinity of the compass needle. In that context, the notion of a "force" seems reasonable. However, hatching baby chicks and getting them to grow within minutes seems to require more than just a force, at least in the sense of a mechanical force of some sort. So, the notion of a "force" could be useful for some phenomena, but not others.

In micro-pk research, Helmut Schmidt was able to show that the complexity of a machine was irrelevant to participants' abilities to influence it; that the effects depended only on participants' goals of doing so. In fact, perhaps one way of directing one's intentions to create a physical change is to visualize in the mind the desired end state of the physical system. "Everything depends on the ability to hold a picture of the desired state, the final outcome, firmly in mind."[209] Such visualization does not need to be literal but can be symbolic. Our psyches work using symbolic representations of whatever it is with which we are involved, as we noted in Chapter 2, "Meaning Beyond the Human." In psychoneuroimmunological research looking at the effects of visualizing the activity of white blood cells, participants did not need to visualize the biological processes themselves, but could visualize them symbolically in order to trigger an immune system response.[210] For instance, a person could visualize police officers being sent out to combat whatever threats the body is facing. More generally, "Symbolic images ... serve to structure and direct certain unconscious energies."[211] One way to think about this is to say that through visualizing a particular end state, we tune to a meaning field that holds the outcome that we seek. And that the result of a person's efforts to create an effect results in choosing a meaning field that has the capability of creating a desired outcome in physical manifestation.

There is another observation that could be critical for understanding some of these phenomena. And that is that, in some of these cases, the people associated with the phenomena claim that they are not responsible for them but, rather, that there is something or someone else, which we cannot see, that has produced the effects or, at least, potentiated them. For William Bengston, the purpose for the cycling was to let the healer get out of the way of the healing process so that whatever it is that has the capacity to heal can do so. In the Scole experiment, the entities speaking through the mediums were the ones who ostensibly knew how to dematerialize and materialize physical matter. And both Thomaz and Ted Owens claimed associations with alien entities of some sort, although Thomaz's contacts just seemed to amplify his abilities and he did not hold them directly responsible for the phenomena that he produced.[212] However, for some of the examples of anomalous transformation, those who seem to have the ability to create the effects have explicitly denied the involvement of any extraneous entities. For instance, Felicia Parise has said: "I feel solely responsible for what I'm doing. In other words, I don't feel like there's a spirit or somebody guiding me or anything."[213] But let us consider in more detail the possibility that some of these cases of anomalous phenomena were produced in some way by extraneous entities of some sort.

Richard Feynman?

At the outset of this book, I described an apparent interaction with the deceased Richard Feynman. In particular, the medium Angie Aristone conveyed information about Richard Feynman that turned out to be correct. At the time, I was talking on the telephone every week with Julia Mossbridge, with whom I was writing the book *Transcendent Mind*. She said that I should ask Richard Feynman some physics questions to see what kind of answers I got. So, the next time Angie came over, I asked her for the value of the fine structure constant, mentioned in Chapter 2, "Meaning Beyond the Human," with which Feynman would have been familiar. Angie said "zero," paused, then said "eight." At that point I cut her off. That was clearly the wrong number. The value of the fine structure constant is approximately .007297 so there was no point in listening to any more digits.[214]

The following week I was telling Julia Mossbridge about the clear miss. As we were talking, Mossbridge found a web site about the fine structure constant and read something from a quotation by Feynman about the value of the "coupling constant" as being point zero eight something. I did not understand what she was saying. As far as I was concerned, Angie had gotten the wrong number and that was the end of that. At that point the phone went dead. I called back Mossbridge, who said that when her phone had died, the number ".08" that she had punched into it earlier, had come on the screen. Aha. Of course. I finally registered the fact that the "zero, eight" was the square root of the fine structure constant, namely, approximately −0.08542455, which, squared, gives the value of approximately 0.007297, the number that I was expecting to hear. And the quotation that Mossbridge had been reading to me was a statement by Feynman asserting his identification of the number −0.08542455 as the value of the fine structure constant contrary to the value used by other physicists.[215]

This is the sort of thing that lends credibility to the survival of consciousness after death. The medium did not know that I would be asking any technical questions but agreed to try to get the answers from Feynman. She herself is not a physicist and does not know these sorts of things. And the answer that she gave is not an answer that an ordinary physicist would have given. But the answer is uniquely consistent with Richard Feynman's ways of thinking about quantum electrodynamics. Furthermore, when I was trying to come up with technical questions to ask, it occurred to me to ask for the value of the fine structure constant. That "just popped into my head" as something to ask. I did not even know what a fine structure constant was and had to look it up in a dictionary of physics, although I am sure I had been exposed to it at some point in my education. Together, these bits suggest (with a little imagination) that Feynman could have prompted me to ask about the fine structure constant in the first place because of the specificity of the answer to him, started to give Angie his answer before I cut her off, and then disabled the phone while I was talking to Mossbridge when it had become apparent that I was going to completely miss the point of the exercise.

For the purposes of this discussion, let me just focus on the fact that the telephone cut out at a critical moment in the conversation with Julia Mossbridge. To understand the significance of this, Mossbridge and I talked on the telephone once a week for about a year. This was the only time that either of us can recall that the phone had cut out in the middle of a conversation. Not only had the phone cut out, but it had cut out at a critical point in our conversation. Mossbridge had tried to tell me that the medium was onto something after all, but what she had said had just gone right by me. Missing what she had said, I had decisively put the matter out of my mind. I thought the medium was wrong and that it was time to move on. At that point the phone cut out. This is what prompts the question of whether some version of Feynman still exists somewhere and is able to interact with the living in real time.

Several days later, I was telling one of my colleagues the fine structure constant story on the phone when the phone cut out. (My phone service is actually quite good, and this is a phone on a land line, not a mobile phone, so, no, this does not happen all the time.) I tried to call him back. I could not get through. I tried to call him back again. Again, I could not get through to him. I called a third time. This time, I got him back on the phone. "What happened?" my colleague asked. "I think it's Richard," I said. I wondered whether Richard had been trying to get my attention by cutting out the phone, so I talked to Angie again. I told her that the phone had died while I had been talking to my colleague and wanted to know whether Richard had done that. "Yes," she said, "three times." I had not told her that I had twice been unable to get through after the phone had cut out. "He says it's easy to do." So, the question is, are these just all coincidences or can discarnate entities affect physical events? According to the ostensible deceased Richard Feynman, the answer is "Yes. It's easy."

Meddling by Discarnate Entities

There is a long history of ostensible interference with telephones by the deceased. In fact, there have been so many accounts of such occurrences that Scott Rogo and Raymond Bayless collected some of them and published them as a book titled *Phone Calls from the Dead*.[216] These days, this apparent telephone interference includes strange text attributed to the deceased that appears on cell phones. The phenomenon is apparently so widespread that I was interviewed in October of 2015 by an editor from *Wired Magazine* who was seeking an explanation for it. My guess is that all of the other experts she consulted told her that people's phones were broken and that I was perhaps the only one offering alternative explanations.

More generally, there is a history of ostensible contact with the deceased through a variety of electronic equipment. Most famously, perhaps, *electronic voice phenomenon* (EVP) is a phenomenon whereby voices attributed to the dead are heard either directly from some electronic source or upon playback from an audio recording.[217] EVP is subsumed by *instrumental trans-communication* (ITC), which refers to communication through any sort of electronic device including computers, radios, telephones, televisions, and so on.[218] Various sorts of ITC phenomena have also been reported during ostensible after-death communication so that there is considerable overlap between those conceptually differentiated domains.

What are we to make of ITC phenomena? First of all, there has been almost no ITC research conducted by academically trained scientists that has been published in academic science journals.[219] In fact, my two studies, one of EVP[220] and one of ITC,[221] both published in the *Journal of Scientific Exploration*, are the only such examples of which I am aware. This research is typically done by amateur scientists reporting their results in specialist publications or web sites.[222] The good thing about that is that such scientists are not constrained by the materialist bias that pervades the academy.[223] The bad thing about that is that such scientists some-times lack the depth and breadth of critical thinking that needs to be brought to such difficult subject matter. Furthermore, pub-lishing the results of such research outside the academy ensures, in effect, that those findings will remain unknown within the academy, so that if anyone within the academy were to take this line of research seriously, she would be starting pretty much from a standstill.

I am not even going to try to summarize or evaluate the ITC research here, beyond making a few comments. The first is that

EVP usually takes the form of brief snippets of apparent speech. For instance, in the EVP study that I conducted, in which we recorded the output from two radios tuned between stations onto audio cassettes, two of three experimenters identified a recorded passage as being the phrase "Tell Peter." This sounded like a woman's voice at regular speed juxtaposed against a cacophony of voices that had faded in and that afterwards faded out again. The experimenter who first identified this passage said that the voice sounded like that of a woman whom she had known "who was now deceased and whose husband's name had been Peter."[224] The problem is that there is no reason to suppose that this is anything other than auditory pareidolia.[225] There is considerable evidence to show that we structure ambiguous sensory experiences, including acoustic experiences, into meaningful perceptions. And the fact that we can agree on what we hear just indicates that those meaning-making processes are hard-wired.[226] So EVP is not particularly evidential and we are left trying to find examples of other forms of ITC that allow us to rule out readily available conventional explanations.

A second comment is that ITC is just an electronic version of poltergeist activity, so we are back to where we started, giving examples of anomalous transformations that may or may not have anything to do with discarnate entities. Poltergeist activity is sometimes separated into *person-centred* and *place-centred*. In other words, the activity appears to attach itself to a person, so that anomalous activity takes place whenever that person is present, or it attaches itself to a place, with no particular person appearing to be necessary for such activity to occur. It is the place-centred version of poltergeist activity that naturally lends itself to a *spirit theory*,[227] that discarnate beings are the source of the disturbance. And the person-centred activity can be attributed to the pk ability of whoever seems to be at the centre of the action. Possibly because any talk of discarnate entities is likely to upset journal editors and referees, some investigators have tried to push all poltergeist phenomena into this second category, renaming it *recurrent spontaneous psychokinesis*, so that it is assumed that there is always a living person who could be identified as being responsible for the occurrence of these types of anomalous events.[228]

However, even person-centred poltergeist activity is not nearly as unproblematical as it seems, as we have already seen in the Philip experiment. Philip was clearly an imaginary ghost created by the minds of the society's members, so that the anomalous raps and table movements can safely be attributed to the macro-pk ability of the people who were present. Perhaps. An alternative hypothesis is that the group members created a meaning field with which they then interacted. The meaning field contained just those ingredients that the group members had placed in it by developing their fictional account of Philip. The raps and table movements could have eventuated from the fact that the Philip meaning field itself lay within the larger meaning field of séance phenomena, so that creating Philip triggered the phenomena that belong to that larger meaning field. There is an alternative way to conceptualize an externalization of Philip that does not explicitly invoke the notion of meaning fields. Through mentally imagining Philip, the members of the group created a discarnate entity (somewhere), a "tulpa," that subsequently interacted with them.[229]

The third comment is that attributing poltergeist activity, of whatever sort, to discarnate entities does not explain the phenomena. All it does is displace the skills needed for producing such phenomena onto beings from another level of reality. But that brings up several questions. During his lifetime Richard Feynman, as far as we know, did not have the ability to anomalously disrupt telephone calls. Upon being dead, he has acquired that ability. How did he learn to do that? And how does he do that? Through what mechanism?

Here is yet another way to think about it. Creating havoc with electronics, including disrupting telephone calls, is sometimes called the *Pauli effect*. People who have had near-death experiences frequently experience the Pauli effect. According to Phyllis Atwater:

> Of the experiencers I interviewed, 73 percent … gave numerous reports of electrical snafus such as microphones that 'fought' them, recorders that began to 'smoke,' computers that 'crashed,' television channels that 'flipped,' electronic memory systems that 'wiped out,' or streetlights that 'popped' as they walked by. None could wear watches anymore without constantly repairing or replacing them.[230]

These people appear to be creating some sort of electronic disturbance in the world around themselves.[231] Is it death itself that gives a person the capacity to affect physical manifestation in these sorts of ways? Is there some type of field that a person encounters during the dying process that changes her physical body in such a way that it creates these effects? Or are these effects being created from a nonphysical level of reality to which a person who has come close to death has been exposed and continues to access?

As a result of coming close to death himself and analysing the effects that that had on him, John Wren-Lewis proposed that near-death experiences knock out a person's normally hyperactive survival mechanism. We live our lives intent on physical survival. During a near-death experience, at some point the awareness that our physical lives are actually over occurs, so that a survival mechanism is no longer relevant. It stops. When we are resuscitated, the survival mechanism resumes activity but is no longer hyperactive.[232] We are no longer locked into physical reality in the same way that we were when the survival mechanism was hyperactive.

During a near-death experience, as we saw with Anita Moorjani, a person often feels connected to everything that exists. Upon returning to life, without resumption of being locked in to physical manifestation, some degree of connectedness remains. Perhaps that connectedness allows the Pauli effect to occur. As

Suzanne Padfield said, it is when she was identified with the processes involved in moving the mobile that she was able to get it to move in the intended direction. Retaining some inner connection to physical manifestation could be an aspect of the mechanism through which watches, telephones, and so on become disabled. To the extent that the deceased, such as Richard Feynman, can experience such connectedness, to that extent perhaps they can create psychokinetic effects.

However, now we have the opposite problem. If the deceased can routinely affect physical manifestation, in part perhaps by virtue of their greater connectedness, then how does physical manifestation remain stable at all, rather than wobbling around like a demented fun house? And what is to stop the deceased from using such abilities not just to cut out phones or move a chest of drawers a few feet over but to torment people for whatever perverse reason? In fact, there is good evidence from some possession cases that such tormenting can sometimes occur.[233] Perhaps the answer with regard to the deceased is the same as it is for the living, namely that only few are able to figure out and master how to create physical effects in spite of their connectedness. But the answer remains unknown.

So, we have three nested questions here. The first is, "Do discarnate entities exist?" If the answer is yes, then the second question is, "Can discarnate entities affect physical manifestation?" And if the answer is yes, then the third question is, "How can discarnate entities affect physical manifestation?" The short answer to the first question is, "Probably yes." The short answer to the second question is, "Probably yes." And the short answer to the third question is, "We do not know." Having spent most of my life seriously thinking about these sorts of things, my sense is that living humans can create various anomalous physical effects, discarnate entities can create various anomalous physical effects, living humans together with discarnate entities can create various anomalous physical effects, and meaning fields can create various anomalous physical effects. The last of these brings us back to the flicker theory. Can it be used as an explanation for these phenomena?

Flicker Theory Revisited

The idea in the flicker theory is that physical manifestation emerges from and disappears into a prephysical substrate over and over again along some deep time. Each emergence constitutes a *now* with its own apparent time, including its own past and future. The problem then is why there is any continuity at all between *nows*. And the answer is that there are implicate meanings in the prephysical substrate which explicate as meaning fields that determine the structure of the *nows*.

Furthermore, the prephysical substrate can also be defined as deep consciousness, a nondual substratum of ordinary consciousness prior to a split into subjective and objective aspects.[234] Deep consciousness has the capacity to modify the implicate meanings, and hence the meaning fields, that structure any given emergent *now*, thereby modulating what shows up. Deep consciousness is shared by human beings, probably other sentient beings, discarnate entities of various sorts, and whoever or whatever else is out there somewhere. What shows up is ultimately determined by a meta-level weighting action. In other words, a *now* that shows up is the result of each being's contribution as to what that *now* should include. And there are some sort of meta-rules as to how much of an effect each being can exert. And all such meta-levels are just more meaning fields.

Consonant with the flicker theory is a cinematic metaphor in which individual frames on a film are laid out in a sequence to give the appearance of the occurrence of various events consistent with whatever rules the screenwriter and director had imagined. In other words, the limitations of the possibilities of what can occur physically are determined by some sort of meta-rules governing who or what gets to modify in what ways the relevant meaning fields. Again, the meta-rules are just more meaning fields. This ability to modify the *nows* becomes important in Chapter 4, "Planetary Transformation." Another obvious analogy is that of dreaming. Dreams are also just made up of *nows*. Levitation, macro-pk, materialization, and dematerialization can all occur in dreams. The provocative contention here is that physical manifestation follows the rules of dreams rather than what we take to be rules of physical events, and that the apparent stability of physical events is due, in part, to the meaning fields that we hold in place for their occurrence.

Now we have a theory that can easily encompass all of the examples we have given above. How do we levitate a coin and place it at the centre of a lime? Easy. There is no coin and there is no lime. The idea is that, in the prephysical substrate, Thomaz has the ability to create a sequence of *nows* in which the projection we call a "coin" levitates and then create a sequence of *nows* in which the projection we call a *lime* is "cut open" to reveal the projection of what we call a "coin" to appear to us at the centre of the projection we call a "lime."

How is it that physical constants change over time? Easy. We have it backwards. The "image" comes first. That is to say, the appearance of reality is what "exists." The physical constants are made-up stuff to keep us happy. They do not exist. The rules can be changed according to some meta-rules along deep time. The meta-rules are just more meaning fields. Although he may or may not agree with my ideas, this is consistent with physicist Lee Smolin's notion about the development of the universe over time.[235]

In a way, the flicker theory offers too much explanatory power for the phenomena that we are trying to rationalize. Is it not possible just to patch things a bit? Perhaps. However, sometimes analysing a few anomalies that lie at the edges of our experience can unravel an entire way of thinking about reality and replace it with a radically different view. That is what I have tried to do here. I will give another example of that in the "Epilogue."

A Practical Approach

What we have done thus far in this chapter is to look at some examples of anomalous transformation and then seek to explain them using various theoretical strategies. Can we turn this around? Can we use our understanding of anomalous transformation to deliberately create changes? Well, there already exist packaged "consciousness technologies" that more or less incorporate some of the ideas associated with these phenomena in a way that can be used practically. In particular, I will say a little bit about my experience with one of them, namely *Matrix Energetics* (ME), developed by Richard Bartlett. I have read several books by Bartlett about ME and attended about a dozen training seminars, each of which has usually lasted for several days.[236]

The idea behind ME, as I understand it, is to engage with the ME field, which we can conceptualize here as a particular meaning field, which then creates the effects. How do I do that? Say I am trying to help someone who wishes to have me help her. The problems the person faces could be anything from feeling anxious to being on the verge of imminent death from some disease. Furthermore, they can be problems in any sphere of life, including health, financial, relationship, academic, existential, or whatever. Or there may not be any specific problems; the person might just "want some." I almost always do this remotely. That is to say, the person is somewhere far away from me. I start by deliberately invoking the ME field. Then I "scan" the person to see what I notice. That could be anything. Sometimes people are struck by the accuracy of what I "see," such as accurately finding pain at the back of someone's neck or correctly describing someone's relationship with her daughter (having never met either of them). Then I do whatever techniques, from a collection of about 50 or 60, I feel like doing. And I do them with a sense of commitment, as though I were carrying out a deliberate action. For instance, I might imagine making a "chiropractic adjustment" to a person's psyche and having an almost tactile feeling of something shifting.

Eventually, I release and go into a nondual state of consciousness. By a "nondual state of consciousness" I mean that I explicitly give up any expectations of whether or not anything should happen or what anything that happens should look like. Moreover, I try to release myself into a deep, quiet inner space. After a few minutes, or sometimes much longer than that, I come back out and "look" to see what is different. The idea is that in the nondual state I am aligned with the deep consciousness at the level of the prephysical substrate. Whatever conditions a person had are naturally dissolved in that state, and that state holds multiple alternative versions of how physical manifestation can occur. The way I think of it is that I am allowing for a shift between meaning fields to take place. I do not try to force a shift; I allow a shift to occur. By looking for what is different, I validate whatever change occurred during the dissolved state. I check an imaginary gauge to see if I am finished, and when I am finished, I deliberately end the session.

I carried out two remote influencing experiments using techniques derived from ME. Both experiments were done entirely over the internet while sitting in front of my computer in my home office. There were 15 volunteers in the first experiment, for whom I carried out a total of 34 remote influencing sessions. I emailed participants telling them the time at which I would begin a session and asked them to report any experiences that they had at that time. Then I would do a session. I just want to mention one interchange from that experiment that I find particularly relevant to the material in this book.

One evening I was doing a session for Participant 03 when I spontaneously thought of Participant 05. Oh, "Why not?" I thought, and for a few minutes I did ME for Participant 05 as well as for Participant 03. Afterwards, Participant 05 told me that she knew exactly what she had been doing at the stated time—she had been brushing her teeth. And she had pictured me doing ME.

Participant 05 also told me at one point that she felt that the ME sessions that I did for her felt like having her battery recharged. So, the question arises for me, "Who did what to whom?" Did I initiate contact with Participant 05, or did Participant 05 somehow "notice" that I was doing ME for someone else and butt in because she wanted some? The analogy I had was that of ME as a shower of water coming down, with Participant 05 noticing that there was ME available and then drawing my attention to her so that she could "get some."[237]

In Experiment 2, I set up a control condition. First, I sent a participant an email saying that I would do a session for her. Then I flipped a coin. If the coin landed heads, I actually carried out a session. If it landed tails, I did nothing further. I also asked participants to indicate their level of agreement, on a six-point scale, with three statements asking whether anything unusual had happened, whether they felt more fatigued than expected, and whether they felt more energized than expected. I had noticed in Experiment 1 that participants reported either getting more fatigued or more energized during the sessions. In this way I introduced a control condition and some self-report measures that could be used for the purposes of statistical analyses, to see if there were any actual effects.

The answer was "Yes," there were actual effects. Over the course of about one year, I carried out a total of 72 experimental sessions and 66 control sessions for 22 participants. The averages for the three items were in the expected direction and the average absolute value of the difference between being more energized and more fatigued was statistically significantly higher for the experimental group than the control group.[238] The idea behind the second measure was that participants were unlikely to be more fatigued and more energized during the same session. And given that the idea was to look for deviations away from expected energy levels, statistical power was increased by looking at the absolute value of the difference between being energized and fatigued. And, indeed, the results support the conclusion that participants' self-reported energy levels were being jiggled during the remote influencing. This was consistent with what I had been reading from participants' descriptions of their experiences in both experiments.

One of the things that I began to notice both in my experiments and when attending ME training seminars was that participants would sometimes go into joyous states of consciousness. In one case, upon my inquiry about her statement that she had felt happy at the time of the session, a participant told me that, at the time of the session (which she did not know was taking place at the time that it occurred), she had felt energy enter the bottom of her feet and rise up through her body. As it did so, she said that she entered a state of bliss that lasted for several days afterwards. In another case, during a class demonstration of ME, a student who was sitting and watching the demonstration entered a deep, transcendent state of consciousness that transformed her life. It was not just that sometimes ME jiggled a person's energy levels or apparently "fixed" some condition, but those who experienced it sometimes entered states of exceptional emotional well-being.

Several years ago, two undergraduate psychology thesis students, along with a research assistant, and I drove to Philadelphia to gather data over three days at one of Richard Bartlett's training seminars. We had a total of 97 participants fill out a battery of paper-and-pencil instruments before the seminar began, at the end of each of the three days, and two months after the end of the seminar through a web site. In addition, we took behavioural measures and conducted 42 structured interviews of individual participants. Perhaps what we found most striking was that "at least some participants at the seminar [were] reporting having had somewhat meaningful, profound, spiritual experiences in altered states of consciousness."[239] So the unsystematic observations of transcendent states were borne out by more systematic observations.

Related to transcendence, participants were shifting into altered states of consciousness in which physical reality appeared to them to have become more pliable. And some of them claimed improved well-being. For instance, one participant claimed that her toothache was better, another one that a chronic backache was gone, a third said that her arthritic knee started popping like popcorn and that she felt taller afterwards. Of the 42 interviews and 457 written comments, only two dysphoric experiences were reported — a transient headache and transient dizziness. Overall, either not much happened for people or there was a movement toward greater well-being. And in some cases there were profound experiences of awakening, as in the case of Participant 76 writing at the time of the two-month follow-up:

> I was absolutely transformed by the Philadelphia Matrix Energetics seminar. I read a lot of books about consciousness and the nature of reality but to actually experience Richard's seminar first hand and observe the effects that were taking place was an amazing experience. I was actually called up to the stage and felt the wave of 'energy' through my body and noticed positive improvements in my health afterwards. It was very rewarding.[240]

Given that these are all self-reports, they are not necessarily evidential, but are suggestive of some type of shift toward well-being that seemed to be occurring at the ME seminar.

We tend to think that physical manifestation is stable, with considerable effortful force required to change anything. The point of this chapter has been to challenge that notion and to look at evidence that physical manifestation is more pliable than we usually think that it is. Then we rationalized such malleability using the flicker theory. Finally, we looked at a particular way of harnessing this information for the purpose of deliberately creating anomalous transformation, which appears to be accompanied, at least some of the time, by alterations of consciousness that can be experienced as being joyful. We will keep these ideas in mind as we move on to look at the global crises that humanity faces at this time in its history. We are going to need all of the resources available to us in order to meet the challenges that we face today.

Chapter 4

Planetary Transformation

It is a near miracle that we have escaped destruction so far, and the longer we tempt fate, the less likely it is that we can hope for divine intervention to perpetuate the miracle.[241]

We started this book with an ostensible quotation from the deceased Richard Feynman, "you guys are barely hanging on | on the brink of destruction." Upon reflection, that warning has two aspects to it, the first of which is a warning of overall degradation of the infrastructure necessary to support life, including the degradation of our biological ecosystem that allows for life to exist in the first place, and the second, a specific threat from the detonation of nuclear weapons. The question is, can anything that we have discussed about the nature of consciousness and reality be useful for understanding and mitigating global crises? The purpose of this chapter is to try to answer that question. I will begin by summarizing what I see as the most critical aspects of the planetary situation and the conventional ways of thinking about it. We are currently in a gridlock that has prevented humanity from effectively resolving planetary threats. Can any of the knowledge about consciousness help us to break that gridlock? I will look at several directions that our inquiry can take and conclude that perhaps we are in a phase of planetary transformation that calls forth precisely the acknowledgment and development of the qualities of consciousness that we have discussed in the earlier chapters.

The Sixth Mass Extinction

Although environmental degradation has been continuously in the background of my mind, I had not intended to write about it in this book. My expertise is in the study of consciousness, not biology, earth sciences, climatology, and other disciplines relevant for understanding the crises that we face on the planet today. However, since these crises span academic disciplines, so that they are inherently interdisciplinary,[242] no one really has the expertise to address them adequately. That means that each of us just has to do the best that we can. So, spurred by Feynman's ostensible warning and encouragement from colleagues, I decided that I had a responsibility to do what I can to address planetary crises.

In reading a couple of palaeontologists, whose job is the "long view" of planetary changes, I was struck by the clear, loud, anxious voice with which they warn about the Sixth Mass Extinction being precipitated by human life on earth.

> A broad body of scientific evidence says that the Sixth Mass Extinction is a very real possibility, but you don't have to be a scientist to realize what's pushed so many species to the brink today. It's us — *Homo sapiens* — and we have done it by changing the very surface of Earth, the climate, the chemistry of the oceans, and the air we breathe as we strive to support seven billion people in the manner to which we have become, or in many cases want to become, accustomed.[243]

So, according to some scientists, the direction we have set is that of extinction — our own and that of many of the species on the planet today.

How are we to address this situation? Perhaps, because of its popularity, the place to start is with James Lovelock's notion of *Gaia*.[244] There are several versions of the *Gaia hypothesis*. According to the minimalist version, *self-regulating Gaia*, life on earth maintains planetary conditions so as to support its own existence. A stronger version, the *optimizing Gaia* hypothesis, is the contention that life improves planetary variables such as "planetary atmospheric and oceanic chemistry, the cycling of elements through the biosphere, and the availability of nutrients to levels *more favorable for life*."[245] A third, over-the-top version, from which scientists seem to distance themselves, is the notion that the earth is a living organism.[246] If the Gaia hypothesis were to be true, by any of these versions of the Gaia hypothesis, then why is there a problem?

The problem appears to arise because humans have somehow overstepped the boundaries of their role on earth. "To rip into the planet's rhythms, cycles, and interconnections, as the civilization we have created is doing, signals human folly not mastery."[247] The idea is that there are *feedback mechanisms* that will restore equilibrium, so that there can be harsh consequences for us as the feedback mechanisms correct the imbalances that we have created. But there are also *feed-forward mechanisms*. Although dynamic systems can respond to perturbations through feedback, thereby restoring a system to its ordinary functioning, if we push a system too far, then we can cross a threshold beyond which feedback mechanisms can no longer restore balance, but give way to feed-forward mechanisms that accelerate whatever changes have been triggered. Such *tipping points* mean that "relatively small changes in input have long-term, large-scale, and often irreversible output."[248] Such is the case, for instance, with climate change. Rising global temperatures cause ice and snow to melt, which leads to the loss of light-reflecting surfaces, which, in turn, means that more heat is trapped on the surface of the planet leading to steeper increases in temperature. The remedy, then, is a *sustainable retreat* to "scale down our consumption, shrink our ecological footprint, and generously share the biosphere with all living beings."[249]

Contrary to the Gaia hypothesis that the earth functions in such a way as to support life, Peter Ward has proposed the *Medea hypothesis*, that life is inherently self-destructive.[250] The earth is like that. Once life appears, it changes "environmental conditions to a point where there can no longer be ... any kind of life."[251] The problem is that each "species innately 'tries' to become the dominant species on the planet, with no regard to other species."[252] And, in the course of its Darwinian evolution, each species thereby exploits whatever resources it can at the expense of the whole of life. The result is that "the killer is life itself. If left unchecked, it will hasten the ultimate death of all life on Earth."[253]

So, which is it? Well, whatever the evidence for and against self-regulation versus self-destruction, there is no getting around the fact that humans are a part of life and that we are catalysing the destruction of all of life on earth. So, the Medea hypothesis certainly applies to human life. More generally, it seems to me that it is a matter of understanding both Gaian and Medean systems on earth along with all of their interactions so as to better assess our own precarious situation. At any rate, the net result is the same, in that we need to address our own extinction and figure out what to do about it.

So, what is that going to be? Perhaps the first thing to note is that biological changes are no longer primarily driven by Darwinian evolution but rather by "an entirely new form of evolution"[254] that has arisen as a result of human beings' ability to transform their own environment. In fact, that is what has created the global crises that we face. We have gone from one period in the history of this earth, into a new one. We have been in the Holocene epoch for about 11,700 years, which was characterized by a stable climate. Since the year 2000, atmospheric chemist Paul Crutzen has "concluded that a new stage had begun in Earth's history, one in which humankind had emerged as the most powerful influence on global ecology."[255] And "the escalation since 1945 has been so fast that it sometimes goes by the name the Great Acceleration."[256] This renaming helps to highlight the depth of the crisis.

> The idea of the Anthropocene ... gives the ecological upheavals of the present day their proper place in the history of the planet. If you want to grasp the force, the scale, and the shape of the catastrophe as it unfolds, look for how it opens a fresh chapter in the long sequences of planetary time.[257]

Is there even anything we can do to stop or slow the Great Acceleration? According to Roy Scranton, the answer is no. "The sooner we confront our situation and realize that there is nothing we can do to save ourselves, the sooner we can get down to the difficult task of adapting, with mortal humility, to our new reality."[258] So, we are, perhaps inevitably, in a period of global transformation whose end-state we do not know.

But our precocious manipulation of our planet could also be the solution. We could try to geoengineer this world back to a more habitable state. For Ward, we have no choice:

> We humans must resort to wholesale planetary engineering if we are to overcome the tendencies of life around us—and those of our own species—to make the Earth a less salubrious (and eventually lethal) abode for life.[259]

It is worth noting that eventually we would need to do this anyway, since the sun is getting bigger and hotter and will heat the planet to temperatures that are unbearable for carbon-based organic life.[260] It is just that we would need to learn to do this much sooner than anticipated. In fact, James Lovelock has proposed that we could catalyse the development of new silicon-based life forms on earth that are better able to survive in a hotter and harsher environment. Life would continue although human beings would not.

If we trash civilization by heedless auto-intoxication, global war or the wasteful dispersal of the Earth's chemical resources, it will grow progressively more difficult to begin again and reach the present level of knowledge. If we fail, or become extinct, there is probably not sufficient time for a successor animal to evolve intelligence at, or above, our level. It is the snail-like speed of natural selection and the slow transfer of information by wet chemical ionic conduction that hampers us and all other forms of animal life. Electronic conduction is 1 million times faster, but it needs our presence for the early and crucial stages of its emergence as a new life form. Our survival is therefore one of the most important steps in the evolution of our planet.[261]

In other words, according to Lovelock, we need to stay alive long enough to create new silicon-based life forms that will succeed us once we are dead.

There are several obvious objections to this line of reasoning. The first is just the natural suspicion that engineering marvels are going to save us once again from problems that we ourselves have created. Our capacity to manipulate the environment keeps increasing but our moral integrity does not, so that we just keep getting better at making life miserable for each other.[262] Is there not a point at which we need to stop to figure out what it is that we are doing?[263] The second objection is the obvious fact that we would need to understand the ecosystem well enough and develop the necessary tools to micromanage it to our specifications. And if we acquire the capability to do that before it is too late, then how do we collectively decide on a course of action? Third, the notion that we can transfer "life" to silicon-based organisms is somewhat naïve, considering how little we know about the relationship of consciousness to its physical substrates. But before considering our situation in greater depth, let us turn to the nuclear threat.

Nuclear Winter

In the scenario that I envisioned, we are precariously balanced, so that we "are barely hanging on." Perturbations in just a couple of spheres of activity could lead to widespread infrastructure collapse. For instance, here is just one scenario. Due to global warming, a deadly virus is able to spread away from equatorial zones to more heavily populated areas so that air travel becomes restricted, thereby driving up the cost of the distribution of food and other goods leading to widespread protests, which in turn provide an opportunity for armed opportunistic attacks against religious targets which then incites widespread violence. (Four years after writing that sentence, I am fact-checking the manuscript of this book during a pandemic lockdown. We will see what repercussions this lockdown creates around the planet.) The problem with such stressors, in addition to their inherent dangers, is that they can lead to sufficient infrastructure collapse to loosen up nuclear weapons caches to the point where they become vulnerable to theft by special interest groups who desperately want to blow up some of these weapons for their own ideological reasons. And once a couple of them are set off, there could be a sequence of devastating counterstrikes. There are thousands of permutations on this scenario, none of which have good outcomes. The point is that as we become increasingly precariously perched, we are less and less able to absorb stressors of various sorts including the ability to secure our nuclear weapons caches.

That is a dark scenario. And there have been warnings against presenting such an apocalyptic version of what could happen. "People should not be persuaded to believe that a terrorist-initiated nuclear attack is the end of the world. We will probably experience such an attack at some point in the future and the world will not end."[264] The nuclear threat is, in fact, complex, and assessing the risk of just what could happen when, leading to what outcome, is itself difficult, so, yes, the probability of my dark scenario cannot be accurately assessed. However, "according to both Reagan and Gorbachev, a major contributing factor to the deep nuclear cuts that they began in the 1980s was the research of [a] handful of scientists who discovered nuclear winter."[265] So there could be practical value in considering this dark scenario.

The nuclear threat includes the accidental breakdown of nuclear reactors;[266] terrorist attacks against nuclear reactors;[267] accidental, unauthorized, or inadvertent use of existing nuclear weapons;[268] the theft of existing nuclear weapons; and the design, construction, and deployment of nuclear weapons by those who plan on using them.[269] Let me first give one example of the threat from inadvertent use.

Inadvertent use would occur if a nuclear weapon were to be launched intentionally by people who have the authority to do so, but who do so on the basis of incorrect information. For instance, on January 25, 1995, a rocket to study the northern lights, the Black Brant XII, was launched jointly by Norway and the United States. Russia's early-warning radars misidentified this launch as a missile attack. Central early-warning stations in Russia were notified of a possible attack. They, in turn, "alerted the highest levels of the Russian command by sending a message to their nuclear suitcases."[270] The president, the defence minister, and the chief of the general staff consulted on the telephone as to what action to take. According to one source, "Russia's command-and-control system was placed in combat mode."[271] There are two things to note. First, this is one of several inadvertent incidents about which we know. How many are there about which we do not know? Second, apparently Russia's early-warning system of a foreign attack has been deteriorating, so the frequency of such incidents is likely to increase.

What is the threat posed by someone who deliberately wants to blow up some nuclear weapons? How realistic is that? Because of the numerous parameters that need to be taken into account, it is difficult to make any estimates. "The variety of nuclear terrorism's scenarios — with the associated contingent require-ments — and the subjective decision process to opt for one of these scenarios enormously complicates the scope and nature of the nuclear threat."[272] However, as I see it, we are in a situation in which we actively need to keep people who would like to blow up nuclear weapons from gaining access to them. The passive default is that they would figure out a way to acquire and detonate them. Up to this point, we have been reasonably good at keeping such people away from obtaining them.[273] But there are a couple of ways that nuclear weapons could end up being detonated: a group of people who want to blow up some nuclear bombs can make some and then use them, and those who already have them can decide to let such people have some or use the weapons themselves. Let us consider these alternatives for a minute.

Many years ago, one of my professors told me that one of her colleagues taught physics on Saturdays to precocious high school students in New York City. Among other things, she taught them how to build a nuclear bomb. And one of the students went home and did just that in her basement. She had no fissile material to put in it, so the device was not harmful, but apparently it was functional. I have not checked with her colleague to verify this story, so it could just be an urban legend, but it speaks to the ease with which such weapons could be built. The reality is that "the basic concepts of weapons design can be found on the Internet" and sophisticated development programs are not necessary to build them.[274] The genie is out of the bottle. We have learned how to make nuclear weapons and, now that we know how to do so, we cannot stop people from making them.[275]

What we need to do, then, is contain access to weapons-grade fissile material; in particular, highly enriched uranium (HEU) and plutonium. Currently there exists enough fissile material in hundreds of buildings with varying levels of security in over 20 countries for more than 100,000 nuclear weapons, so that "managing the dangers posed by plutonium and HEU is one of the greatest challenges our species will face for decades—perhaps centuries—to come."[276] And, in fact, there have been "multiple documented cases of thefts of kilogram quantities of highly enriched uranium."[277] It does not take a great deal of imagination to suppose that someone, at some point, will get away with such theft.

What about those who already have such weapons? The idea, during the Cold War, was that nuclear weapons provided a deterrent to other countries not to take military action. Initially only two countries had nuclear weapons, then five, then nine;[278] and now it is not clear how many more have joined them, with increasingly unstable regimes trying to gain access to such weapons.[279] Also, whereas previously nuclear weapons were accumulated for their deterrence value, the rigid world order that supported such a strategy has crumbled, giving way to more amorphous regional alignments, so that "nuclear deterrence is no longer effective and may become dangerous," and such weapons are more likely to be deployed strategically.[280] For instance:

> The most alarming form of a nuclear nightmare could be described this way: a hair-trigger, opaque nuclear arsenal controlled by a dispensation that has embraced tactical use under decentralised military control, is steered by an ambiguous doctrine, and is guided by a military strategy that carouses with non-state actors.[281]

In simpler language, when military commanders, who are no longer tightly bound to civilian authorities, who cooperate with special interest groups, and who have their own ideas about what to do, control a hidden nuclear arsenal that they would consider using for tactical purposes, then there is cause for alarm. And that situation apparently already exists.[282]

The detonation of 100 small bombs of 15 kilotons each (i.e. the equivalent of 100 Hiroshima bombs) in a regional conflict would result not only in a large number of immediate fatalities, but would send so much smoke into the middle and upper atmosphere that the growing season in countries around the world would be substantially shortened, degrading agricultural productivity and causing widespread famine. Such climate anomalies have been predicted to persist for at least a decade after such a nuclear exchange.[283] If a "moderate" to "large"[284] portion of the world's arsenal is released, then the climate consequences are more severe with an average cooling of 7°C to 8°C for years afterwards and cooling of more than 20°C for much of North America and 30°C for much of Eurasia, "including all agricultural regions." In particular, for instance, in Iowa, United States, an important grain-growing region, minimum daily temperatures "would plummet below freezing and stay there for more than a year."[285] That would be a nuclear winter.[286]

Human Factors in the Global Crises

What are we going to do? Perhaps the first thing to note is the role of human factors, both through social institutions as well as at the personal psychological level, that maintain the current predicament and inhibit the implementation of effective solutions. "The problem is that the problem is too big. The problem is that different people want different things. The problem is that nobody has real answers. The problem is that the problem is us."[287]

An overarching contributing factor that gets a lot of ink is that of a capitalist economy.[288] The goal of accumulating wealth is not always consonant with the goal of maintaining life on earth and often, in fact, conflicts with it. For instance, capitalist enterprises typically conceptualize the ecological effects of their activity as "cost-shifting" or as "externalities" for which capital does not have to pay. For example, pollution can get unloaded on the environment without monetary cost.[289] And it can be strategically dispersed. As noted by David Harvey, according to a previous chief economist at the World Bank, Africa is "under-polluted" so that "it would make sense to use it to dispose of the advanced countries' wastes."[290]

> Deaths from starvation of exposed and vulnerable populations
> and massive habitat destruction will not necessarily trouble
> capital (unless it provokes rebellion and revolution) precisely
> because much of the world's population has become
> redundant and disposable anyway. And capital has never
> shrunk from destroying people in pursuit of profit.[291]

With regard to climate change in particular, "the problem is that global decarbonization is effectively irreconcilable with global capitalism."[292]

The proportion of the population that enjoys the benefits of the accumulation of wealth is declining, with an increasingly greater gap between the rich and the poor. For example, by one measure of wealth distribution, from 1968 to 2010 there was a 20% increase in the gap between the wealthy and the impoverished in the United States,[293] leading to a dominant ruling class. "This new ruling class is aided by a security and surveillance state that is by no means loath to use its police powers to quell all forms of dissent in the name of anti-terrorism."[294] Thus, in addition to creating problems with environmental degradation, the accumulation of capital, as it is currently practiced, creates social inequality that can lead to strife. In fact, there is a coincidence between growing numbers of the poor and the failure of states to provide their citizens with bodily security, a functioning justice system, basic services, and economic opportunities. In 2006 there were 28 fragile or failed states; in 2013 that number had risen to 47. Over the same time period "the percentage of the world's poor in such nations has doubled from 20.5 percent to 40.8 percent."[295]

Furthermore, capital moves to monetize as much of nature as it can, so that "life forms, genetic materials, biological processes," and so on, become commercialized.[296] And there is no room for the protection of nature in its exploitation.

> Systemic risk in the financial system can be remedied by the
> taxpayer, but no one will come to the rescue if the

environment is destroyed. That it must be destroyed is close to an institutional imperative. Business leaders who are conducting propaganda campaigns to convince the population that anthropogenic global warming is a liberal hoax understand full well how grave is the threat, but they must maximize short-term profit and market share. If they don't, someone else will.[297]

Furthermore, this creep of commercialization replaces other ways of conceptualizing nature. In particular, attributes that we might otherwise value as part of what it means to be human, such as compassion, altruism, aesthetics, wisdom, and so on, are only relevant to capital to the extent that they can be co-opted in the service of accumulation. Otherwise they stand to be simply crushed in the advance of commodification. "This idea that capital mandates the destruction of a decent and sensitive human nature has long been understood."[298]

At the personal level, the human factor in planetary crises that appears to be discussed most frequently is that of denial.[299] We deny that there is anything wrong, or that there is anything sufficiently wrong such that we would actually have to do something, or that there is anything that we can do anyway to make a difference, and so on. Denial is a standard defence mechanism that we use when confronted with something disturbing that we would rather not experience.[300] And it can take a number of forms.

For instance, it can be in the financial interests of some large corporations, such as companies that extract, process, and distribute fossil fuels, to deny playing a role in planetary crises. Corporations have been granted some of the rights that usually only attach to individuals, such as the right to free speech, which can be used to promote a version of reality through the media that is sympathetic to a corporation's interests.[301] Furthermore, a version of reality can be politicized, so that, for instance, climate change can be perceived to be a political issue being promoted for political gain, rather than an actual matter of life and death.[302] The problem in such cases is exposure to lopsided information that interferes with a person's ability to adequately understand a situation.

But there is a more insidious version of denial. Even those who have adequate exposure to scientific information about global crises can deny that anything needs to be done and fail to act. Those in a position to act effectively are those who have a sufficiently high standard of living so as to have access to avenues of power that could potentially make a difference in the world. But that very relative affluence is "directly yet invisibly linked to the hardships and poverty of people in other parts of the world." The social and environmental costs of our lifestyles get displaced "onto other people (and species), and across time (through extinction, sea-level rise, and future weather scenarios) and space (through melting polar ice caps, floods, food scarcity, and disease in tropical nations)."[303] So there is a lot to deny.

Perhaps the simplest way of understanding the dynamics of our denial is through the use of Martin Heidegger's notion of *inauthenticity*. Faced with the existential threat of our own death, we uproot ourselves so that we are no longer in touch with our own being, and busy ourselves with mundane activities that keep us preoccupied, all the while talking past each other so as to mutually support one another's evasion.[304] Given that the slide toward extinction is an existential threat, it is not surprising that our response is an inauthentic one. And this is precisely what was found in a field study of denial about climate change among educated people living comfortably in a stable society. It was found that conversation norms define socially organized denial so that "public nonresponse to global warming is *produced* through cultural practices of everyday life."[305] And the conversation norms are shaped through the "engineering of consent" so that people are "diverted from dangerous efforts to think for themselves and challenge authority."[306]

A number of years ago I taught an undergraduate course about humanistic psychology in which I had students consider the ways in which we can address existential issues and engage in self-development for the purposes of reaching states of exceptional psychological well-being. As the last topic in the course, I had students read Roger Walsh's book *Staying Alive: The Psychology of Human Survival*. Walsh has argued that our planetary crises are rooted in our psychological natures and he has used different psychological perspectives as lenses through which to understand the risks that we face. For instance, Walsh has pointed out that our "normal" is psychological immaturity, marked by "fear, greed, aversion, ignorance, unwillingness to delay gratification, defensiveness, and unconsciousness"[307] and held in place by "a shared conspiracy against self-knowledge and psychological growth in which we collude together to protect one another's defenses and illusions."[308] Such dysfunctional behaviour can be understood as inauthenticity from the perspective of existential philosophy, immaturity in the context of humanistic psychology, or compliance with social norms when addressed scientifically in social psychology.[309]

I had also collected magazine articles, pamphlets, and other material about different global crises. This was before the widespread availability of the internet. I gave a pile of material about a single topic to each student and told her that she had to give a 10-minute presentation the following week to the class about that topic. Topics included the population explosion, global warming, deforestation, chemical contamination of freshwater, decimation of large mammals in Africa, illegal whale hunting, disappearance of humane communities, the global weapons trade, the threat of nuclear war, and so on. During the following class, each student got up and presented a summary of the information that I had given her. The students had had no idea that so many things were going wrong. And there was little opportunity for denial. By the end of the three-hour class, the students appeared to be notably depressed.

The following week we discussed how the things that we had learned in the class about self-development could be applied to the global situation. Year after year, with different groups of students, we reached the same conclusion, namely, that these planetary problems needed to be urgently addressed. Furthermore, by the end of our deliberations, it was clear that there could only be one lasting solution: human beings needed to grow up and start behaving like responsible adults.

A quarter century has passed since teaching students this material. Unsurprisingly, I have seen no overall maturation in the world. As I understand it, for maturation to occur, people first need opportunities to develop conceptual and critical thinking skills. This means that appropriate opportunities for learning need to be available. That is not the case if someone is co-opted to be a child soldier[310] or shot through the head on the way home from school.[311] And critical thinking skills are just the beginning. Considerable self-development is required in order to become free of one's conditioning in order to be able to learn to think freely and to move toward states of exceptional well-being.[312] And there need to be opportunities for such development to take place.

In fact, the opposite seems to be the case. There has been a rise of fundamentalism of various sorts. And this has not just occurred in vulnerable or failed states. As part of its 2012 platform about education, the Republican Party of Texas wrote: "We oppose the teaching of Higher Order Thinking Skills …, critical thinking skills and similar programs that … have the purpose of challenging the student's fixed beliefs and undermining parental authority."[313] Large segments of our society are sliding deeper into immaturity and ignorance, and as they do so, a feed-forward mechanism makes it increasingly difficult to reverse that slide, as we can see from the previous example. So, for those of us who actually have the ability, education, and "leisure" time to read and think about this, what are we to do?

Subtle Activism

Thus far I have summarized the situation in which we find ourselves from a conventional point of view. And it is bleak. What happens if we bring in the material from the earlier parts of this book? Does any of that shed light on the circumstances in which we find ourselves? We recall from Chapters 2 and 3 that psychokinetic effects are possible. In particular, we noted that experiments with intercessory prayer, non-contact healing, remote healing, and remote influencing have shown statistically significant results. In laboratory studies, the effect sizes are typically small, with larger effects, apparently occurring sporadically, noted in some field studies. So, can we simply fix the planet using remote influencing?

There has been considerable effort to do so. David Nicol has used the expression *subtle activism* to refer to the intentional use of "consciousness-based practices" for the purpose of changing the world for collective benefit.[314] Such practices could include "meditation, prayer, ritual, chanting, ecstatic dance, mindful movement, shamanic journeying—any spiritual or consciousness-based practice, really, from any tradition."[315] And how would these work? For Nicol, it is possible that these practices are affecting subtle aspects of reality that underlie physical manifestation from which their effects trickle down to create positive changes. "These activities ... transform ... what we might call the collective psychical context out of which ideas themselves, and, therefore, decisions and actions, arise."[316] Or, to use the ideas developed in this book, we could change the meaning fields underlying human activity on this planet to allow for healthier outcomes.

Does subtle activism work? By its very nature, the effects of subtle activism are difficult to study empirically. The best-known series of studies are those involving Transcendental Meditation (TM). TM is a meditation practice that was introduced to California by Maharishi Mahesh Yogi in 1959, and from there became widespread in North America and Europe. The basic practice consisted of repeating a word over and over again silently to oneself for twenty minutes. When one's thoughts strayed from the word, one simply returned to saying the word. This practice was to be done twice a day. Physiological measures taken of participants engaged in this meditation practice have revealed that it can trigger a relaxation response in which a person's body is in a state of low arousal with lowered metabolism, lowered heart rate, and so on. As such TM, and other similar techniques with similar effects, has been used as a treatment for stress reduction.[317]

In the early 1960s, Maharishi predicted that if 1% of a particular population practiced TM, then there would be measurably increased harmony in that population. And, indeed, in two separate studies, it was found that there were lower crime rates in 24 US cities that met that requirement than control cities that did not. With the introduction of more advanced techniques in the late 1970s, Maharishi predicted that a group of only the square root of 1% of a population was required for beneficial change if that group practiced the more advanced techniques in a group setting. Improvements in "crime rates, auto accidents, fires, war deaths, and other measures" have been shown in over 40 published studies.[318] The main criticism of this research has been that it has been carried out entirely by investigators who are part of the TM movement. Although no substantial errors have been found with this research, readers would have greater confidence in it if some studies were to have been done by investigators who were not identified with TM. However, much of the data used for the statistical analyses were gathered by people who have not been part of the movement.[319]

As an example, in a prospective study in August and September of 1983 during the Israel–Lebanon war, around 200 TM practitioners were brought to a hotel in Jerusalem to augment the approximately 38,000 TM practitioners living in Israel and 2,000 in Lebanon who would also ostensibly be contributing to any effects. Although the goal was to have over 200 participants in the hotel, for practical reasons the actual number of participants fluctuated irregularly. However, that allowed investigators to look at the correspondence of the number of participants on quality of life measures. And, indeed, there was a negative correlation of $r = -.48$ between group size and war intensity and a positive correlation of $r = .57$ between group size and an overall composite index of quality of life. While causality cannot be inferred from these correlations, given that group size was only partially under experimenter control, the analyses did factor out potentially confounding variables such as trends in the dependent measures, effects of holidays, temperature, and so on, making these results suggestive.[320]

In this system, consciousness is conceptualized as having field effects, so that when individuals in a group of people enter transcendent states of consciousness, the positive qualities of their experience radiate outward to others in their vicinity, thereby creating harmony. That harmony shows up on a number of dependent measures that then sum to create a large change in the composite indices.[321] This is consistent with David Nicol's notion that what is being affected is a subtle level of reality from which changes can occur.

One way to think about this is to suppose that the meditators were applying a meaning field. Some people have the idea that 1% of the population meditating and the square root of 1% engaged in advanced meditation could have a harmonizing effect on a surrounding population. That is a meaning field. This would imply that those who are affected are not necessarily those who are in close physical proximity, but those who fit the criteria for inclusion. And because the effects are not expected for populations that fall below the critical numbers, we would not expect the carry-over effect that was found in William Bengston's studies. It would be helpful to carry out similar studies using other types of meditation practices to try to tease out the relevant parameters. I think that the beneficial effects could be due to creating meaning fields that are consistent with one's goals. Before pursuing this line of inquiry further, toward the end of this chapter, there is another wrinkle to the global crises that I want to introduce.

Alien Agenda

Several decades ago, I was at a scientific meeting held at a hotel in the American southwest. The banquet on the final night of the conference was winding down when one of my colleagues came up to me and told me that there was a person with whom I really needed to talk who was sitting in the hallway outside the banquet room. When I got out to the hallway, there was someone, neatly dressed, sitting in a chair. I introduced myself, pulled up a chair and sat down, and we started talking. We talked for three or four hours well into the early morning. They said that they had worked for an intelligence organization and had been involved in some of the then covert military remote viewing activities.[322]

In the course of our discussion, they said that, early on in the remote viewing program, the remote viewers had seen spaceships coming to earth. When they tracked the source, they found that the spaceships were coming from Mars. According to my informant, aliens lived underground inside Mars. In fact, at the time, there was a National Aeronautics and Space Administration (NASA) satellite on its way to Mars expected to arrive in a couple of months. I was told that the aliens did not want the satellite there and would shoot it down. Several months later, I was listening to the radio when I heard a news announcement that NASA had lost the signal from its Mars Observer just days before it was to enter Mars orbit. The cause for the loss of contact was not known, although there was subsequent speculation that there could have been a fuel line rupture.[323] I thought that was an interesting coincidence in light of the earlier prediction.

There was more—a lot more. About alien colonies on earth inside mountains. About aliens implanting abduction scenarios in people's minds. And so on. By the time we were finished, and I had gone upstairs to my hotel room, I was terrified. My room had double doors opening out onto a balcony. And, even though I was dead tired, I could not let myself fall asleep because I kept imagining aliens coming in through those doors. To this day I have a rule for myself that I will not read anything about aliens after dinner.

So, what are we to make of this? There are a number of interpretations. One is that this was all true, that there really are aliens, that they live inside Mars, that they are here on earth, and so on. A second possibility is that my informant was unhinged and a little out of touch with reality, so that there is not much point in paying attention to anything that they said, no matter who they said they were. A third possibility is that they were a disinformation agent making up stories about aliens to be leaked into the Zeitgeist.

Let me just consider the third of these possibilities. Why would anyone do that? Here is one idea. Suppose that the powerful military-industrial complex needs to keep humming along,[324] so there need to be wars. The problem is that globalization has created so much commercial interdependence between nation states that regional wars are starting to cause too much financial disruption. What are needed are off-planet wars against something from somewhere else. To that end, through various sources, disinformation is "leaked" that there are hostile aliens coming to this planet doing nasty things to people, ensuring that the public will pay for "star wars"-style defence systems in space. There could even be a staged invasion in which some subdivision somewhere within the military-industrial complex[325] creates "aliens" in "spaceships" that attack earth, just to show how much we need to boost weapons development in order to protect ourselves from "them." In fact, there have been claims that alien abduction experiences are clandestine government experiments that have nothing to do with actual extraterrestrials, or false memories, or mental illness, and so on.[326]

For the next 15 years or so, I tried to learn what I could about UFOs and the abduction phenomenon. I read papers, books, and newsletters. I talked to some *experiencers*, as they prefer to be called, about the details of their abductions. I talked to several physicians who treated experiencers. I expected that with a little investigation I would quickly figure out what was happening. While there was good evidence for the existence of UFOs, those could be pretty much anything, such as military hardware. Alien abductions, it seemed to me, had to be some sort of hallucinations, or delusions, or mental illness of some sort. That sort of thing. In fact, the usual strategy by scientific investigators is to assume that what people said happened to them did not happen and that there must be some more conventional explanation.[327] However, the more I learned, the more it became clear that none of the superficial explanations could account for the complexity of the events that occurred for some of the people who were having these experiences and the more enigmatic these occurrences became.[328] I will not try to capture the richness of the phenomena here, but will just stay close to their relevance for planetary crises. The evidence for what I do say is convoluted and difficult to evaluate, so let me just tell this as a story to think about, with references to some of the key writings.

In a typical alien abduction scenario, experiencers report having been taken by aliens to a spaceship where they underwent some sort of physical procedure, often involving the genitals.[329] And prior to their return, they were sometimes shown apocalyptic scenarios of the end of the earth either through degradation of the ecosystem or a nuclear holocaust, with the aliens impressing upon the experiencers the importance of protecting the earth from destruction.[330] In some scenarios, sperm is extracted from men and women are impregnated, with the idea, in some versions, that the aliens are creating hybrid human-alien beings. By some accounts, the purpose of the hybridization program is to create life forms that are better adapted to the harsher environmental conditions that we are going to face on this planet.[331] By other accounts, the hybridization is not for our benefit, but that of the aliens, so that once the hybridization process has been completed the aliens will reveal themselves and kill the rest of us so that only the hybrids, that is to say, themselves, remain. For instance, according to David Jacobs, "abduction evidence points to a single goal: global integration resulting in takeover. It does not point to other goals."[332]

By yet other accounts, the hybridization program is the default if the planet cannot be saved in its present form; that the primary purpose of the alien abduction experience is to create an *ontological shock*[333] so as to get people to wake up and start to take care of the planet. As psychiatrist John Mack has said about working with experiencers who appear to have been abducted:

> I was astonished to discover that, in case after case, powerful messages about the human threat to the Earth's ecology were being conveyed to the experiencers in vivid, unmistakable words and images. The impact of these communications is often profound and may inspire the experiencer to work actively on behalf of the planet's life. Indeed, it seems to me quite possible that the protection of the Earth's life is at the heart of the abduction phenomenon.[334]

Mack's conclusion, as he told me once in conversation, was that the aliens' purpose was to "crack us open" so that we would wake up.[335] Indeed, alien abduction experiences frequently serve as contemporary *conversion experiences* in which experiencers "find religion"[336] and dedicate themselves to planetary healing.

It is important to note that the experience of conversion is independent of whether or not people really are being abducted by aliens. In fact, in her study of experiencers, Susan Clancy has come to the conclusion that the purpose for the alien abductions is precisely that of finding meaning in one's life even though the "alien-abduction memories are best understood as resulting from a blend of fantasy-proneness, memory distortion, culturally available scripts, sleep hallucinations, and scientific illiteracy, aided and abetted by the suggestions and reinforcement of hypnotherapy."[337] According to Clancy, "the contact these people have had with aliens doesn't just feel real—it feels transformative,"[338] with the result that people find "meaning, reassurance, mystical revelation, spirituality, transformation."[339]

In the case of this last scenario, we have exactly that which we were seeking. We already said that the only long-term solution to planetary problems is to have people wake up and start taking responsibility for their actions. Sometimes alien abduction experiences can do that irrespective of whether or not aliens actually exist or what our final explanation of alien abduction experiences will turn out to be. So how many people fall into that category? Is there an equivalent to Maharishi's square root of one of awakened experiencers needed to turn around the planetary crises?

There are no good estimates of the incidence of alien abduction experiences, with numbers ranging from .04% to 2% of the population.[340] Given that this has been generally acknowledged to be a worldwide phenomenon, using just the lowest of these figures that would mean that approximately three million people have had experiences of apparently having been abducted by aliens. Some estimates give a figure of 3.7 million for the United States alone.[341] That is a lot of people.[342] But clearly not enough since we are still sliding toward extinction. Some research would be helpful here, to find out how many people are having alien abduction experiences that are convincing them to become planetary activists of some sort, and how effective their activism actually is.

However, there is another relevant twist to the alien story that I think is worth mentioning, not because it is necessarily factually true, but because it could serve as a way of helping us to break the gridlock of the ways in which we think about global crises. There are two avenues of access to this speculative twist. One of those avenues of access is to ask the obvious question: "How is a hybridization program even possible with alien beings? How could their exobiology and DNA (if they have any) possibly be compatible with human biology and DNA to even create hybrid beings in the first place?"

The second avenue of access is to look at the transformations that occur of the terror that experiencers initially feel. Experiencers often start by being terrified and outraged at being physically violated against their will. Some successfully resist abduction.[343] In the course of some sort of traumatic bonding, perhaps, such feelings sometimes change to those of acceptance and deep love toward the alien beings[344] as experiencers "realize" that the aliens have a right to do this to them. Why do they have that right? Because we are the aliens. In one variation, aliens are us from the future.[345] In another variation, the aliens created human beings at the dawn of civilization from their own material.[346] And, given the ostensible ability of extraterrestrials to manipulate matter[347] it is not difficult to imagine a more extreme variation in which aliens terraformed this planet and seeded it with life in the first place. The idea is that we are an alien project, and the current hybridization program is just an upgrade to what they have already created.

Whatever the truth value of this twisted alien story, it presents a somewhat different way of thinking about our planetary situation. Academics usually assume that life arose by accident and that natural selection led to the intellectual capabilities that we enjoy, as we saw in the quotation from James Lovelock. But what if that were not how we got to this point in our history? And if there are alternative versions of how we got to where we are, whatever they might be, then are there alternative ways of moving forward? From the point of view of the Gaia hypothesis, we have tampered with nature and are creating too much disruption, so our only recourse is to repent and make a "sustainable retreat." But if we are not nature's product in the first place, then it might make little sense to retreat to "nature" and trust "nature" to fix the situation. We might need to fix our way out of this ourselves. Of course, we can reach the same conclusion without positing an alien agenda, but doing so gives us a stark contrast with the way in which we ordinarily think about our situation.

What if there really are aliens doing things to us and possibly having done things to us in the past? The obvious question is "Where is the evidence?" In particular, where is the physical evidence? Well, there is enough physical evidence to convince "believers" but not enough to convince "skeptics."[348] For instance, there have been physical lesions, so-called "scoop marks," and other biological anomalies that have occurred for experiencers that are consistent with their reports of alien abduction.[349] But we can imagine other ways of explaining such physiological aberrations. To firm this up, it has been suggested that the locations from which people claim to have been abducted be treated as crime scenes and systematically examined for forensic evidence.[350] In other words, if we want physical evidence, it helps to actually look for it.

If there really are aliens tampering with us, for whatever purpose, then it does not appear that they are necessarily squishy things in tin cans physically flying to earth from another star system. For instance, the French scientist Jacques Vallée thought that alien abduction accounts were consistent with accounts of abduction by odd creatures throughout human history[351] and that these creatures emerge from other dimensions of being and then disappear back into them.[352] John Mack held a similar view. Several mediums have told me in conversation that they not only channel the deceased, but sometimes "aliens" come through as well. They have told me that they do not mention this to others, so as not to have the veracity of their channelling called into question. And there are those who claim to be able to contact aliens at will. As we have seen already, this was a claim made by Ted Owens. And there have been others as well.[353] Aliens could be liminal beings who are able to cross the boundary between physical manifestation and other levels of reality and with whom we could interact either "here" or "there."

There is one last relevant apparent incident that I want to bring to the discussion. On March 16, 1967, at two of the Echo Flight Minuteman Intercontinental Ballistic Missile launch facilities for nuclear weapons in the United States, "*all* the maintenance and security personnel present at both sites reported seeing UFOs hovering over the silos."[354] One of the missiles went offline. Then more followed until "all ten ... missiles went offline and became inoperable." It turned out that "all the missiles had suffered a guidance and control fault."[355] However, the missiles were independent of one another, so they should not all have been affected. A week later the same thing happened at another launch facility about 20 miles away. An investigation apparently revealed that "all of those missiles were clean and did not shut themselves down, it had to have come from outside."[356] In general, UFOs appear to have been frequently sighted around nuclear facilities.[357] This leads to the question of whether aliens could disable nuclear weapons so that they could not fire, and, therefore, that such weapons would not pose a threat to human survival. And this leads to the further, speculative question of whether they have already done so.

Planetary Transformation

I think it is clear from our analyses of global crises that our planet has already changed. It is not a matter of going back to a state of natural innocence, but, rather, of acknowledging that we are in the midst of a process of transformation and, thus, of trying to take as much control of events as possible so as to direct them toward a beneficial outcome. In addition to the numerous ordinary strategies that have been available to humanity all along, the following is a list of additional resources that could be useful to us:

1. *Self-development.* The existential crisis precipitated by global crises can prompt self-development that itself is the key to the resolution of our global problems.

2. *Strengthening desirable meaning fields.* Through the way in which we think, we can strengthen desirable meaning fields so as to structure harmonious change.

3. *Anomalous transformation.* Through subtle activism, we can use meditation, ME, and whatever methods are used by Thomaz and others with macro-pk abilities to manipulate physical manifestation toward desirable outcomes.

4. *Cooperation with non-human beings.* It is possible that we have access to discarnate beings of various sorts who could potentially help us to solve the problems that we face by providing knowledge or directly manipulating physical manifestation in beneficial directions.

Let us consider each of these resources in turn.

Self-Development

Is there any reason to even try to do anything, if we are on a collision course with extinction? Is denial our best option? Not so, for Roy Scranton, as we have already noted. He has spoken provocatively of the need to interrupt our usual patterns of activity in order to confront the situation that we face. "The rub now is that we have to learn to die not as individuals, but as a civilization."[358] Facing our own extinction raises existential questions: What is the purpose of human life? Why are we here in the first place? What is going on? These are questions that are awakened by the prospect of extinction. It is in extreme situations, when the usual routines of our everyday lives are stripped away as we confront our mortality, that a quest for meaning can arise.[359] Crises consume our attention and can lead to a psychological reorientation whereby we begin to seek answers to existential questions. And that seeking can be the beginning of self-development.[360] And, as we noted previously in this chapter, it is self-development that we need in order to mitigate these crises.

War correspondent Sebastian Junger noticed that sometimes during war time and other extreme situations, the people who are affected find greater meaning in their lives. For instance, 30,000 people were killed by German bombs dropped on London during World War II. The British Government was prepared for mass psychiatric casualties, but they did not materialize. Rather, admissions to psychiatric wards declined during the bombing and went back up when the bombing stopped. "And later, many civilians said that they actually missed the war. And what they missed was the sense that they all belong to this group that was struggling to survive."[361] We live in a horrific world. In the words of Roy Scranton, who fought in Iraq and saw its horrors first-hand:

> People are fighting and dying in ruined cities all over the planet. Neighbors are killing each other. Old women are bleeding to death in bombed rubble and children are being murdered, probably as you read this sentence. To live in that world is horrific. Constant danger strains every nerve. The only things that matter are survival, killing the enemy, reputation, and having a safe place to sleep. The experience of being human narrows to a cutting edge.[362]

It should not have to take such horror to awaken us to our humanity, yet, sometimes, during extremis, the people who are affected are empathically drawn together with a sense of belonging.[363] The patina of ordinary life disappears, and the genuine expression of meaningful human feelings sometimes emerges.

As the planetary crises deepen, either gradually through infrastructure collapse, or suddenly through a nuclear incident, humanity is coming under increasing psychological pressure. And that pressure could lead to a re-examination of what it means to be human and what, exactly, we would collectively like to be doing here on this planet. If sufficiently profound, such re-examination could lead to ontological awakening. We saw such awakening in the context of alien abduction experiences.

Awakening can also occur during a near-death experience or upon witnessing dramatic anomalous transformations such as those that occurred during the Scole experiment or during Thomaz's demonstrations. Although I am not in any way advocating the ingestion of psychedelic drugs, their use has sometimes also been associated with a degree of awakening. For instance, my undergraduate thesis student, Paula Rayo, spent four weeks in the Amazon gathering data from participants at ayahuasca ceremonies and found that self-reported existential meaning increased with participation in the ceremonies.[364] Arguably, without diminishing the need for a responsible relationship with nature, we could allow the global situation to act as a catalyst for our own conversion. An accelerator of our own self-development.

Strengthening Desirable Meaning Fields

In Chapter 2, "Meaning Beyond the Human," we discussed the notion of meaning fields with which we can interact, which structure our reality. These meaning fields encode the rules by which nature works, including *Gaian* and *Medean* processes. We can interact with meaning fields by "thinking" about them the right way, whatever that might be. If physical constants can change with time, then biological processes can also change. We can weaken them or strengthen them. Recall that one of the versions of the Gaia hypothesis was that the earth is a living organism. If the earth were not already a living organism that supported life, then, by creating that construct, we have given nature a way to structure our experience of the earth. This would be similar to what occurred in the Philip experiment. In other words, it is irrelevant how "scientific" the notion of a living planet is, what is relevant is that by using that notion we might be able to shift the planet toward optimizing processes that support life.

Anomalous Transformation

In Chapter 3, "Radical Transformation of Physical Manifestation," we discussed radical transformation. In particular, we considered some examples of radical biological transformation. In this chapter, Chapter 4, we considered calls for geoengineering to bring our planet back to a state of equilibrium. Is geoengineering enough? Do we also need "consciousness technologies?" Are "consciousness technologies" on their own enough? Notice that we are back to the marvels of a technological fix; it is just that this technological fix is more outlandish than geoengineering. We need better understanding of how such processes work if we are to use them for practical purposes.

In Chapter 1, "Consciousness Unplugged," I introduced a flicker theory of reality, which I developed further in Chapters 2 and 3. Perhaps we can put the theory to the test of global transformation. According to the theory, each *now* that we experience emerges from a prephysical substrate complete with its own past and future in apparent time. The structure of events in any given now is determined by meaning fields. Radical transformation is explained as a replacement of a *now* that is structured by one set of meaning fields with a *now* that is structured by a set of meaning fields that were not in the first *now*'s apparent future. In other words, the limits of change from one *now* to the next, along deep time, are the limits of our (and other embodied or disembodied entities') ability to manipulate the meaning fields that give rise to the structure of physical manifestation in each *now*. We are back to the question of how such meaning fields can be effectively altered. It may be that, through the pursuit of self-development, we could enter states of consciousness that might give us the capability to alter reality at that fundamental level.

Cooperation with Non-Human Beings

This brings us back to where we started this book, with the story about Richard Feynman. If we have access to discarnates of various sorts and aliens (incarnate or discarnate), can they help us to solve the problems that we face and turn our planetary crises into planetary transformation? If so, who else is out there? Are there "experts" of some sort who know how to create physical changes, such as the discarnates in the Scole experiment who apparently had the skill to dematerialize and rematerialize a crystal? Can we call on some experts to "dematerialize" some greenhouse gases? Or materialize more crops to feed the expanding population? Or defuse nuclear weapons so that they will not fire? Or manipulate the minds of people who are trying to kill other people so that they will stop killing? Wait a minute. Where does this end? And who gets to decide what gets done? If we start taking the existence of discarnates seriously, then lots of questions are raised.[365]

We have already considered the following question: "Is this already happening?" In other words, has there already been interference by non-human entities in human affairs? We have speculated about meddling by discarnates through poltergeist activity and instrumental transcommunication, and the manipulation of human biology by aliens. In addition, various historical figures have claimed to have had not only access to information from nonphysical sources but received assistance from such sources.[366] To give just one simple example, Charles Lindbergh, the first person to fly non-stop across the Atlantic Ocean in 1927, claimed to have been assisted by beings whose presences he could sense in the cockpit of his aeroplane, "The Spirit of St. Louis."[367] It could be productive to comb through the history of such claims to look for patterns and then to see whether any of the results of such an investigation could be useful for deliberately accessing whatever are the sources of such assistance for the purpose of dealing with planetary crises.

Another obvious question is to ask whether there are discarnate beings who are deliberately making matters worse. We already considered this when discussing apparent alien intrusions. There are also cases of possession, in which a person's mental health is ostensibly compromised by the presence of entities that have taken over a person's body.[368] So, there could be direct interference by discarnates with motives to mess things up as much as possible. And there could also be indirect interference by providing assistance to people who are messing things up. Clearly, it is not only those who are trying to improve planetary quality of life but those with specific agendas who are acting contrary to planetary interests, who could access resources from hidden aspects of reality. Is there any evidence for any of these types of interference or are we the sole agents of our self-destruction? In fact, is there a "war" between discarnates or aliens trying to help us and those trying to destroy us? That has been one of the claims about the alien agenda, that there are "good" aliens, sympathetic to human life on earth, and "evil" aliens who are trying to destroy us and take away our planet.[369] By their nature, these are difficult questions to answer. But I do not think that we should regard them as ridiculous questions. We need some systematic research to look for the effects of both positive and negative influences to try to understand what the forces are with which we need to reckon if we are to move our survival forward.

Conclusion

What I have done in this chapter has been, first, to rationally and dispassionately summarize some of the crises that we are confronting on our planet today. And I tried to show how the seriousness of our situation continues to increase as the structures that have given rise to these crises continue the indomitable exertion of their influence. Efforts to mitigate our headlong rush toward extinction have been gridlocked. We need practical solutions that work. And thus far, we have not found them.

Second, I showed how knowledge at the cutting edge of consciousness research could be useful for breaking the gridlock. In particular, could subtle activism be effective? This draws on the discussion about meaning fields and the relative effect that any given person can have on modifying the meaning fields that are controlling the expression of planetary unfoldment. Can we strengthen meaning fields that lead to a harmonious outcome? I also discussed various examples of anomalous transformation. Have we reached a point where we necessarily need to supplement conventional geoengineering with anomalous terraforming? Can planetary crises compel us to seek to study anomalous transformation? Can our deteriorating situation force us to examine the possibility that there could be discarnate beings to whom we could have access? Who might be able to work together with us to resolve our problems? And, perhaps most importantly, are there ways in which we can precipitate ontological awakening? Can the threat of annihilation itself draw forth a re-examination of our purpose in being alive on this planet? Can we start to take our situation seriously and collaborate together to create a smooth transition into a healthy future? Those are some of the issues that I have tried to address in this chapter.

I want to end this discussion with a couple of reflections. First, we usually think that for there to be any effective change, we will need to mobilize the appropriate channels through which effective action can be taken. But in a nonlocal universe, there could be ways of exercising influence that bypass the usual power structures. Working mentally toward harmonious planetary reconstruction could actually help. Second, it seems to me that waiting until our situation has deteriorated to the point where we are compelled to witness various atrocities before we address their causes is not a wise course of action. It would be less painful to motivate ourselves to grow into greater maturity without being forced to do so. And, it seems to me, beneficial planetary change requires personal self-transformation for its realization. Let us have a closer look at this theme in the next chapter, "Radical Self-Transformation."

Chapter 5

Radical Self-Transformation

Then all my earlier ways of grasping naturally faded away, and I came to rest in the great, spontaneous vastness of the originally pure ground of being. All things that arose as its creative expressions naturally released themselves in their own expanse. This essential nature – together with its creative expressions, which are free of modification, antidote, meditation practice, memory, grasping, and identification – is called path *pristine awareness. At that time, with the absence of mental activity, there was ultimate reality.*[370]

About 50 years ago I had a spontaneous mystical experience. It occurred on a sunny afternoon while I was visiting two friends who were planning a trip to northern Africa. I was kneeling by a large map that was spread out on the floor. As one of my friends came over to point out an oasis that they were planning to visit, I went into an interesting state of consciousness.

Perhaps the most salient feature of the experience was the apparent knowledge that perfection was inevitable. The only question was one of timing, whether it would occur sooner or later, and the apparent knowledge that the more I could release that which was imperfect, the more quickly perfection would arrive. This was accompanied by an apparent expansion of consciousness whereby I could see that all the difficulties that were occurring in my life were part of a greater pattern that was itself perfect. My suffering was due solely to the limitations of my restricted vision. Third, I was in a state of exceptional emotional well-being that could be characterized as bliss. Yet at the same time, I did not feel as though I were somehow "high" but, rather, the opposite. I felt more grounded than I had ever felt previously in my life; completely at peace with myself.

This experience lasted for at least several minutes. But it did not interfere with my interaction with my friends, which continued uninterrupted, asking questions about the oasis and listening to the details of their planned trip. The inner profundity that was occurring had no impact on my ability to behave in a completely ordinary manner.

I did recognize the experience as a mystical experience. For several years by then I had been studying the world's religious traditions and learning and practicing numerous forms of meditation and self-development. However, none of that had been on my mind as I chummed with my friends. In that sense, this is an example of a spontaneous mystical experience.[371] Since that time, I have become an academic with a research interest in transcendent states of consciousness, so I know more about them intellectually. I know the details of the range of explanations for them, from "brain burps" to "enlightenment."[372] And having had that experience myself has been helpful for understanding and articulating them in my teaching and writing. At a minimum, whatever the explanation for them, I know that such states do occur.

I want to focus on the juxtaposition of the emotional well-being that I was experiencing with my ability to interact in an ordinary way with my friends. My state of consciousness did not incapacitate me in any way. Rather, it simply set a highly desirable subjective tone for myself as a backdrop for my behaviour. So, I have some questions. Why not live one's life in such a state of consciousness on an ongoing basis? Is it possible to do that? And is there any reason not to live in such a state? Let us explore some answers to those questions. This will take us to research about persistent transcendent states and then a somewhat detailed examination of the nature of subjective experience in an effort to identify mental techniques that could be useful for precipitating such states. We will end with some reflections on this material.

Persistent Transcendent
States of Consciousness

Perhaps the place to start is to acknowledge that living blissfully in a persistent state of mental expansion would be regarded as an altered state of consciousness by the definition of an altered state that we used in Chapter 1, "Consciousness Unplugged." It is clearly not the normative, ordinary waking state with its customary ongoing stream of pleasures and worries. I will usually use the expression "transcendent state of consciousness" as a generic term to denote such euphoric states.

Would such an altered state not, somehow, be inappropriate or strange? I find the response given by Bernadette Roberts, a former Carmelite nun who has found herself in some such state, to be apposite. According to her, there is nothing strange about living one's life in such a state. Rather, it is the beginning of living a life that is truly human.[373] Roberts' argument makes sense to me based on the fact that, during my experience, I felt naturally grounded with intact faculties that allowed me to participate in our usual shared reality.

In fact, the opposite case could be made that the ordinary waking state is a strange state of unnecessary misery. Sometimes the analogy of sleep is used for the ordinary waking state, and shifting to a mystical state regarded as awakening.[374] More dramatically, the ordinary waking state has also been characterized as a pathological state of delusion, as I intimated in Chapter 1, "Consciousness Unplugged," with the mystical state being regarded as a state of sanity.[375]

By mentioning Roberts, I have intimated that there are people who appear to live their lives in transcendent states of consciousness. In the case of Roberts, these experiences occurred in a religious context, although she has stated that the members of her religious community did not really understand what had been happening to her.[376] I have also previously written extensively about the ongoing transcendent states of consciousness that occurred for the American mystic Franklin Wolff in the context of his spiritual development.[377] So, is that it? A few people, here and there, in religious and spiritual settings? So I thought.

For all that has been written and said about spiritual development, and for all that a wide range of techniques has been put into practice, the expectation seems to be that nothing much will actually occur. This brings to mind the religious studies scholar, Huston Smith, who has said that thirty years of Zen meditation practice led nowhere.[378] Only a tiny fraction of any system's practitioners appear to end up in a persistent transcendent state, and even then, we are suspicious of whether they have actually transcended anything or whether they are just behaving as though they have.[379] So I thought as well.

It turns out that there are a good number of people living in persistent states of consciousness. And there have been two recent studies carried out independently by Steve Taylor and Jeffery Martin, to find these people and to determine the nature of their psychological states. Let us consider them in turn.

Characteristics of the Awakened State

Steve Taylor has noted a number of perceptual, emotional, cognitive, and behavioural characteristics of a transcendent state relative to the ordinary waking state. The following is an abbreviated list.[380]

1. *Aliveness.* An increased sense of being alive so that the world seems fresh and filled with wonder and beauty.

2. *Interconnectedness.* A sense that everything is connected and works together harmoniously.
3. *Silence.* Mental chatter is attenuated, and inner silence strengthened.
4. *Euphoric mood.* Feelings of compassion and bliss become the baseline of one's daily life.
5. *Improved relationships.* One's relationships with others become deeper and more authentic.

For Taylor, there are two metacharacteristics of *wakefulness*, as he prefers to designate these states. The first is *openness*, which includes psychological fluidity and lack of boundaries, so that a person can experience connection rather than separation. The second metacharacteristic is that of *silence*. Without constant mind chatter we can settle down and enjoy what there is to experience by simply being present to whatever it is that is going on for us, allowing us to move through liminal states into a greater connection with a deeper underlying reality.

Taylor has several observations about his list. One of those is that not everyone experiences all of the characteristics on his longer list, although he has found it striking that those who are permanently awakened experience most of them at about the same degree of intensity, although the overall intensity of wakefulness varies. Another observation that he has made is that the perspective that is held by those who are in this state is more valid than that of those who are still asleep. Why? The answer is that these are the people who are more alive, with a broader view of reality than those who are still asleep.[381]

The latter point is one that I have raised several times previously in my writing, namely, that transcendent states appear to be noetically inclusive. The idea is that knowledge is synthetic, so that whoever knows more has a better understanding of the nature of reality. During my mystical experience, I realized that I was aware of everything that I ordinarily knew, that knowledge had not been obliterated to be replaced with something else, but that there was additional information that had been added so that, for a few minutes, my cognitive abilities were expanded so as to be able to integrate a greater amount of material at once. A common metaphor for expressing this synthetic aspect of the noetic quality of transcendent states is to say that the difference is that of no longer seeing in black-and-white, but of being able to see in colour. Nothing has been removed from the black-and-white view but, rather, it has been enhanced in ways that someone who is colour blind cannot appreciate. In other words, the idea is that there is a psychological shift, in such a way that one's experience has been changed so as to result in the characteristics noted above, without removing anything substantive from a person's understanding of reality.[382]

Wakefulness seems to be a desirable state, given that it includes exceptional psychological well-being, so how does someone get to be in a perpetual transcendent state? Taylor classified the pathways into three categories: there are those who are born awake; those who "wake up gradually over a long period of time, through a commitment to spiritual practice;" and those whose awakening is sudden, often apparently as a consequence of "intense psychological turmoil."[383] Taylor found the last of these, "posttraumatic transformation," to be the most common.[384] For instance, upon being diagnosed with stomach cancer and told that he would die soon, the musician Wilko Johnson apparently said "I felt an elation of spirit. You're walking along and suddenly you're vividly alive. ... I've spent most of my life moping in depressions and things, but this has all lifted."[385] But what is a person to do if they would deliberately like to be in such a state? This takes us to Jeffery Martin's research.[386]

The Finders

Similar to what Taylor has done, Martin investigated people who appeared to be living in a state of exceptional well-being, which he has called *persistent non-symbolic experience* (PNSE). Initially he had his participants complete various psychological self-report measures so as to be able to determine the characteristics of their states of mind. This was followed by extensive interviews to try to determine what it was that made these people different from others. As he followed this trail, he increasingly encountered "ordinary" people who had never publicly spoken about their state of well-being and whose behaviour was apparently indistinguishable from what it had been prior to their transition to PNSE.[387]

As he gathered his data, Martin noticed that there were differences between the states in which his participants found themselves. In particular, he identified four "locations" with numerous "sublocations," which seemed to progress from location 1 to location 4 along a continuum of well-being with the intimation of additional locations beyond 4. Perhaps the primary characteristic of this continuum is the increasing disappearance of the "narrative self;" the part of a person's psyche that creates mental chatter about who one is and what is going on with one's life. Furthermore, participants did not simply remain in a single location but moved around within locations as well as between them, with some doing so more than others.[388]

Location 1 is characterized by a deep sense that everything is okay. There is a sense of existential satisfaction and completion with a diminished need to seek answers to life's perplexing questions. Worries and fears, including the fear of death, are attenuated. There is greater inner silence and those who find themselves in this location are less attached to life's dramas than they were previously. They are less interested in their own or others' stories. There is a greater focus on the present rather than past or future. Peace and contentment surface in their psyche, with finders in this location seeking to optimize their occurrence.

Location 2 appears to be largely a deepening of the features of Location 1, with decreased thoughts related to the narrative self and an increased sense of well-being. Negative emotions become increasingly rare, being replaced with positive ones. There is decreased need for approval from others. Psychological boundaries become more porous so that one sometimes experiences nonduality, wherein the distinction between oneself and everything else disappears. It can feel as though something greater than oneself were acting through oneself and making one's decisions.

Those who find themselves in location 3 appear to have the qualities that are archetypally associated with spiritual enlightenment. They experience an impersonal positive emotion that is a mixture of love, joy, and compassion. Rarely do thoughts related to the narrative self distract them from their equanimity. There is a sense of deep connection to something other that is greater than themselves. For them, the world is profoundly perfect, although they are still likely to be engaged in activism aimed at its improvement. They are a delight to be with because of the value they place on being of service to others even though they have even lower levels of need for approval than finders in location 2.

The experience of location 4 is quite different from that of previous locations, in the sense that not only has the narrative self pretty much disappeared, but so has the experience of any emotions, positive or negative. This location is characterized by a deepened sense of well-being that is regarded as being significantly greater than that experienced in any of the previous locations. There is also a feeling of freedom which seems to be associated with an apparent loss of agency, so that finders at this location have the experience of not making any decisions themselves, but of having the universe, with which they are identified, act through them. Their state of nonduality is greater than that which occurs in location 2. There appear to be memory deficits in location 4, which interfere with finders' ability to remember to get things done, and which seem to be related to an intensification of living in the present. Some finders are "Fluid 4's" who have the ability to move between location 4 and earlier locations, as necessary for different aspects of their professional and personal lives.

Are there four such locations, with clearly demarcated boundaries, or are there just variations of an awakened state due to individual differences, such as those described by Taylor? What come to my mind are the transcendent experiences of Franklin Wolff, whose philosophy we have considered previously. Wolff found himself in a nondual state that could reasonably be identified with Martin's location 3. He had not been expecting anything further, but then found himself being overtaken by an "overwhelming power that required all the active phase of the resources of consciousness to face it."[389] He called this a state of *High Indifference* in which all opposites were reconciled. In particular, "this state is not characterized by an intensive or active feeling of felicity" as he found himself "on a level of consciousness where there is no need of an active joy." Nor does such a state seem attractive to those who have not experienced it. For Wolff:

> if this state had been outlined to me … as an abstract idea, it could not by any possibility have seemed attractive. But while fused with the state, all other states that could formerly have been objects of desire seemed flaccid by comparison.[390]

While the preceding descriptions of states of consciousness are based on Martin's work without independent verification, there is support in the mystical literature for at least some of the distinctions that Martin has found between the locations.

The Finders Course

One of the questions that Martin says that he had asked his participants was what they had done that had precipitated a shift into PNSE.[391] It turned out that there had been only a half-dozen or so techniques that they had found that had worked. So, Martin put together an 18-week online course during which students taking the course would practice versions of these techniques. He front-loaded the course with positive psychology exercises so as to set a positive tone, and took various self-report measures to track psychological changes.[392] After nine iterations of the course, Martin has claimed that consistently 73% to 74% of participants who complete the course have transitioned to these higher states of consciousness.[393] If true, this is a remarkable level of achievement.

At this point, the technical information about the methodology and results of Martin's studies have not been published in academic journals and, until they have, this is all quite interesting but difficult to evaluate. For instance, which criteria, exactly, were used for determining whether a person had transitioned to one of the four locations? Was it just a subjectively reported feeling of "okayness?" Was it more precise than that? And what about those who experienced only temporary transcendent states of consciousness? And those who do not appear to fit into any of the locations?

Finders Course Alumni Survey

In 2017, one of my students, Kelsey Thomas, and I decided to survey Finders Course alumni to see if we could determine some of the psychological aspects of their state of being. At that point, there were about 500 members of the Finders Course alumni organization. We created a survey on Western University's server, and invited Finders Course alumni to log in to answer our questions. We included three commonly used psychological self-report measures along with 36 Likert-type items and eight open response items that we created ourselves. The three psychological measures consisted of Ron Pekala's Phenomenology of Consciousness Inventory (which can be used to assess the state of consciousness in which a person finds herself), Carol Ryff's Scales of Psychological Well-Being, and a Global Motivation Scale. The items that we created ourselves were about the frequency of thoughts, presence of the self, nonduality, knowledge about reality, and feelings of okayness, joy, and satisfaction. We also asked for basic demographic information and the location in which participants would place themselves using Martin's scheme.

We received 55 completed questionnaires, 23 from women and 30 from men, with an average age of 55; 33 of whom had completed a postgraduate degree and others of whom had less education. They were fairly evenly spread out with regard to Martin's locations including eight who were not in any location and nine who were beyond location 4.

We began by cluster analysing 18 of the items that we had developed and chose a solution with two clusters. We labelled the first cluster "Okayness" and found that it contained items about nonduality, joy, and understanding of reality, in addition to feelings of okayness. The second cluster we labelled "Self," which included feeling the presence of a "self" and feeling that one knows what is happening. We turned these two clusters into scales that ended up having good reliability[394] and that had a small negative correlation between them, with 16% of the variance being shared.[395] So the first, somewhat surprising observation is that feelings of okayness are not necessarily tied to losing the sense of self.

Martin's locations, as reported by our respondents, proved to be a key variable in the data. In particular, Okayness increased with location and Self generally decreased with location. Four of the six Scales of Psychological Well-Being increased overall with location, namely Positive Relations with Others, Environmental Mastery, Self-Acceptance, and Personal Growth. The Global Motivation Scale did not have a statistically significant relationship with location but it did have a strong correlation with Purpose in Life, from the Scales of Psychological Well-Being.

At the beginning of the survey, we asked participants to sit silently for a minute and then asked them to fill out the Phenomenology of Consciousness Inventory, which consists of 53 items measuring 21 dimensions of consciousness. In general, participants scored above the normative values for positive experiences and below normative values for dysphoric ones.

Cognitive dimensions suggested that the mind seemed to be clearer with greater absorption and less internal dialogue, imagery, and awareness of the self, compared to normative values. Furthermore, scores depended on location. Thus, sadness, fear, and anger flattened to zero for location 2 and above. The numerical values of love and joy peaked at location 3 and then dropped for locations 4 and beyond location 4, although only some of those fluctuations were statistically significant. It appears that, for some participants, emotional experience is attenuated or takes on a different form in location 4 and beyond location 4. This was reflected in some of the written comments. When asked about the detrimental effects of transitioning to PNSE, Participant 11 wrote that his "lack of emotions" impacted his relationship with his family who did not understand.

Overall, our data confirm the general characteristics of Martin's descriptions of the psychological states of participants in the Finders Course who have transitioned to one of the locations. It seems as though the psyche resets from the ordinary waking state to a state of compassion and joy in location 3 and then a state of "high indifference" in location 4. At the same time, the role of the "self" in such transitions appears to be more complicated than a simple loss of self and requires more research to untangle. Certainly, it is premature to think that simply transitioning to one of the locations would solve our planetary predicament. The impact of persistent transcendent states of consciousness on global transformation needs to be carefully investigated.

So, what are the techniques that are likely to lead to transitioning to PNSE? In my conversations with him, Martin has revealed that the most effective methods appear to be self-awareness practices in which there is an effort to invert consciousness. So, let us consider some of these strategies outside the context of Martin's work.

Phenomenology of Consciousness

Our approach in this book is a scientific one. What that means is that truth-claims are grounded in empirical observations. The prototype of empirical observation is sensory perception. Consciousness, as we have defined it, is about interior experiential events. Looking inward, rather than outward, is usually defined as *introspection*, to which we have alluded already several times in this book. But what is that? How does one use it? How reliable is it? Perhaps the first thing to note is that introspection has had a tumultuous history.[396] And the second thing to note is that any discussion of introspection already involves some conceptualization of the nature of the mind that is both the observational tool being used as well as the object being examined. So, it seems to me, we need to consider at least three relevant aspects of the mind to even figure out our methodology: introspection (also mindfulness and inquiry), will (including self-determination and decisiveness), and intentionality (including attention and the notion of self). And there is no obvious entry point into this material.

However, there are a few initial remarks that I think are important to make. The first is that in reading the relevant academic literature in preparation for writing this chapter, I was struck by how little agreement there is among philosophers, psychologists, and other academics about any of these three aspects of the mind. The second is the observation, already made in Chapter 1, "Consciousness Unplugged," that much of the theorizing about the nature of the mind is based on a sample size of one—the theorist who is doing the theorizing, usually without explicit reference to her own observations. This raises the question of the extent to which one's own experience should influence one's ideas about the nature of consciousness.[397] But perhaps more to the point, if the subject matter is ongoing experience and we do not explicitly refer to our own experience, and only allow nonconscious biasing of our ideas by our experience, then are we cutting off access to critical data? In fact, the relevant data largely consist of third-person accounts of first-person accounts of first-person data, so why not explicitly include a first-person account of first-person data?[398] Third, research about the mind is usually based on information about the ordinary waking state of consciousness, although there has been increasing respect for deviations from normative functioning resulting from pathological states such as depersonalization or Cotard's syndrome.[399] And fourth, how useful are theories of mind based on the ordinary waking state for understanding the functioning of the mind in persistent transcendent states where the structure and dynamics of the mind appear to be fundamentally different from what they are during the ordinary waking state? In spite of these methodological difficulties, let us proceed as best we can.

Intentionality

Let me start with intentionality. In common usage, the word "intentionality" refers to the intention to do something. That is not the meaning in this context. Rather, the meaning of "intentionality" in philosophy and consciousness studies has to do with the structure of conscious mental acts. When I teach students what this is, I draw the following picture on the chalkboard: I write the word "Self," then draw an arrow from the word "Self" pointing to the right and write the word "Object" at the tip of the arrow. I explain that *intentionality* refers to the characteristic of the mind whereby there are "objects" for a "self" along with the directionality of the objects being the focus of attention for whatever it is that is the subject, which I am calling a "self." I try to clarify this by saying that the term "aboutness" is sometimes used as a rough equivalent for "intentionality," in the sense that thoughts are always about something, and, more generally, that our experience consists of ongoing contents. Something goes on for us within the privacy of our experience. I make it clear that this has nothing to do with whether or not the "objects" have any correspondence in physical manifestation; that they are simply part of the structure of conscious mental acts. If I am thinking about a unicorn, then the unicorn is an object for whatever is the subject. This is the definition of intentionality that I use, which is based on Edmund Husserl's notion.[400] More generally, "Intentionality ... has to do with the directedness, aboutness, or reference of mental states ... and is sometimes seen as equivalent to, what is called 'mental representation.'"[401]

A flood of questions arises. Do all thoughts have intentional structure? Does consciousness necessarily entail intentionality? What is the self? How do we know any of this? And so on. The answers to these questions are all over the place. But let us plough on as though we knew what we were doing.

Suppose that we can shift our emphasis, however that might be possible, along this arrow of intentionality. What I mean by that is that we are usually somewhere in middle of the arrow, in that there is a sense of stuff going on for us without our being overly identified with either the self or the objects. But suppose now that we shift the emphasis onto the objects. In my diagram on the chalkboard, that would be a shift toward the right. We would call that *absorption*. We forget about our selves and lose ourselves in whatever activity with which we are engaged. Those can be euphoric experiences; in which case we call those *flow* states. One of the characteristics of flow is precisely a loss of awareness of the self.[402] In *concentrative meditation*, one restricts attention to a single object, or to semantically related objects. The idea is that as we succeed in doing so, we shift our awareness away from the self into the object, possibly becoming identified with it.[403] So the shift in emphasis could potentially be a shift of *identity*.

Now suppose we go the other way. In my diagram, we would be shifting to the left, back toward the self. So, suppose we dissociate from the objects of our experience. We recognize the objects of thought as objects. We *disidentify* from the contents of our experience.[404] And we can deliberately assume an internal posture of watching the flow of contents of experience, such as in the practice of *mindfulness*.[405] Euphoric variations of experiences can include stillness of the contents so that awareness itself remains as an existential quale.[406] And dysphoric variations can include derealization and dissociative disorders.[407] I will also use the terminology of *dissociation* for disidentification.

The Self

What about this subjective aspect of intentionality that I have called a "self." Is there a self? Three distinctions about subjectivity are sometimes made. First we have the notion of a self as simply the one for whom anything occurs at all, called "for-me-ness."[408] This can be interpreted minimally as an aspect of the occurrence of experience that fixes it to a particular individual as her experience rather than someone else's. A second type of subjectivity is that of there somehow being awareness of the subject herself in the act of having experiences, "me-ness."[409] Third, we have "mineness" whereby there is explicit awareness of both for-me-ness and me-ness.[410] In other words, a person takes ownership of the experiences that occur for her. It is not clear at the outset whether any of these "exist" and what the relationships are among them.

So what are we to make of this? For some theorists, we have ongoing awareness of the subjective aspect of experience so that

> each of us is permanently aware of him- or herself in a pre-reflective and pre-conceptual way in any moment of his or her conscious life. The general concept of an experiencing subject is acquired on the basis of that omnipresent pre-reflective self-awareness.[411]

For other theorists, we are simply victims of the *refrigerator-light illusion*, whereby we attribute properties to the mind that appear to be there whenever we look, without realizing that the looking could be creating the appearance of those properties.[412] Thus, we have contradictory opinions that range from the notion that we have ongoing awareness of the subjectivity of experience to denial that such subjectivity is a structural feature of the mind. But we plough on.

To what extent do we identify with the self? In other words, how rigid is our identification with whatever is the subject of experience? There is a fairly superficial layer to this, what William James called the "me," that consists of the characteristics that we attribute to ourselves, such as our gender, age, that we are a nice person, smart, and so on. These can be regarded as conceptual accretions gained from our life-long interactions with the world or something of that sort. We could well be identified with that, but what is at issue here is the for-me-ness triad, the sense of being a subject for objects of thought. What James called the "I."[413] How rigidly are we a self in that regard?

It was when I was trying to understand the experiences of people with dissociative identity disorder (DID) that I slowly started to realize that the rigidity of identification with a "self," that I had taken for granted, might not be there. In the usual version of the aetiology of DID, a person learns to deal with traumatic events by dissociating from whoever it is that is experiencing the trauma. For instance, while being assaulted, a person could imagine themselves as being a crack in the wall of the room in which they find themselves and looking back at the scene from that vantage point.[414] I interpreted such dislocation to mean that the identification with the subject of experience was still located within the person's physical body, but that the determination to escape the situation resulted in an imaginative fantasy of looking back at the scene from the vantage point of the crack in the wall. But that crack in the wall persona can become an alternate personality. So, then, where is the self-identity? The answer is that it is possible that a person with DID does not have a reference for the self. Such a person learns to use the word "I" appropriately as a child but does not actually know what it means.

What started to slowly dawn on me was that the sense of self, which I had assumed was rigidly fastened to the subjective tail of intentionality, might not be so securely fastened after all. In particular, it seemed to me that it could be dislocated, from the body to the wall, for instance. Or from the self to the object, in the case of concentrative meditation. Or smeared out from the self to include everything in nondual states of consciousness. This could result in the experience of being "headless" or being the entire universe looking out through one's eyes.[415]

Introspection

So, how are we going to "look" inside to figure out what is happening? That looking would be introspection. And what is that? That ranges from the idea that there is no such thing to some form of actual inner observation.[416] And if there is some form of inner observation, is it analogous to sensory perception or is it just a form of cognition? For instance, "Conscious states are often held to be in some sense self-intimating, in that the mere having of them involves, requires, or implies some sort of representation or awareness of those states."[417] In fact, what exactly is the difference between perceptions and thoughts anyway?

Let us go one step further and start by thinking of introspection as the literal sensory perception of our own bodies. This includes touch, proprioception, balance through the vestibular system, nociception, and interoception. So, for instance,

> Interoception provides information about the physiological condition of the body in order to maintain optimal homeostasis, namely, cardiovascular, respiratory, energy (feeding and glucose), and fluid (electrolyte and water) balances. The parasympathetic system is sensitive to mechanical, thermal, chemical, metabolic, and hormonal status of skin, muscle, joints, teeth and viscera.[418]

The activity of these senses results in richly textured bodily experiences that likely contribute to the development of a notion of a self and what that self is like.[419]

Does this perception have intentional structure? In some cases, such as a stomach-ache, yes. In other cases, such as losing one's balance, maybe not so much. But there is also the notion that deliberately inwardly directed attention during some mystical practices can result in a loss of intentionality. Olga Louchakova-Schwartz has studied the "introspective space" of over 5,000 participants who have reported the occurrence of religious experiences.[420] According to Louchakova-Schwartz, we can "see and act inside in the same way as externally, not physically but by intention and focus."[421] Such seeing and acting creates its own "field of consciousness" which "includes compounds of impressions of the internal senses, images, thoughts, and feelings; vague representations of the internality of the anatomical body, and perhaps, even of the brain ... also, there are memories integrated into the body schema."[422] According to Louchakova-Schwartz, with such practices, two states are possible. In one of them, intentionality is preserved. In the other state, there is an unveiling of intentionality "as if awareness is digging into, folding onto, or being sucked into the phenomenologically material 'stuff' of the meditating subject"[423] giving access to a "fundamental mode of appearing that is precisely *non-* and even *pre-*intentional and that therefore essentially differs from intentionality."[424]

As an example, Louchakova-Schwartz has noted the phenomenology resulting from following St. Simeon the New Theologian's instructions to monks in the tenth century to "search inside yourself with your intellect so as to find the place of the heart where all the powers of the soul reside."[425] The result, as deduced from over 300 contemporary practitioners, is that

the outgoing thrust of intentionality is weakened, but self-awareness, on the contrary, becomes more prominent and intensified. ... Between the initial reversal of intentional consciousness onto the self, and the full cessation of intentional consciousness when it becomes absorbed in the core of self-awareness, there emerges a whole field of phenomena 'inside' embodied self-awareness.[426]

And what are these phenomena? According to St. Simeon, initially "darkness and impenetrable density" and later "unceasing joy" and the intellect beholding "itself entirely luminous and full of discrimination,"[427] whatever that might mean.

What are we to make of this? If we direct our attention "inward" rather than "outward," then we find a mixture of bodily awareness and what appears to be imaginal activity, initially having intentional structure, but sometimes resolving itself into non-intentional "self-awareness" and a variety of non-intentional phenomena. We have already discussed Wolff's notion of introception—knowledge through identification with that which is known. For Wolff, subject–object duality breaks down and, as it does so, it permits a new type of knowledge to emerge, which does not have intentional structure. The various introspective techniques studied by Louchakova-Schwartz could trigger similar shifts into nondual states with their non-intentional knowledge.

We have considered introspection as a perceptual process, but is it actually a cognitive process of self-knowledge? And is knowledge itself sufficiently rich to intimate to itself its own properties,[428] including intentional structure and for-me-ness, me-ness, and mineness? What exactly is the difference between cognition and perception? Are they aspects of a single property of the mind that entails both of them? This is suggested by the occurrence of "transcendental awareness," a form of remote viewing that sometimes occurs during near-death experiences, which seems to be an amalgamation of perception and knowledge.[429] We have discussed remote viewing throughout this book; let us now consider its possible relevance to introspection.

Introspective Remote Viewing

The notion of remote viewing opens up another possibility. Can introspection be remote viewing? In other words, can we turn remote viewing onto ourselves to "look" at our own minds? I do not recall having ever seen anything in the remote viewing literature about this. Ostensibly remote viewing the interiors of bodies occurs[430] and can certainly be applied to one's own body. But what if we remote view the mind?

I want to bring in James Carpenter's First Sight theory of remote viewing and influencing. For Carpenter, these anomalous experiences are not isolated events that sometimes occur for whatever reason but, rather, the surfacing of nonconscious, ongoing, psychological processes. For Carpenter, we are already always directly interacting with our "environment" without the mediation of our physical senses. Julia Mossbridge and I made the same point in *Transcendent Mind*.[431] Everything is deeply interconnected so that we are influencing and being influenced by everything that has ever happened, will ever happen, or is happening now. In addition,

A person's psychological transactions with the universe are best understood in terms of personal meaning rather than impersonal process. Even in regard to unconscious processing of reality, things are essentially what they mean to an individual in the context of the individual's concerns. These transactions extend beyond the physical boundaries of the person and cannot be adequately represented by reductionistic accounts in the impersonal language of chemistry and physics.[432]

In other words, our deeply interactive experience is structured according to our meanings, which extend beyond the human into the universe. This is, of course, also a characteristic feature of the proposed meaning fields discussed in Chapter 2, "Meaning Fields." And we have already noted that such a conception of reality is frequently held by those who have transitioned to transcendent states of consciousness.

Is remote viewing intentional? Clearly yes, for much of it. In fact, the early research entailed the identification of a physical object or locale.[433] Is it always intentional? It is not clear that it would necessarily need to be intentional. Is it cognitive or perceptual? Perhaps it is fundamentally transcendental awareness which has features of both perception and knowledge. Can we apply it to introspection? Are we already automatically applying it to introspection without knowing that we are doing so? Is it possible that the segue apparently identified by Louchakova-Schwartz from intentional to non-intentional introspection corresponds to gaining access to the usually nonconscious level at which remote viewing is already occurring? And then, at that level, something shows up as a result of using whatever are the psychological mechanisms of remote viewing.

There is another twist to introspection. In his research about hypnagogic and hypnopompic states, Andreas Mavromatis found that hypnagogic imagery is sometimes autosymbolic. What he meant by that is that the images that occurred for a person would be symbolic representations of what she had just been thinking about.[434] For instance, my worrying showed up as an image of a fly buzzing around the room and my reasoning about how we cannot escape from the mind showed up as a wall of mirrors encircling me.[435] In fact, such symbolization need not only occur as one is falling asleep. It appears to be occurring during dreams.[436] And it can be deliberately evoked, such as with the use of free drawing exercises, as a way of accessing nonconscious parts of one's psyche.[437] What is notable here is that the psyche seems to have the capacity to convert cognition into perception; not literally, but symbolically.[438]

The question now is whether this symbolization capacity of the psyche is being activated during introspection. Is that the process underlying some of the phenomenal contents of introspection found by Louchakova-Schwartz? Also, remote viewing itself is not always literal, but can be symbolic. In particular, in my case, my precognitive dreams are usually symbolic rather than literal.[439] So, as we seek to look at or know our own minds, are the results of such investigation sometimes showing up in symbolic form? Is it that introspection is not revealing a literal image of whatever is the underlying reality, but rather a symbolic representation of that underlying reality? Or is introspection just producing a symbol of our mind's activity as we seek introspective knowledge? These are important questions, which need to be addressed theoretically and empirically as we move forward with our understanding of introspection.

Will

The final aspect of the psyche, in addition to intentionality and introspection, that is relevant to any discussion about fundamental shifts of consciousness is the will. Materialism usually comes with determinism,[440] the idea that the occurrence of all events in reality is strictly determined through some cause and effect interactions of matter. There is no room for free will in such a conceptualization of reality and, hence, no need to help people to develop their wills. So, for a determinist, believing that one has a free will and choosing to use it are just determined events.[441] However, those are determined, or not so determined, events that turn out to be conducive to well-being. Self-determination has been correlated with a number of variables associated with well-being.[442] From a practical standpoint, unless a person is in Location 4, there is usually a felt sense of will, whatever that will might end up being as an aspect of the psyche. And it is useful to use it to the best of one's ability.

The will plays an important role in the dynamics of the mind. One of the things we can do is to direct our attention to different objects of thought. So, I am attending to the string of text emerging on a white page on my computer screen as I type but I can shift my attention to an imaginary unicorn. In fact, there is a range of possible targets of my attention at any given time. And, by definition, it is the will that allows me to shift my attention between them. And we can do that more or less effectively.[443] I usually conceptualize attention using the arrow of intentionality. That arrow gets pointed at different objects. But does attention require such intentional structure?

All three of these qualities of mind — directing attention, introspection, and the will — are used when meditating. For instance, in concentrative meditation, the idea is to restrict one's attention to a single object. For example, a common practice is to pay attention to one's breathing. So, breathing becomes the contents of experience, introspection is used to monitor whether or not one is paying attention to breathing, and the will is engaged in returning attention back to breathing if one notices that one is no longer paying attention to breathing. For all the theoretical difficulties with intentionality, introspection, and the will, there are no practical issues with using them in such a meditation practice.

Inverting Consciousness

Now that we have this somewhat cursory preparation, we can address the issue of self-awareness techniques, which seem to be the most effective for transitioning to persistent transcendent states of consciousness. For Franklin Wolff, "the whole value of the objective development of consciousness lies in the arousing the consciousness of being conscious."[444] In other words, we can become aware of our own awareness. For Wolff, pain and suffering have a positive value insofar as they force awakening. We have seen this already, directly, with Taylor's notion of posttraumatic transformation to persistent transcendent states of consciousness. OK, so we have become aware of our awareness. Then what?

For Wolff, there needs to be an inversion of consciousness.

Recognition and Liberation is attained by an inversion of the vector of consciousness. This means that the focus of attention must be turned toward the subjective pole and away from the objective content of consciousness. The effort must be to attain a consciousness without objective content.[445]

Wolff has conceptualized consciousness as flowing outward from an apparent subject toward an object. Our task is to turn it back through 180 degrees "so that it returns toward its source without projecting an object in consciousness, no matter how subtle."[446]

How is that possible? The structure of intentionality is such that there is a subject for which there are objects. Here we are asked to turn our attention to the subject without regarding it as an object. My interpretation of this, for a long time, was to suppose that this meant that we are to sink back into the subject, so to speak; to stay with the awareness of the subjectivity of our conscious mental acts. This corresponds to moving toward the subjective pole of the subject–object arrow of intentionality, as described previously, which is to say, dissociation from the objects of experience. In other words, we are not actually turning anything around, but rather allowing ourselves to be subjects in the sense of abiding with the sense of existence.[447]

Cutting Through to Pristine Awareness

It was while taking an online course taught by the religious scholar Alan Wallace[448] about Dzogchen, a type of Tibetan Buddhism, that I started to see the inversion technique somewhat differently. The following is my interpretation. In Tibetan Buddhism, a distinction is made between *substrate consciousness* and *pristine awareness*. My understanding is that substrate consciousness is the domain of the ordinary waking state, with its intentional structure. Pristine awareness is a transcendent, yet immanent, reality from which substrate consciousness emerges. If we just dissociate in the process of inverting our consciousness, then all that happens is that we isolate ourselves from the objects of experience and move back into the subject. *But we have not left the ordinary mind.* We are still within the structure of subject–object duality. We are substrate consciousness. We have not left the room. And I think that this may be the state of consciousness of many people who appear to be enlightened.

In order to realize the transcendent state of pristine awareness, we need the *cutting through* practice of Trekchö. And what is that? According to my interpretation of Wallace, much of Tibetan Buddhist practice consists of inquiry. We are to query the nature of the mind and then look at the mind to "see" what there is to "see." The mind, by this account, is whatever we find to be the mind. This is introspection with an emphasis on its perceptual aspects. We look at the mind to see what we can see. So, the practice is to deliberately invert our awareness in order to try to see that which is doing the observing. And, no, according to Wallace, this is not an impossible task. It is an actual practice. Sustaining such inward focus can be exhausting, so we can release the inward directedness of our attention outward for a while and then focus back inward again. Done rhythmically, this can result in a "chopping" action that chips away at confinement in substrate consciousness.[449]

There is another, more demonstrative variation of inverting consciousness, called "the headless way."[450] I point at something in front of me. This would be the arrow of intentionality. What am I pointing at? Clearly there is an "I" directing attention toward some object in the environment. Then I point at my foot. What am I pointing at? I am directing attention toward my foot. I point at my torso. What am I pointing at? Well, that would be my torso. Then I point my finger eye-level, straight back at my face. What am I pointing at? When people do this exercise, sometimes they apparently transition into a persistent transcendent state. When I do the exercise, nothing happens. I am just left staring at my finger wondering what it is that is supposed to happen.

One way of thinking about these exercises is that their purpose is to get the location of for-me-ness to move away from being positioned apparently in the centre of my head.[451] If I am the object, then where is the subject? Not where I think it is. When I make the self an object of attention, is this the same attention that I use when I am paying attention to an imaginary unicorn? To use an expression that we have already introduced, is mineness self-intimational? Is there a secondary attention that can be used for "observing" the self? Another way to conceptualize these exercises is to regard them as challenging the notion of intentionality itself. What if there were to be no arrow? What if there were to be just contents and a subjective sense that attaches to some of them? In other words, what if there are no vectors that need to be turned back on themselves? And that this is why such an exercise works. We are simply correcting a misunderstanding. The idea, perhaps, is to stress the intentional structure to the point where it starts to destabilize and then collapse. For Düdjom Lingpa,

> I ardently meditated on luminosity and cognizance. Consequently, at times it seemed as if that which appeared and that which was aware nondually dispersed outward ... and then converged inward again. On other occasions, that which appeared and that which was aware were nondually and spontaneously objectified and then naturally disappeared. At other times appearances and awareness were nondually self-emergent and self-dissolving, such that I understood that they were not projected out from within the body. I knew that these experiences were attributable to grasping at the ground of being as an object.[452]

"Luminosity," as I understand it, refers to the "light" of consciousness, existential qualia, which would be the sense that anything is going on at all. "Cognizance" I interpret as understanding, the ability to know. Consciousness seems to have a blend of both existential qualia and understanding. In this quotation, I find it interesting that intentionality is warped and twisted as though Lingpa were struggling to free himself of intentionality. And, more specifically, to free himself from continuing to regard the "ground of being" as the sort of thing that can be objectified by the mind.

There is one other way to think about this exercise and, for that, I want to go back to the distinction between the perceptual and the cognitive. According to Franklin Wolff, the spiritual traditions of the East were based on an aesthetic reorientation from the discrete to the universal. As I understand it, what this means is that an effort is made to shift away from perceiving the particulars of a sensory image toward the transcendent ground of there being the capacity for any perception at all. In the West, we have developed a powerful capacity for theoretical thinking, so that movement from the discrete to the universal consists of moving from concrete thoughts toward the "transcendent ground of knowledge."[453] And Wolff has claimed that his contribution to our understanding of spiritual transformation has been that of pointing out this shift of method away from the aesthetic to the theoretical. So now, applying Wolff's suggestion, rather than "looking" at what there is to see when the arrow of consciousness is turned back to its source, what if we just *understand* what there is to *know* when we enact the reversal? In other words, what happens if we do a straight substitution of knowledge for perception? Does that work?

Not for me. At least, not so far. I have been able to direct attention to the sense of existence that goes on for me. And to conceptualize the emergence of contents for a subject. But that is as far as I get. At one point, an image arose spontaneously, possibly autosymbolically, of the transparent surface of a hollow sphere, like a soap bubble, empty inside. The idea was that contents of experience emerge in an ongoing stream as though on the surface of an empty bubble, and that is all. The nature of the subject for whom they emerge remains unknown. So that it is not that there is no "self" but that knowledge of the presence or absence of a "self" is unavailable to me.

Waking Up

We have been considering Dzogchen as practiced in the Nyingma tradition, but it is also available in a second Tibetan tradition, that of Bön.[454] So, from the point of view of a Bön practitioner, what is to be done?

> The practitioner of best capacity does not need to meditate or contemplate, but needs to make a decision. By this firm decision he or she is liberated. This is the method of the Trekchö system.[455]

So, there seem to be different Trekchös around. But maybe I have been placing emphasis in the wrong place, namely, on technique. Maybe the meditative contortions to wrap consciousness back on itself are unnecessary, whether or not an arrow of intentionality exists. Perhaps the active ingredient is the will, with which we can decisively switch from the ordinary waking state of consciousness to a transcendent state.[456]

Our earlier notion of meaning fields may be helpful as a way of understanding this. We can be in one of a number of stable states of consciousness. One of those is the ordinary waking state. Another is sleep. Through a physiological mechanism, we transition from the waking state to the sleep state. Suppose, now, that we are asleep, having a bad nightmare. Some people, when they become aware of the fact that they are asleep, can will themselves to wake up. So, through the activation of the will, whatever psychological resources that implies, we can force ourselves to awaken. Do we have an analogous situation here? We realize that we are "asleep" during the ordinary waking state. Our life has become a "nightmare." As Wolff noted, suffering can arouse a desire for awakening. Can we will ourselves to "wake up" into a state of pristine awareness? And if we decide to awaken, is there a further effort of the will that is required in order to bring our decision to manifestation?

There is just such a practice in Dzogchen. According to Padmasambhava:

> At this time, powerfully imagine that your environment, city, house, companions, conversation, and all activities are a dream; and even say out loud, 'This is a dream.' Continually imagine that this is just a dream.[457]

In this exercise, one creates a template of what reality is like in the imagination, and then mindfully holds that template in one's mind as an object of attention. The idea is that by doing so, "your imagination may open up, break down the barriers that are preventing you from seeing what is already there—that you are dreaming."[458] This is reminiscent of Suzanne Padfield's method of visualizing the desired end state of a mobile.

In practicing Matrix Energetics (ME), I noticed that a practitioner can usually forgo some complicated technical sequence of actions, and simply manipulate a symbol that stands for that complicated technical sequence. We can think of this as bumping up to the meta-level. For instance, I can imagine that there is some sequence of actions that will create greater well-being in any given situation. I do not know what that sequence is. Perhaps I have insufficient ability to bring that knowledge into explicit awareness. Or I am too "lazy" to do so. No problem. I just imagine that I have access to that sequence and that I am instantiating it for the person with whom I am playing. Does that work? It seems to, sometimes.

So, is it possible to simply imagine being at a meta-level and deciding to shift to a transcendent state of consciousness? To tune out the meaning field for the ordinary waking state and tune in the meaning field for the transcendent state of consciousness that interests me? To tune it in by thinking about it? And to use a symbol to stand in for what I want but have not accessed in my experience? To select the meaning field that I want? Does that work? Perhaps.

These techniques are somewhat similar to not doing anything. In Dzogchen, one of the techniques is to eschew technique and to not do anything except remain in the desired state.

> Activity can not bring Buddhahood because all activities are material and therefore impermanent. Nature and final truth are like the sky; no activity can bring emptiness. ... Whoever wants to get into this nature should not make any kind of action — only remain in the final truth.[459]

There is nothing to do except to "remain" in the transcendent state as though it were already present. This could explain some of Steve Taylor's cases of naturally occurring awakening. However, for most people, this is not enough, since most people are not already awakened. For most people, "doing nothing" just leaves them with nothing. Rather, it seems to me that this is actually just another example of choosing a meaning field of interest. After all, "remaining" implies an activity of some sort determined by the will. And that activity could simply be imagining oneself to be in the desired state based upon some conception that one already has of what that state would be like.

Preparation

So why is not everyone awakened? Or, more specifically, awakened into a healthy state of transcendence, by some reasonable meaning of "healthy?" One way to think about a transition from the ordinary waking state to a persistent transcendent state is to consider that some sort of preparation is necessary for such a transition to be possible. And, certainly, some preparation may be needed for it to occur safely. If the capacity for switching from one state to another is not there, then a shift cannot occur in spite of one's best efforts. On the other hand, one's best efforts could bring about the conditions necessary for developing the necessary qualities. The task, then, becomes one of self-development for the purposes of creating the capacity for transcendence. Let us consider two different ways of thinking about such preparation.

I have previously written extensively about the need for the development of authenticity prior to any effort to transition to transcendent states of consciousness.[460] A way to think about this is to consider that all of the aspects of personality development need to have reached mature expression. In particular, different motivations, tendencies of thought, moods, and behaviours need to be integrated so that a person can act effectively in the world in which she finds herself. And she needs to have freed herself from social influence so as to be able to act freely on the basis of her own understanding. The idea is that when that level of development has reached fruition, then the next one, involving expansions of consciousness, can safely begin. Without such integration, expansions of consciousness could be disruptive.

Another way to think about such personality preparation is to consider the difference between getting rid of the personality and shaping it to be an effective aspect of one's psyche once one has awakened. For Martin, one of the key differences between the ordinary waking state and PNSE is the attenuation of the narrative self, the mind chatter about oneself that goes on continuously for many people. In some conceptualizations of transcendence, "mind chatter" is negatively valued. If so, then perhaps we can just locate the narrative self within ourselves and then, using some technique from some tradition, we simply delete it. Presto. No more mind chatter. Peace.

However, research about mind wandering has revealed that one of many beneficial purposes of spontaneous thinking is that it reminds us of current concerns. Current concerns are goals that we would like to realize. And our spontaneous thinking reminds us of those goals and the things that we need to do in order to realize them.[461] So if we get rid of the narrative self with its attendant mind chatter, then we might also lose a psychological resource. Is this what is happening for those people with memory impairment who have transitioned to Jeffery Martin's Location 4? Is there a connection? Perhaps.

What if we figure out how to retain an efficiently organized personality so that we can continue to use its resources for living our lives? Then the idea is not to get rid of the narrative self, but simply to disidentify from it so that one is not being pulled into whatever dramas eventuate. Rather, one deliberately chooses one's interactions with one's environment.[462] Could this distinction of approaches to the self also explain the disconnection between Okayness and Self that Kelsey Thomas and I found? Perhaps losing the "self" simply leaves one confused; whereas disidentification from the "self" with synthesis of its elements into some expanded version of the "self" is congruent with okayness.

A second way of thinking about preparation comes from the notion that there is an "energy body" underlying the physical body. In some variations of this notion, that energy body has seven energy centres in it aligned with the spine, from its base to the crown of the head. Ostensibly these centres need to be properly progressively awakened from the bottom up. Once awakened, a type of energy called *kundalini*, rises from the base of the spine to the crown of the head with corresponding expansions of consciousness.[463] This is consistent with Steve Taylor's observation that those who are in persistent transcendent states seem to have access to a universal force that can enhance their sense of aliveness.[464] However, apparent premature awakening of kundalini can create considerable disruption, including the occurrence of uncontrolled body movements.[465]

In 1980 Christina and Stanislav Grof created a spiritual emergency network, later called the "spiritual emergence network," made up of professionals who made themselves available to help people who had had some sort of disruptive spiritual awakening.[466] While the prototypical disruptive spiritual awakening would be an experience of prematurely rising kundalini, "spiritual" disruption can also occur with psychedelic drug use, near-death experiences, and other events involving expansions of consciousness for which people are not adequately prepared. In other words, there is work to be done while one is waiting to transition to a persistent transcendent state of consciousness.

Reflections

A recurrent theme that seems to emerge from the transcendence literature is the notion that the key ingredient for transformation from the ordinary waking state to a transcendent state is that of surrender. As we cease grasping, radical transformation becomes possible. Ironically, that includes grasping at transcendent states of consciousness. "Practitioners have no hope to achieve nirvana nor are they frightened to fall down to samsara. ... They do not wish to do good things. Those practitioners who have this capacity do not doubt any longer."[467] The word "samsara" refers to ordinary human life without enlightenment. In our survey, Thomas and I asked participants what actions they would take if they were to lose the state in which they found themselves. All but one who responded to this question articulated strategies that they would use for regaining a transcendent state. From the point of view of High Indifference, an enlightened state does not have greater value than the ordinary waking state. One ceases to strive for states of greater well-being, and we end up where we began. Lousy states of well-being suffice. However, the response by Participant 35, in Location 3, is instructive: "I don't know, this state always seems to be present below any surface disturbance." Simply by resting in whatever state we find ourselves could unexpectedly deepen into a more expansive state.

We have separated out luminosity and cognizance, or perception and understanding. A person can have an experiential shift to a transcendent state of consciousness without much understanding about what happened. I have found in my experience that understanding is important for those who have had anomalous experiences of any sort. And I think that understanding itself may have soteriological value. Understanding, not just in the sense of information about some subject matter, but understanding in the sense of embracing inherent meaning, as discussed in Chapter 2, "Meaning Beyond the Human." The development of understanding has value that appears not to disappear in transcendent states of consciousness. And, in fact, understanding itself could be a "practice" for the eventuation of transcendent states of consciousness.[468] And understanding has, of course, intrinsic value as understanding.

Finally, is transition to persistent transcendent states helpful for resolving planetary crises? We discussed earlier that self-development was necessary for their resolution, and persistent transcendent states appear to be the peak of self-development. We would think so, given the sense of connection and altruism that appear to be characteristics of at least some such states. However, in addition to the reservations already expressed, Jeffery Martin has found that people's conditioned tendencies frequently carry on into PNSE,[469] so that global activism will not necessarily be triggered if it were not already present. In fact, if, in a persistent transcendent state of consciousness, everything is regarded as already being perfect, then what need is there to change anything? Especially if one feels that one has no agency anyway? The fact is that the resolution of global crises does not require persistent transcendent states of consciousness; it just requires people awakening to an ordinary state of responsibility for their own actions. Clearly, the relationship between our planetary dilemmas and the farther reaches of self-development is a complicated one and needs considerably more research to understand it.

Epilogue

*At the very least we need to do more to be more proactive and less
reactive in doing ethics. We need to learn about the technology as
it is developing and to project and assess possible consequences of
its various applications.*[470]

I have always been interested in anomalies, phenomena that do
not fit with conventional versions of thinking about reality,
because they are gateways beyond our current understanding.
For instance, as a sailing ship comes into port, at first only the
masts and sails are visible so that a ship can be described as "hull-
down." As it gets closer to port, the hull becomes visible as well as
the mast and sails, so that a ship can be regarded as being "hull-
up." Most of the early Greek thinkers, such as Ptolemy,
Pythagoras, and Parmenides, knew that the earth was round. The
exceptions were the materialists, Leucippus and Democritus.[471]
Now suppose that we think that the earth is flat. Then this
transition of a sailing ship from hull-down to hull-up as it comes
into port would be an anomaly. It would make no sense. Perhaps
the water bunches up between the ship and port. Perhaps the
explanation is not a physical one, but a perceptual one. Perhaps
we cannot see properly when we look across water. We are
deluded. Or the people reporting such observations are simply
lying. Overall, however, such an anomaly does not change our
everyday experience that the earth is manifestly flat. And yet,
recognizing that the anomaly is caused by the curvature of a

spherical earth makes all the difference in the world. It is difficult to imagine going back to thinking that the world is flat, once we know that it is round, even though it makes little practical difference in our everyday lives which version we believe. That is why I am interested in anomalies. Anomalies force us to re-conceptualize reality.

Pierre Gassendi has frequently been credited with resuscitating Greek atomism in the early 1600s,[472] leading to contemporary materialism. But then, an anomaly arises that fails to fit a materialist theory and makes us wonder. For instance, a medium correctly gives us the first two digits of Richard Feynman's version of the fine structure constant. That could have been a coincidence. Or she might have cryptomnesia and simply not remember that she had previously seen it somewhere. And even if this is anomalous, so what? That need not change our faith in materialism. This would be analogous to noticing that a sailing ship coming to port goes from hull-down to hull-up but figuring that there must be some conventional explanation for it, and certainly no reason to give up a flat-earth theory. But now the anomalies multiply: remote viewing, remote influencing, William Bengston's non-contact healing data, quantum eraser experiments, Thomaz's macro-pk, the effects of meditation on quality of life, people popping into persistent transcendent states of consciousness, and so on. While any one of these phenomena can perhaps be discounted and forced back into Procrustes' materialist bed, their cumulative weight calls materialism itself into question. Maybe materialism is not the correct interpretation of reality. Maybe the earth is not flat after all.

From a materialist point of view, the universe is a mechanical system that runs in the dark. There are tiny pinpoints of the light of consciousness that arise, somehow, from the brains of human beings—themselves, clearly, for a materialist, by-products of the mechanical processes undergirding them. What I have done is in this book is to look at the cumulative implications of a number of anomalies, and, in doing so, found that nature embodies meaning and, probably, elements of consciousness itself. And there appear to be discarnate beings out there somewhere, also possibly conscious, with whom we can interact. And I theorized that we emerge from a prephysical substrate that is itself deep consciousness that carries meaning. And now we have restored the notion that the universe could well be inherently suffused with consciousness — that the light of consciousness is not just an incidental aberration in an otherwise dark universe, but the essence of its fabric.

It is worth remembering that Pierre Gassendi was a Catholic priest. For him, atomism could only explain so much. The human passions, for example, were amenable to materialist analysis, yet "these are ultimately governed, however, by the rational and immaterial soul."[473] So, in a way, I am going back to the roots of materialism, whereby materialism is a somewhat useful heuristic for explaining some of our experiences in our everyday state of consciousness. But these experiences are embedded within a larger framework that is nonlocally interconnected and may itself be conscious. And it is from that expanded viewpoint that new solutions to old problems can emerge. If our viewpoint flips to a postmaterialist perspective, triggering a vigorous race to develop applications of our knowledge about consciousness, then new problems coincident with the new solutions can also emerge. I want to consider some of the ethical concerns that could arise.

Ethical Concerns

As we develop our ability to engage in remote viewing, remote influencing, after-death communication, and self-transformation, we are, in effect, developing new technologies — consciousness technologies. I have been using the expression "consciousness technologies" loosely thus far but let me make that moniker more precise. For James Moor, technological revolutions entail three aspects: a technological paradigm, technological devices, and the social impact that such devices have.[474] In the case of the consciousness technologies, the technological paradigm is the dynamic, nonlocal, mental interconnectivity of reality; the technological devices are trained, possibly neurotechnologically enhanced, individual psyches; and the social impact stems from any person's ability to mentally interact with anything anywhere. Note that I regard properly trained "psyches" rather than properly trained "brains" as technological devices, since our psyches could entail nonphysical aspects of reality. However, the neurotechnological enhancement would, likely, only apply to our brains.

For Moor, technological revolutions proceed through three stages: introduction, permeation, and power stages. In the introduction stage, there are some people who are fascinated by the technology and "explore its capabilities."[475] There is little impact on society as few people are aware of its existence, and the applications are limited and expensive. In the permeation stage, the technology undergoes standardization, more people become aware of it, access to its availability increases, and training programs are set up to educate people about its uses. There is a noticeable impact on society. In the power stage, the technology proliferates, and its use becomes integrated in such a way that most people are directly or indirectly affected by it. Examples of such technologies would be automobiles, electricity, and computers. I think that the consciousness technologies are on the cusp of moving from the introduction stage to the permeation stage. For instance, in Chapter 5, "Radical Self-Transformation," I reviewed Jeffery Martin's development of the Finders Course, a standardized series of exercises which allows some individuals to shift from an ordinary waking state of consciousness to a persistent transcendent state. Similarly, in my lab, we have been trying to identify the psychological parameters associated with the successful ability to influence a random event generator, so as to standardize the methods that a person could use in order to do so.

But there is a basic ethical problem with humanity's development of any technology, namely, that our technological prowess keeps increasing, but not our moral integrity. This is starkly illustrated with the release of energy from the atom. Not only did we learn how to harness nuclear energy, but we built nuclear weapons. And, not only did we build nuclear weapons, but we promptly used them against large populations of people for dubious reasons.[476] And we have been living in the nuclear shadow ever since, as spelled out in Chapter 4, "Planetary Transformation." Any technology that we develop can be deliberately used for beneficial or malicious purposes. Furthermore, any technology that we develop can have unintended, harmful consequences. Let me address the second of these for a minute, before coming back to the first.

There is a *precautionary principle* in the development of new technologies, whereby an effort is made to anticipate potential harm without having the scientific evidence necessary to know that it will materialize.

> The absence of full scientific certainty should not inhibit action if otherwise severe damage could be caused. The later society takes action to minimize a risk, the higher the cost of prevention or repair. Furthermore, while society is waiting for full scientific proof of causality before deciding to take measures, irreversible developments may take place.[477]

In a study conducted by the European Environmental Agency, it was found that we tend to underestimate rather than overestimate risks when there is uncertainty. Add to that the fact that we are increasingly outrunning our ability to anticipate consequences[478] and we are, already, facing increasing jeopardy. As we develop and implement consciousness technologies, can we step back and consider the consequences of our actions? Where are we going with this? Where are we likely to end up? And is that a place where we would want to be?

Technologies can be deliberately used to harm someone. Nuclear weapons are one example. Automobiles can be driven on sidewalks or transformed into tanks. And we are increasingly confronted by ongoing cyberwarfare.[479] In our context of consciousness technologies, remote influencing could be used, not only for promoting health, but, on the contrary, for bringing physical harm to someone. And I am not just raising a hypothetical spectre of malevolence. According to a Gallup Poll taken in 1994, 5% of Americans have admitted to having prayed for the purpose of bringing harm to others.[480] In Chapter 3, "Anomalous Transformations of Physical Manifestation," we considered the case of Ted Owens, some of whose apparent influences were ethically ambiguous at best. And in Chapter 4, "Planetary Transformation," we explicitly considered the possibility that subtle activism, with the possible assistance of unseen entities, could be both benevolent and malevolent. Is this sufficient reason to back off and leave the consciousness technologies alone?

But the ethical imperative can also be applied backwards, to argue that it is necessary to develop the consciousness technologies and to mitigate any detrimental effects as they arise. If our moral purpose is to increase the well-being of others, including future generations (for as long as there are future generations), and there were resources for doing so that could be developed, then is there not a moral imperative to proceed with their development? Perhaps, more directly, if there were to be ways of increasing moral integrity among humanity, then would there not be a moral imperative to attempt to do so? In ways that would not violate the human rights that we are trying to protect? This is a tangled thicket. I am not able to untangle it here; and leave it to others to do so. But I do want to raise these issues for consideration. The scientific understanding of consciousness is undergoing a seismic shift, consciousness technologies are in the process of development, we are in the midst of planetary crises, and we have a practical need to figure out an appropriate course of collective action. What we do know is that radical transformation does occur, and that we have an opportunity at this historical time point to seek to understand and harness it for the benefit of humanity.

Endnotes

1 Noam Chomsky, *Who Rules the World?* (New York: Metropolitan Books, 2016), 4.

2 Albert Einstein, as quoted in W.F. Bynum and Roy Porter, eds., *Oxford Dictionary of Scientific Quotations* (Oxford, UK: Oxford University Press, 2005), 199.

3 See Imants Barušs and Julia Mossbridge, *Transcendent Mind: Rethinking the Science of Consciousness* (Washington, DC: American Psychological Association, 2017).

4 Ibid.

5 See Richard P. Feynman, *Perfectly Reasonable Deviations from the Beaten Track: The Letters of Richard P. Feynman* (New York: Basic Books, 2005).

6 See Patricia Pearson, *Opening Heaven's Door: What the Dying May Be Trying to Tell Us About Where They're Going* (Toronto: Random House Canada, 2014).

7 See Erlendur Haraldsson, *The Departed Among the Living: An Investigative Study of Afterlife Encounters* (Guildford, UK: White Crow, 2012), 1.

8 Ibid., 3. The percentages do not add up to 100% because about 20% of the cases involved more than one modality.

9 Barušs and Mossbridge, *Transcendent Mind.*

10 Julie Beischel et al., "Anomalous Information Reception by Research Mediums Under Blinded Conditions II: Replication and Extension," *EXPLORE: The Journal of Science & Healing* 11 (2015): 136–142.

11 See, for example, James Gleick, "Richard Feynman Dead at 69; Leading Theoretical Physicist," http://www.nytimes.com/1988/02/17/obituaries/richard-feynman-dead-at-69-leading-theoretical-physicist.html.

12 Richard P. Feynman, *Perfectly Reasonable Deviations*; also see Gabe Mirkin, "Richard Feynman, Physicist and Humorist," http://www.drmirkin.com/weekly-ezine-page/richard-feynman-physicist-and-humorist.html.

13 See Gabe Mirkin, "Richard Feynman, Physicist and Humorist."

14 See Lawrence Krauss, *Quantum Man: Richard Feynman's Life in Science* (New York: W.W. Norton & Company, 2012).

15 See Peter Ward, *The Medea Hypothesis: Is Life On Earth Ultimately Self-Destructive?* (Princeton, NJ: Princeton University Press, 2009), 143.

16 See Eleanor Ross, "The Nine Countries That Have Nuclear Weapons,"

http://www.independent.co.uk/news/world/politics/the-nine-countries-that-have-nuclear-weapons-a6798756.html.

17 See William Langewiesche, *The Atomic Bazaar: The Rise of the Nuclear Poor* (New York: Farrar, Straus & Giroux, 2007).

18 Ibid., 12.

19 Ibid., 19.

20 See Peter L. Berger, *A Rumor of Angels: Modern Society and the Rediscovery of the Supernatural* (Garden City, NY: Anchor Books, 1970), 42.

21 See Imants Barušs and Robert Woodrow, "A Reduction Theorem for the Kripke-Joyal Semantics: Forcing Over An Arbitrary Category Can Always Be Replaced By Forcing Over a Complete Heyting Algebra," *Logica Universalis* 7, no. 3 (2013): 323–334.

22 See Michael Rescorla, "The Computational Theory of Mind," http://plato.stanford.edu/archives/win2015/entries/computational-mind/, and Zenon Pylyshyn, *Computation and Cognition: Toward a Foundation for Cognitive Science* (Cambridge, MA: A Bradford Book, 1984).

23 See Michael Rescorla, "The Computational Theory of Mind," and Gualtiero Piccinini, "Functionalism, Computationalism, and Mental States," *Studies in History and Philosophy of Science* 35 (2004): 811–833.

24 See Verena Huber-Dyson, *Gödel's Theorems: A Workbook on Formalization* (Stuttgart, Germany: B.G. Teubner Verlagsgesellschaft, 1991), 35–37.

25 See Crossley et al., *What is Mathematical Logic?* (Oxford, UK: Oxford University Press, 1972); Rescorla, "The Computational Theory of Mind."

26 Piccinini, "Functionalism, Computationalism, and Mental States;" and see also Susan Schneider, *The Language of Thought* (Cambridge, MA: MIT Press, 2011).

27 For example, Daniel Dennett, *Brainstorms: Philosophical Essays on Mind and Psychology* (Montgomery, VT: Bradford Books, 1978), 93.

28 Rescorla, "The Computational Theory of Mind."

29 See Walter J. Freeman, "Brains Create Macroscopic Order from Microscopic Disorder by Neurodynamics in Perception," in Århem et al., eds., *Disorder Versus Order in Brain Function: Essays in Theoretical Neurobiology* (Singapore: World Scientific Publishing, 2000), 205–219.

30 See Roger Young, *How Computers Work: Processor and Main Memory*, http://www.fastchip.net/howcomputerswork/bookbpdf.pdf.

31 See Jerry Fodor, *The Mind Doesn't Work That Way: The Scope and Limits of Computational Psychology* (Cambridge, MA: A Bradford Book, 2000), 2.

32 See Warren S. McCulloch and Walter H. Pitts, "A Logical Calculus of the Ideas Immanent in Nervous Activity," *Bulletin of Mathematical Biophysics* 5 (1943): 115–133.

33 Rescorla, "The Computational Theory of Mind."

34 See Pauli Pylkkö, *The Aconceptual Mind: Heideggerian Themes in Holistic Naturalism* (Amsterdam: John Benjamins, 1998).

35 Rescorla, "The Computational Theory of Mind."

36 See R. Douglas Fields, *The Other Brain: The Scientific and Medical Break-*

throughs That Will Heal Our Brains and Revolutionize Our Health (New York: Simon & Schuster, 2011).

37 See Paul Smolensky, "On the Proper Treatment of Connectionism," *Behavioral and Brain Sciences* 11 (1988): 1–23; Stephen José Hanson and David J. Burr, "What Connectionist Models Learn," *Behavioral and Brain Sciences* 13 (1990): 471–518.

38 See Owen Flanagan, *Consciousness Reconsidered* (Cambridge, MA: A Bradford Book, 1992), 5.

39 See my "Metanalysis of Definitions of Consciousness," *Imagination, Cognition and Personality* 6 (4) (1987): 321–329; "Beliefs About Consciousness and Reality," *Journal of Consciousness Studies* 15 (10–11) (2008): 277–292.

40 For example, Christof Koch, *Consciousness: Confessions of a Romantic Reductionist* (Cambridge, MA: MIT Press, 2012), 27.

41 Barušs and Mossbridge, *Transcendent Mind*, 15.

42 See David J. Chalmers, "Facing Up to the Problem of Consciousness," *Journal of Consciousness Studies* 2 (3) (1995): 201.

43 See John Searle, *Intentionality: An Essay in the Philosophy of Mind* (Cambridge, UK: Cambridge University Press, 1983), ix, emphases in original.

44 See David Skrbina, "Introduction," in David Skrbina, ed., *Mind That Abides: Panpsychism in the New Millennium* (Amsterdam: John Benjamins, 2009), xi–xiv; also Avshalom Elitzur, "What's the Mind–Body Problem with You Anyway? Prolegomena to any Scientific Discussion of Consciousness," in Alexander Batthyany et al., eds., *Mind and Its Place in the World: Non-Reductionist Approaches to the Ontology of Consciousness* (Frankfurt: ontos verlag, 2006), 15–22.

45 Barušs and Mossbridge, *Transcendent Mind*.

46 Koch, *Consciousness: Confessions of a Romantic Reductionist*, 119.

47 See Karl R. Popper and John C. Eccles, *The Self and Its Brain* (Berlin: Springer International, 1981), 96; also see Donald E. Watson and Bernard O. Williams, "Eccles' Model of the Self Controlling Its Brain: The Irrelevance of Dualist-Interactionism," *NeuroQuantology* 1 (2003): 119–128.

48 See William James, "Does 'Consciousness' Exist?" *The Journal of Philosophy, Psychology and Scientific Methods* 1(18) (1904): 477–491.

49 Dennett, *Brainstorms*, 173.

50 Barušs and Mossbridge, *Transcendent Mind*.

51 See my *Alterations of Consciousness: An Empirical Analysis for Social Scientists* (Washington, DC: American Psychological Association, 2003); also "What We Can Learn about Consciousness from Altered States of Consciousness," *Journal of Consciousness Exploration and Research* 3 (7) (2012): 805–819.

52 This list has been adapted from a previous paper: "What We Can Learn about Consciousness from Altered States of Consciousness." See also my *Alterations of Consciousness*.

53 See Robert Waggoner, *Lucid Dreaming: Gateway to the Inner Self* (Needham, MA: Moment Point, 2009).

54   See Michael Nahm and Bruce Greyson, "Terminal Lucidity in Patients with Chronic Schizophrenia and Dementia: A Survey of the Literature," *The Journal of Nervous and Mental Disease* 197 (12) (2009): 942–944.

55   See Raymond Moody Jr., *Glimpses of Eternity: Sharing a Loved One's Passage from This Life to the Next* (New York: Guideposts, 2010).

56   See Roger N. Walsh, "Journey Beyond Belief," *Journal of Humanistic Psychology* 24 (2) (1984): 30–65; Judith R. Malamud, "Becoming Lucid in Dreams and Waking Life," in B.B. Wolman et al., eds., *Handbook of States of Consciousness* (New York: Van Nostrand Reinhold, 1986), 590–612; Düdjom Lingpa and Pema Tashi, *Heart of the Great Perfection: Düdjom Lingpa's Visions of the Great Perfection*, Translated by B. Alan Wallace (Somerville, MA: Wisdom Publications, 2016).

57   For example, Waggoner, *Lucid Dreaming*.

58   See Lance Storm, "Foreword," in A.J. Rock, ed., *The Survival Hypothesis: Essays on Mediumship*, 1–4 (Jefferson, NC: McFarland & Company, 2013), 2.

59   See Etzel Cardeña, "A Call for an Open, Informed Study of All Aspects of Consciousness," *Frontiers in Human Neuroscience* 8 (17) (2014): 1–4; Baruss, *Authentic Knowing: The Convergence of Science and Spiritual Aspiration* (West Lafayette, IN: Purdue University Press, 1996); Baruss and Mossbridge, *Transcendent Mind*.

60   Baruss and Mossbridge, *Transcendent Mind*.

61   See Julie Beischel et al., "Anomalous Information Reception by Research Mediums Under Blinded Conditions II: Replication and Extension," *EXPLORE: The Journal of Science and Healing* 11 (2) (2015): 136–142.

62   Baruss and Mossbridge, *Transcendent Mind*.

63   For example, Stephen E. Braude, *Immortal Remains: The Evidence for Life After Death* (Lanham, MD: Rowman & Littlefield, 2003); David Fontana, *Is There an Afterlife? A Comprehensive Overview of the Evidence* (Winchester, UK: O-Books, 2005).

64   Baruss, *Authentic Knowing*.

65   See Janice Miner Holden, "Veridical Perception in Near-Death Experiences," in Janice Miner Holden et al., eds., *The Handbook of Near-Death Experiences: Thirty Years of Investigation* (Santa Barbara, CA: Praeger, 2009), 185–211; also, for example, Titus Rivas and Rudolf H. Smit, "A Near-Death Experience with Veridical Perception Described by a Famous Heart Surgeon and Confirmed by His Assistant Surgeon," *Journal of Near-Death Studies* 31 (3) (2013): 179–186; and Titus Rivas, Anny Dirven, and Rudolf H. Smit, *The Self Does Not Die: Verified Paranormal Phenomena from Near-Death Experiences* (Durham, NC: International Association for Near-Death Studies, 2016).

66   See Sam Parnia et al., "AWARE—AWAreness During Resuscitation—A Prospective Study," *Resuscitation* 85 (12) (2014): 1802.

67   Ibid., 1803.

68   Holden, "Veridical Perception in Near-Death Experiences."

69   See Michael Sabom, *Recollections of Death: A Medical Investigation* (New

York: Harper & Row, 1982); and Penny Sartori, *The Near-Death Experiences of Hospitalized Intensive Care Patients: A Five Year Critical Study* (Lewiston, NY: Edwin Mellen Press, 2008).

70 See Peter Safar, "Resuscitation from Clinical Death: Pathophysiologic Limits and Therapeutic Potentials," *Critical Care Medicine* 16 (10) (1988): 929.

71 Safar, "Resuscitation from Clinical Death."

72 Gideon Lichfield, "The Science of Near-Death Experiences: Empirically Investigating Brushes with the Afterlife," http://www.theatlantic.com/magazine/archive/2015/04/the-science-of-near-death-experiences/386231/; see also Madeleine M. Grigg, Michael A. Kelly, Gastone G. Celesia, Mona W. Ghobrial and Emanuel R. Ross, "Electroencephalographic Activity After Brain Death," *Archives of Neurology* 44 (1987): 948–954.

73 See Ashleigh Sherrington and Martin Smith, "International Perspectives in the Diagnosis of Brain Death in Adults," *Trends in Anaesthesia and Critical Care* 2 (1) (2012): 48–52.

74 Barušs and Mossbridge, *Transcendent Mind*.

75 Holden, "Veridical Perception in Near-Death Experiences."

76 See Emily W. Kelly et al., "Unusual Experiences Near Death and Related Phenomena," in Edward F. Kelly et al., eds., *Irreducible Mind: Toward a Psychology for the 21st Century* (Lanham, MD: Rowman & Littlefield, 2010), 386.

77 Lichfield, "The Science of Near-Death Experiences: Empirically Investigating Brushes with the Afterlife."

78 See Simon Kochen and Ernst P. Specker, "The Problem of Hidden Variables in Quantum Mechanics," *Journal of Mathematics and Mechanics* 17 (1) (1967): 59–87.

79 See Anthony Sudbery, *Quantum Mechanics and the Particles of Nature: An Outline for Mathematicians* (Cambridge, UK: Cambridge University Press, 1986), 192; see also Itano et al., "Quantum Zeno Effect," *Physical Review A* 41 (5) (1990): 2295–2300.

80 See my "Characteristics of Consciousness in Collapse-Type Quantum Mind Theories," *Journal of Mind and Behavior* 29 (3) (2008): 255–265.

81 John Wren-Lewis, "The Darkness of God: A Personal Report on Consciousness Transformation through an Encounter with Death," *Journal of Humanistic Psychology* 28 (2) (1988), 116; emphases in original.

82 See David Bohm, *Wholeness and the Implicate Order* (London: Ark, 1983), 149.

83 Ibid., 208.

84 See my "Characteristics of Consciousness in Collapse-Type Quantum Mind Theories," and "Beyond Scientific Materialism: Toward a Transcendent Theory of Consciousness," *Journal of Consciousness Studies* 17 (7–8) (2010): 213–231.

85 See my "Quantum Mechanics and Human Consciousness," *Physics in*

Canada/La Physique au Canada 42 (1) (1986): 3–5; also "Speculations about the Direct Effects of Intention on Physical Manifestation," *Journal of Cosmology* 3 (2009): 590–599; and "Beyond Scientific Materialism: Toward a Transcendent Theory of Consciousness."

86 Baruš and Mossbridge, *Transcendent Mind.*

87 See Lee Smolin, *Time Reborn: From the Crisis in Physics to the Future of the Universe* (Toronto: Alfred A. Knopf Canada, 2013).

88 Baruš and Mossbridge, *Transcendent Mind.*

89 See Julian Barbour, *The End of Time: The Next Revolution in Physics* (New York: Oxford University Press, 2000).

90 See Alan W. Watts, *The Joyous Cosmology: Adventures in the Chemistry of Consciousness* (New York: Vintage Books, 1965), 33.   '

91 See Franklin Merrell-Wolff, *Transformations in Consciousness: The Metaphysics and Epistemology* (Albany, NY: SUNY Press, 1995), 132.

92 Baruš and Mossbridge, *Transcendent Mind.*

93 See Aldous Huxley, *The Doors of Perception and Heaven and Hell* (London: Grafton Books, 1977), 20.

94 Baruš, *The Personal Nature of Notions of Consciousness: A Theoretical and Empirical Examination of the Role of the Personal in the Understanding of Consciousness* (Lanham, MD: University Press of America, 1990); Imants Baruš and Robert J. Moore, "Notions of Consciousness and Reality," in Joseph E. Shorr et al., eds., *Imagery: Current Perspectives* (New York: Plenum, 1989), 87–92.

95 Imants Baruš and Robert J. Moore, "Measurement of Beliefs about Consciousness and Reality," *Psychological Reports* 71 (1992): 59–64; and Baruš, "Beliefs about Consciousness and Reality."

96 Baruš, *The Personal Nature of Notions of Consciousness,* 125.

97 Imants Baruš and Robert J. Moore, "Beliefs about Consciousness and Reality of Participants at 'Tuscon II'," *Journal of Consciousness Studies* 5 (4) (1998): 483–496.

98 See Emily Pronin and Kathleen Schmidt, "Claims and Denials of Bias and their Implications for Policy," in Eldar Shafir, ed., *The Behavioral Foundations of Public Policy* (Princeton, NJ: Princeton University Press, 2013), 195–216.

99 Baruš, *Authentic Knowing;* Baruš and Mossbridge, *Transcendent Mind.*

100 William F. Lyons, *The Disappearance of Introspection* (Cambridge, MA: MIT Press, 1986).

101 Düdjom Lingpa and Pema Tashi, *Heart of the Great Perfection: Düdjom Lingpa's Visions of the Great Perfection.*

102 Baruš and Mossbridge, *Transcendent Mind.*

103 Baruš, *The Personal Nature of Notions of Consciousness,* 125.

104 See my *Science as a Spiritual Practice* (Exeter, UK: Imprint Academic, 2007).

105 See Eduardo Kohn, *How Forests Think: Toward an Anthropology Beyond the Human* (Berkeley, CA: University of California Press, 2013), 21–22.

106 Baruš, *The Personal Nature of Notions of Consciousness,* 175.

107 Ibid., 120.

108 As quoted in Steve Paulson, "On Reconciling Atheism and Meaning in the
    Universe," http://www.theatlantic.com/health/archive/2012/08/on-
    reconciling-atheism-and-meaning-in-the-universe/261627/.

109 See David Skrbina, *Panpsychism in the West* (Cambridge, MA: MIT Press,
    2005), 1.

110 See Richard Menary, ed., *The Extended Mind* (Cambridge, MA: A Bradford
    Book, 2010); also Kohn, *How Forests Think*; Skrbina (2005); and Skrbina,
    "Introduction."

111 See William Bengston, *The Energy Cure: Unraveling the Mystery of Hands-on
    Healing* (Boulder, CO: Sounds True, 2010); also see William F. Bengston
    and David Krinsley, "The Effect of the 'Laying On of Hands' on Trans-
    planted Breast Cancer in Mice," *Journal of Scientific Exploration* 14 (3) (2000):
    353–364; Margaret M. Moga and William F. Bengston, "Anomalous Mag-
    netic Field Activity During a Bioenergy Healing Experiment," *Journal of
    Scientific Exploration* 24 (3) (2010): 397–410; Sarah Beseme, William
    Bengston and Dean Radin, "Transcriptional Changes in Cancer Cells
    Induced by Exposure to a Healing Method," *Dose-Response* 16 (3) (2018): 1–
    8, https://doi.org/10.1177/1559325818782843.

112 See S.P. Walborn et al., "Double-Slit Quantum Eraser," *Physical Review A* 65
    (033818) (2002), https://doi.org/10.1103/PhysRevA.65.033818.

113 See Peng et al., "Delayed-Choice Quantum Eraser With Thermal Light,"
    Physical Review Letters 112 (180401), https://doi.org/10.1103/PhysRevLett.
    112.180401.

114 See William F. Bengston, "Commentary: A Method Used to Train Skeptical
    Volunteers to Heal in an Experimental Setting," *The Journal of Alternative
    and Complementary Medicine* 13 (3) (2007): 329–331; also Bengston, *The
    Energy Cure*, 233–235.

115 Bengston and Krinsley, "The Effect of 'Laying on of Hands' on Trans-
    planted Breast Cancer in Mice."

116 Ibid.

117 Margaret M. Moga, in a personal communication with the author from
    February 9, 2016, emphases removed.

118 Bengston, *The Energy Cure*; Margaret M. Moga and William F. Bengston,
    "Anomalous Magnetic Field Activity During a Bioenergy Healing
    Experiment."

119 Bengston and Krinsley, "The Effect of 'Laying on of Hands' on Trans-
    planted Breast Cancer in Mice," 359.

120 Ibid., 360.

121 Ibid.

122 Ibid., 360–361, emphases in original.

123 Ibid., 360.

124 Ibid., 361.

125 William F. Bengston and Margaret Moga, "Resonance, Placebo Effects, and
    Type II Errors: Some Implications from Healing Research for Experimental

Methods," *The Journal of Alternative and Complementary Medicine* 13 (3) (2007): 317–327.

126   See Stefan Gerlich et al., "Quantum Interference of Large Organic Molecules," *Nature Communications* 2 (263) (2011): 1–5, https://doi.org/10.1038/ncomms1263.

127   Richard P. Feynman, *QED: The Strange Theory of Light and Matter* (Princeton, NJ: Princeton University Press, 2006), 80.

128   The claim that entangled particles do not carry information about their states with them clearly requires experimental evidence. I give a straightforward but technical discussion of the evidence in endnotes 2 and 3 on pages 127–128 of *Science as a Spiritual Practice*; see also Evan Harris Walker, *The Physics of Consciousness: Quantum Minds and the Meaning of Life* (Cambridge, MA: Perseus, 2000).

129   See Albert Einstein et al., "Can Quantum-Mechanical Description of Physical Reality Be Considered Complete?", in John Archibald Wheeler et al., eds., *Quantum Theory and Measurement*, 138–141 (Princeton, NJ: Princeton University Press, 1983), 141.

130   Walborn et al., "Double-Slit Quantum Eraser;" also see M. Holden et al., "The Double Slit Experiment with Polarizers," https://arxiv.org/pdf/1110.4309v1.pdf; and Peng et al., "Delayed-Choice Quantum Eraser with Thermal Light."

131   Anton Zeilinger as quoted in Dennis Overbye, "Quantum Trickery: Testing Einstein's Strangest Theory," https://www.nytimes.com/2005/12/27/science/quantum-trickery-testing-einsteins-strangest-theory.html.

132   See Dean Radin et al., "Psychophysical Interactions with a Single-Photon Double-Slit Optical System," *Quantum Biosystems* 6 (1) (2015): 82–98.

133   See Dean Radin et al., "Psychophysical Interactions with a Double-Slit Interference Pattern," *Physics Essays* 26 (4) (2013): 555.

134   Ibid.

135   See Dean Radin et al., "Psychophysical Modulation of Fringe Visibility in a Distant Double-Slit Optical System," *Physics Essays* 29 (1) (2016): 14–22.

136   Or at least, for an observer in the immediate proximity of the apparatus. Given that the events in path *p* and path *s* are spatially separated, by the special theory of relativity there is an observer somewhere in the universe for whom the order of events would be reversed (that is to say, in the "right order"), so that photon *p* encounters the polarizer cancelling out the information before photon *s* has been detected. If the experiment were to be done with entangled particles moving slower than the speed of light, it should be possible to find a configuration of an experiment in which the cancellation along the *p* path is in the future light cone of the detector in the *s* path, so that the eraser effect appears to be retrocausal for all observers. That experiment has not yet been done.

137   See Iris M. Owen, *Conjuring Up Philip: An Adventure in Psychokinesis* (Toronto: Fitzhenry & Whiteside, 1976), 30.

138   See *Philip: The Imaginary Ghost*, produced by 835850 Ontario Limited, 1974.

DVD, 15 min. Available from the Visual Education Centre, http://www. visualed.com.

[139] Owen, *Conjuring Up Philip*, 28.

[140] Ibid., 41.

[141] Bengston and Moga, "Resonance, Placebo Effects, and Type II Errors: Some Implications from Healing Research for Experimental Methods," 322.

[142] Ibid., 323.

[143] Ibid., 323.

[144] Smolin, *Time Reborn*, 161.

[145] See Rupert Sheldrake, *Science Set Free: 10 Paths to New Discovery* (New York: Deepak Chopra Books, 2012), 100.

[146] Ibid., 99.

[147] Stephen E. Braude, *The Gold Leaf Lady and Other Parapsychological Investigations* (Chicago, IL: University of Chicago Press, 2007), 142.

[148] Stephen E. Braude, *Crimes of Reason: On Mind, Nature, and the Paranormal* (Lanham, MD: Rowman & Littlefield, 2014).

[149] Bengston and Moga, "Resonance, Placebo Effects, and Type II Errors: Some Implications from Healing Research for Experimental Methods."

[150] Bengston, *The Energy Cure*.

[151] Braude, *Crimes of Reason*, 42.

[152] See Imants Barušs and Vanille Rabier, "Failure to Replicate Retrocausal Recall," *Psychology of Consciousness: Theory, Research, and Practice* 1 (1) (2014): 88.

[153] Dick J. Bierman, "On the Nature of Anomalous Phenomena: Another Reality between the World of Subjective Consciousness and the Objective World of Physics?," in Philip van Loocke, ed., *The Physical Nature of Consciousness* (Amsterdam: John Benjamins, 2001), 269–292.

[154] Barušs, *Alterations of Consciousness*.

[155] See my *The Impossible Happens: A Scientist's Personal Discovery of the Extraordinary Nature of Reality* (Alresford, UK: Iff Books, 2013).

[156] Barušs and Mossbridge, *Transcendent Mind*.

[157] Ibid.

[158] Barušs, *Alterations of Consciousness*, 221.

[159] See Kenneth Ring and Sharon Cooper, "Near-Death and Out-of-Body Experiences in the Blind: A Study of Apparent Eyeless Vision," *Journal of Near-Death Studies* 16 (2) (1997): 101–147.

[160] See Rosemary E. Guiley, *Harper's Encyclopedia of Mystical and Paranormal Experience* (New York: HarperSanFrancisco, 1991), 616.

[161] Owen, *Conjuring Up Philip*, 127–129.

[162] Dean Radin et al., "Psychophysical Modulation of Fringe Visibility in a Distant Double-Slit Optical System."

[163] As a first approximation, the strength of a meaning field could be conceptualized as a linear combination of weighted parameters, i.e.

$$M(x,t) = \sum_{i=1}^{n} \alpha_i p_i$$

where $M(x, t)$ is the strength of the meaning field at a point in space and time, p_i is a parameter, and a_i is the weight associated with that parameter.

[164] See John D. Barrow and John K. Webb, "Inconstant Constants: Do the Inner Workings of Nature Change with Time?" *Scientific American* 292 (6) (2005): 56–63.

[165] See my "Questions About Interacting with Invisible Intelligences," *EdgeScience* 18 (2014): 18–19.

[166] See Richard Panek, *The 4 Percent Universe: Dark Matter, Dark Energy, and the Race to Discover the Rest of Reality* (Boston, MA: Houghton Mifflin Harcourt, 2011).

[167] Merrell-Wolff, *Transformations in Consciousness*, 170.

[168] Ibid.

[169] As quoted in Paulson, "On Reconciling Atheism and Meaning in the Universe."

[170] See my "Meaning Fields: Meaning Beyond the Human as a Resolution of Boundary Problems Introduced by Nonlocality," *EdgeScience* 35 (2018): 8–11.

[171] See my "Categorical Modelling of Conscious States," *Consciousness: Ideas and Research for the Twenty-First Century* 7 (7) (2019): 1–10.

[172] Niels Bohr, as quoted by Freeman J. Dyson, "Innovation in Physics," in Jong Ping Hsu et al., eds., *JingShin Theoretical Physics Symposium in Honor of Professor Ta-You Wu* (River Edge, NJ: World Scientific, 1998), 84.

[173] See Harvey J. Irwin, *An Introduction to Parapsychology* (Jefferson, NC: McFarland & Company, 1994).

[174] See Stephen E. Braude, "Macro-Psychokinesis," in Etzel Cardeña et al., *Parapsychology: A Handbook for the 21st Century* (Jefferson, NC: McFarland & Company, 2015), 258.

[175] See Pamela Rae Heath, *The PK Zone: A Cross-Cultural Review of Psychokinesis (PK)* (New York: iUniverse, 2003), xxv.

[176] Braude, "Macro-Psychokinesis;" Heath, *The PK Zone: A Cross-Cultural Review of Psychokinesis (PK)*.

[177] See Stephen E. Braude, Review of *The Man Who Could Fly: St. Joseph of Copertino and the Mystery of Levitation*, by M. Grosso, *Journal of Scientific Exploration* 30 (2) (2016): 275–278.

[178] See Michael Grosso, *The Man Who Could Fly: St. Joseph of Copertino and the Mystery of Levitation* (Lanham, MD: Rowman & Littlefield, 2016), 70.

[179] Ibid., 70.

[180] Ibid. 72.

[181] Ibid., 70, emphases in original.

[182] Ibid., 82

[183] Ibid., 180.

[184] Ibid., 26.

[185] Ibid., 183.

[186] See Suzanne Padfield, "Mind–Matter Interaction in the Psychokinetic Experience," in Brian D. Josephson et al., eds., *Consciousness and the Physical*

World: Edited Proceedings of an Interdisciplinary Symposium on Consciousness Held at the University of Cambridge in January 1978 (Oxford, UK: Pergamon Press, 1980), 167.

[187] See Charles Honorton, "A Moving Experience," *Journal of Scientific Exploration* 29 (1) (2015), 72.

[188] See Montague Keen et al., "The Scole Report: An Account of an Investigation into the Genuineness of a Range of Physical Phenomena Associated with a Mediumistic Group in Norfolk, England," *Proceedings of the Society for Psychical Research* 58 (220) (1999): 149–392, 191. I have spoken to Montague Keen personally about the Scole investigation to verify the authenticity of the phenomena.

[189] Montague Keen, as quoted in *The Afterlife Investigations* (2011), available on DVD from UFO TV. See also Montague Keen, "The Scole Investigation: A Study in Critical Analysis of Paranormal Physical Phenomena," *Journal of Scientific Exploration* 15 (2) (2001): 167–182.

[190] Ibid. The account given by Robin Foy (one of the people involved in managing the sessions) differs from that of Montague Keen, in that Foy infers that each of the investigators initially had an opportunity to handle the solid crystal. Then "moments later, the scientists were invited to pick it up again. One by one, they tried — and failed — as their hands went straight through the visible crystal." And, finally, according to Foy, each of the investigators was asked to pick it up for a third time, at which point the crystal was sensed to be solid again (Foy, *Witnessing the Impossible*, 310). I am favouring Montague Keen's version of events for two reasons. First, on November 7, 1996, according to Robin Foy, he and his wife Sandra (the other person managing the sessions) had been asked to put their hands in the bowl to feel the crystal, only to find that their hands went right through it, and that that memory could have colored the reporting of the scientists' experiences two days later. Second, both have reported that Arthur Ellison had had his face almost inside the bowl so as to convince himself that there could be no human interference with the demonstration, and this would only have made sense if he were to then have attempted to grasp the crystal in consecutive trials himself without giving way to the others.

[191] See Anita Moorjani, *Dying to Be Me: My Journey from Cancer, to Near Death, to True Healing* (Carlsbad, CA: Hay House, 2012).

[192] Ibid., 75.

[193] Ibid.; also see Larry Dossey, "Dying to Heal: A Neglected Aspect of NDEs," *Explore: The Journal of Science and Healing* 7 (2) (2011): 59–62.

[194] See Lee Pulos and Gary Richman, *Miracles and Other Realities* (Vancouver, BC: Omega Press, 1990), xvi.

[195] Ibid., 173.

[196] See ibid., 181; also see Imants Barušs and Julia Mossbridge, "Mind-Boggling Chicks. Response to Broderick," *Journal of Scientific Exploration* 32 (1) (2018): 159–160.

[197] Pulos and Richman, *Miracles and Other Realities*, 106.

198 See Jeffrey Mishlove, *The PK Man: A True Story of Mind Over Matter* (Charlottesville, VA: Hampton Roads Publishing Company, 2000).

199 Ibid., 135.

200 Ibid., 139.

201 Ibid., 138.

202 Ibid., 105.

203 Ibid.

204 Ibid.

205 Ibid., 225.

206 Ibid., 226.

207 Baruš and Mossbridge, *Transcendent Mind*.

208 As quoted in Grosso, *The Man Who Could Fly*, 88. By a "new force" Crookes was referring to the discovery of forces rather than the coming into existence of a force that had previously not existed.

209 Grosso, *The Man Who Could Fly*, 180.

210 See John Schneider et al., "Guided Imagery and Immune Systems Function in Normal Subjects: A Summary of Research Findings," in Robert Kunzendorf, ed., *Mental Imagery* (New York: Plenum, 1990), 179–191.

211 See Piero Ferrucci, *What We May Be: Techniques for Psychological and Spiritual Growth through Psychosynthesis* (Los Angeles, CA: Jeremy P. Tarcher, 1982), 127.

212 Pulos and Richman, *Miracles and Other Realities*.

213 As quoted in Rosemarie Pilkington, "Interview with Felicia Parise, August 6, 2013," *Journal of Scientific Exploration* 29 (1) (2015): 82.

214 See Mark Srednicki, *Quantum Field Theory* (Cambridge, MA: Cambridge University Press, 2007), 351, for the value of the fine structure constant; also see Baruš and Mossbridge, *Transcendent Mind*.

215 Baruš and Mossbridge, *Transcendent Mind*.

216 See D. Scott Rogo and Raymond Bayless, *Phone Calls from the Dead* (Englewood Cliffs, NJ: Prentice-Hall, 1979).

217 See my "Failure to Replicate Electronic Voice Phenomenon," *Journal of Scientific Exploration* 15 (3) (2001): 355–367; also see Mark R. Leary and Tom Butler, "Electronic Voice Phenomena," in Cardeña et al., eds., *Parapsychology: A Handbook for the 21st Century* (Jefferson, NC: McFarland & Company, 2015).

218 See my "An Experimental Test of Instrumental Transcommunication," *Journal of Scientific Exploration* 21 (1) (2007): 89–98.

219 Leary and Butler, "Electronic Voice Phenomena."

220 Baruš, "Failure to Replicate Electronic Voice Phenomenon."

221 Baruš, "An Experimental Test of Instrumental Transcommunication."

222 Leary and Butler, "Electronic Voice Phenomena."

223 Baruš and Mossbridge, *Transcendent Mind*.

224 Baruš, "Failure to Replicate Electronic Voice Phenomenon," 363.

225 Leary and Butler, "Electronic Voice Phenomena."

226 Baruš, "Failure to Replicate Electronic Voice Phenomenon."

227 Irwin, *An Introduction to Parapsychology*, 201.

228 Ibid.

229 See Owen, *Conjuring Up Philip*. There are precedents for the creation of tulpas. While in Tibet, the French orientalist Alexandra David-Neel has claimed to have deliberately created a tulpa that became physically visible and interacted with her so that she sometimes "felt as if a robe was lightly rubbing against" her and, on one occasion, that "a hand seemed to touch [her] shoulder." The imaginary entity seemed to develop a mind of its own so that she felt compelled to dissolve it. It was not clear to her whether her phantom had taken on an actual material form or whether it was a hallucination that was visible to others as well as to herself (Alexandra David-Neel, *Magic and Mystery in Tibet* (New York: Dover Publications, 1971), 315).

230 See P.M.H. Atwater, *The Big Book of Near-Death Experiences: The Ultimate Guide to What Happens When We Die* (Charlottesville, VA: Hampton Roads, 2007), 109.

231 Atwater, *The Big Book of Near-Death Experiences*; also Atwater, *Near-Death Experiences: The Rest of the Story; What They Teach Us about Living, Dying, and Our True Purpose* (Charlottesville, VA: Hampton Roads, 2011); also see Penny Sartori, *The Wisdom of Near-Death Experiences: How Understanding NDEs Can Help Us Live More Fully* (London: Watkins, 2014).

232 See John Wren-Lewis, "Aftereffects of Near-Death Experiences: A Survival Mechanism Hypothesis," *Journal of Transpersonal Psychology* 26 (2) (1994): 107–115.

233 Baruss and Mossbridge, *Transcendent Mind*.

234 Baruss, "Characteristics of Consciousness in Collapse-Type Quantum Mind Theories;" also see my "Speculations about the Direct Effects of Intention on Physical Manifestation," and "Beyond Scientific Materialism: Toward a Transcendent Theory of Consciousness."

235 Smolin, *Time Reborn*.

236 Baruss, *The Impossible Happens*.

237 Ibid.

238 Average value experimental condition = 2.08 (sample size = 60; standard deviation = 1.58), average value control condition = 1.56 (sample size = 57; standard deviation = 1.59), z = 1.78, p = .04, one-tailed).

239 See Imants Baruss, Carolyn van Lier, and Diana Ali, "Alterations of Consciousness at a Self-Development Seminar: A Matrix Energetics Seminar Survey," *Journal of Consciousness Exploration and Research* 5 (11) (2014): 1078.

240 Ibid., 1081–1082.

241 Chomsky, *Who Rules the World?*, 188.

242 See Roderick J. Lawrence, "Interdisciplinary Science: A Coming of Age?" *The New York Academy of Sciences Magazine* (Spring 2016): 18.

243 See Anthony D. Barnosky, *Dodging Extinction: Power, Food, Money, and the Future of Life on Earth* (Berkeley, CA: University of California Press, 2014), x.

[244] James Lovelock, "Our Sustainable Retreat," in Eileen Crist et al., eds., *Gaia in Turmoil: Climate Change, Biodepletion, and Earth Ethics in an Age of Crisis* (Cambridge, MA: MIT Press, 2010), 21. James Lovelock proposed the notion of a self-regulating earth and the novelist William Golding proposed the name "Gaia" for it (See Lovelock, "Our Sustainable Retreat.").

[245] See Peter Ward, *The Medea Hypothesis: Is Life On Earth Ultimately Self-Destructive?* (Princeton, NJ: Princeton University Press, 2009), xviii–xix, emphases in original.

[246] Ibid., xix.

[247] See Eileen Crist and H. Bruce Rinker, "One Grand Organic Whole," in Crist et al., eds., *Gaia in Turmoil*, 13.

[248] Ibid., 14.

[249] Ibid., 15.

[250] In Greek mythology, Medea married the Argonaut Jason, bore him children, and then killed them all, hence the choice of Medea as the name of this hypothesis (Ward, *The Medea Hypothesis*).

[251] Ward, *The Medea Hypothesis*, xx.

[252] Ibid., xxi.

[253] Ibid., xv.

[254] See James Lovelock, *A Rough Ride to the Future* (London: Allen Lane, 2014), 12.

[255] See J.R. McNeill and Peter Engelke, *The Great Acceleration: An Environmental History of the Anthropocene Since 1945* (Cambridge, MA: Belknap Press, 2014), 1.

[256] Ibid., 2.

[257] See Jeremy Davies, *The Birth of the Anthropocene* (Oakland, CA: University of California Press, 2016), 2.

[258] See Roy Scranton, *Learning to Die in the Anthropocene: Reflections on the End of a Civilization* (San Francisco, CA: City Lights Books, 2015), 23.

[259] Ward, *The Medea Hypothesis*, xx.

[260] See Jack O'Malley-James et al., "Swansong Biospheres II: The Final Signs of Life on Terrestrial Planets Near the End of Their Habitable Lifetimes," *International Journal of Astrobiology* 13 (3) (2014): 229–243.

[261] Lovelock, *A Rough Ride to the Future*, 163.

[262] See David Nicol, *Subtle Activism: The Inner Dimension of Social and Planetary Transformation* (Albany, NY: SUNY Press, 2015).

[263] Also see Scranton, *Learning to Die in the Anthropocene*.

[264] See Robert C. Harney, "Inaccurate Prediction of Nuclear Weapons Effects and Possible Adverse Influences on Nuclear Terrorism Preparedness," *Homeland Security Affairs: The Journal of the NPS Center for Homeland Defense and Security* 5 (3) (2009): 17.

[265] See Max Tegmark, "Nuclear War from a Cosmic Perspective," (2015): 4–5, https://arxiv.org/pdf/1505.00246v2.pdf.

[266] See Kristin Shrader-Frechette, "Fukushima, Flawed Epistemology, and

Black-Swan Events," *Ethics, Policy and Environment* 14 (3) (2011): 267–272.

267 See Brecht Volders and Tom Sauer, "Introduction," in Brecht Volders et al., eds., *Nuclear Terrorism: Countering the Threat* (London: Routledge, 2016), 6.

268 See Nathan E. Busch, *No End in Sight: The Continuing Menace of Nuclear Proliferation* (Lexington, KY: University Press of Kentucky, 2004).

269 Volders and Sauer, "Introduction," 6.

270 Nathan E. Busch, *No End in Sight*, 116.

271 Ibid.

272 Volders and Sauer, "Introduction," 6.

273 See Kier A. Lieber and Darryl G. Press, "Why States Won't Give Nuclear Weapons to Terrorists," *International Security* 38 (1) (2013): 80–104; also see Matthew Bunn, "Bombs We Can Stop," review of *The Atomic Bazaar: The Rise of the Nuclear Poor*, by William Langewiesche, *American Scientist* 95 (5) (2007): 452–454; Wood et al., "The Future of Nuclear Archaeology: Reducing Legacy Risks of Weapons Fissile Material," *Science & Global Security* 22 (2014): 4–26.

274 See Owen B. Toon et al., "Consequences of Regional-Scale Nuclear Conflicts," *Science* 315 (2007): 1224.

275 Langewiesche, *The Atomic Bazaar*.

276 Bunn, "Managing the Bomb's Supply Side," review of *Unmaking the Bomb, A Fissile Material Approach to Nuclear Disarmament and Nonproliferation*, by Harold A. Feiveson, Alexander Glaser, Zia Mian, and Frank N. von Hippel, *Physics Today* 68, no. 5: 50.

277 Bunn, "Bombs We Can Stop."

278 Eleanor Ross, "The Nine Countries That Have Nuclear Weapons," http://www.independent.co.uk/news/world/politics/the-nine-countries-that-have-nuclear-weapons-a6798756.html.

279 Langewiesche, *The Atomic Bazaar*.

280 Toon et al., "Consequences of Regional-Scale Nuclear Conflicts," 1225.

281 See Vijay Shankar, "Subcontinental Nuclear Stability: The Spiralling Nightmare," *International Journey of Nuclear Security* 1 (1) (2015): 5.

282 Ibid.

283 Toon et al., "Consequences of Regional-Scale Nuclear Conflicts," 1224.

284 See Alan Robock et al., "Nuclear Winter Revisited with a Modern Climate Model and Current Nuclear Arsenals: Still Catastrophic Consequences," *Journal of Geophysical Research* 112 (D13107) (2007): 1.

285 Ibid., 6.

286 Tegmark, "Nuclear War from a Cosmic Perspective."

287 Scranton, *Learning to Die in the Anthropocene*, 68.

288 See, for example, Naomi Klein, "Capitalism and the Climate," *Nation* 293 (22) (2011): 11–21; and *This Changes Everything: Capitalism vs. the Climate* (New York: Simon & Schuster, 2014).

289 David Harvey, *Seventeen Contradictions and the End of Capitalism* (London: Profile Books, 2014).

290 Ibid., 255.

[291] Ibid., 249.

[292] Scranton, *Learning to Die in the Anthropocene*, 43.

[293] Barnosky, *Dodging Extinction*, 158.

[294] Harvey, *Seventeen Contradictions and the End of Capitalism*, xiii.

[295] Barnosky, *Dodging Extinction*, 157.

[296] Harvey, *Seventeen Contradictions and the End of Capitalism*, 262.

[297] Chomsky, *Who Rules the World?*, 56.

[298] Harvey, *Seventeen Contradictions and the End of Capitalism*, 262.

[299] For example, Paul Ehrlich and Anne Ehrlich, *One with Nineveh: Politics, Consumption, and the Human Future* (Washington, DC: Shearwater Books, 2004); also see Kari Marie Norgaard, *Living in Denial: Climate Change, Emotions, and Everyday Life* (Cambridge, MA: MIT Press, 2011).

[300] See Roger N. Walsh, *Staying Alive: The Psychology of Human Survival* (Boulder, CO: New Science Library, 1984); also George Vaillant et al., "An Empirically Validated Hierarchy of Defense Mechanisms," *Archives of General Psychiatry* 43 (8) (1986): 786–794.

[301] Paul Ehrlich and Anne Ehrlich, *One with Nineveh: Politics, Consumption, and the Human Future*; also Chomsky, *Who Rules the World?*

[302] Norgaard, *Living in Denial*.

[303] Ibid., 221.

[304] See Martin Heidegger, *Being and Time*, translated by John Macquarrie and Edward Robinson (New York: Harper & Row); Baruš, *Authentic Knowing*; and Walsh, *Staying Alive: The Psychology of Human Survival*.

[305] Norgaard, *Living in Denial*, 207, emphases in original.

[306] Chomsky, *Who Rules the World?*, 88.

[307] Walsh, *Staying Alive: The Psychology of Human Survival*, 41.

[308] Ibid., 42.

[309] Baruš, *Authentic Knowing*.

[310] Alpaslan Özerdem et al., eds., *Child Soldiers: From Recruitment to Reintegration* (New York: Palgrave Macmillan, 2011).

[311] See Jaclyn Chai et al., "Malala Yousafzai: A Young Female Activist," http://caseresources.hsph.harvard.edu/files/case/files/2014_malala-tcs.pdf.

[312] See my *The Impossible Happens*; and *Authentic Knowing*; also Ferrucci, *What We May Be*.

[313] As quoted by Valerie Strauss, "Texas GOP Rejects 'Critical Thinking' Skills. Really." https://www.washingtonpost.com/blogs/answer-sheet/post/texas-gop-rejects-critical-thinking-skills-really/2012/07/08/gJQAHNpFXW_blog.html.

[314] Nicol, *Subtle Activism*, 1.

[315] Ibid., 31.

[316] Ibid., 37.

[317] Baruš, *Alterations of Consciousness*.

[318] Nicol, *Subtle Activism*, 55.

[319] Ibid.

320 See David W. Orme-Johnson et al., "International Peace Project in the Middle East: The Effects of the Maharishi Technology of the Unified Field," *Journal of Conflict Resolution* 32 (4) (1988): 776–812.

321 Ibid.

322 See H.E. Puthoff, "CIA-Initiated Remote Viewing Program at Stanford Research Institute," *Journal of Scientific Exploration* 10 (1) (1996): 63–76; see also Jim Schnabel, *Remote Viewers: The Secret History of America's Psychic Spies* (New York: Dell Publishing, 1997).

323 See National Aeronautics and Space Administration, "Mars Observer (NSSDCA/COSPAR ID: 1992-063A)."

324 See Dwight D. Eisenhower, "Farewell Radio and Television Address to the American People," in *Public Papers of the Presidents of the United States: Dwight D. Eisenhower: 1960–61* (Washington, DC: Office of the Federal Register, National Archives and Records Service, General Services Administration, 1961).

325 See Come Carpentier de Gourdon, "The Global Crisis and the Ultimate Secret of the Empire," *Exopolitics Journal* 3 (2) (2009): 65–83.

326 See Jacques Vallée, *Revelations: Alien Contact and Human Deception* (New York: Ballantine, 1991); also see Bridget Brown, *They Know Us Better Than We Know Ourselves: The History and Politics of Alien Abduction* (New York: New York University Press, 2007).

327 For example, see Katherine J. Holden and Christopher C. French, "Alien Abduction Experiences: Some Clues from Neuropsychology and Neuro-psychiatry," *Cognitive Neuropsychiatry* 7 (3) (2002): 163–178; also see Susan A. Clancy, *Abducted: How People Come to Believe They Were Kidnapped by Aliens* (Cambridge, MA: Harvard University Press, 2005); Brown, *They Know Us Better Than We Know Ourselves*; and Stuart Appelle et al., "Alien Abduction Experiences," in Etzel Cardeña et al., eds., *Varieties of Anomalous Experience: Examining the Scientific Evidence* (Washington, DC: American Psychological Association, 2014), 213–240.

328 Richard Grossinger, "Giving Them a Name," *ReVision: The Journal of Consciousness and Change* 11 (4) (1989): 43–48.

329 See Andrea Pritchard et al., eds., *Alien Discussions: Proceedings of the Abduction Study Conference Held at MIT, Cambridge, MA* (Cambridge, MA: North Cambridge Press, 1994); David Michael Jacobs, ed., *UFOs and Abductions: Challenging the Borders of Knowledge* (Lawrence, KS: University Press of Kansas, 2000).

330 See John E. Mack, *Passport to the Cosmos: Human Transformation and Alien Encounters* (New York: Three Rivers Press, 1999); Clancy, *Abducted*.

331 See Christopher F. Roth, "Ufology as Anthropology: Race, Extraterrestrials, and the Occult," in D. Battaglia, ed., *Anthropology in Outerspaces* (Durham, NC: Duke University Press, 2005), 83.

332 David M. Jacobs, *Walking Among Us: The Alien Plan to Control Humanity* (San Francisco, CA: Disinformation Books, 2015), 235.

333 Mack, *Passport to the Cosmos*, 55.

334 Ibid., 94.
335 Ibid.
336 See Ralph W. Hood Jr. et al., *The Psychology of Religion: An Empirical Approach*, 5th ed. (New York: Guilford Press, 2018).
337 Clancy, *Abducted*, 138.
338 Ibid., 146.
339 Ibid., 154.
340 Barušs, *Alterations of Consciousness*.
341 Appelle et al., "Alien Abduction Experiences," 216.
342 In fact, according to some, too many for these to be actual physical abductions because of the logistical implausibility of surreptitiously abducting that many people (see Holden and French, "Alien Abduction Experiences: Some Clues from Neuropsychology and Neuropsychiatry").
343 See A. Druffel, "Resistance Techniques Against UFO Abduction as Reported by Credible Witnesses," in Andrea Pritchard et al., eds., *Alien Discussions: Proceedings of the Abduction Study Conference Held at MIT, Cambridge, MA* (Cambridge, MA: North Cambridge Press, 1994), 508–512; and Ann Druffel, *How to Defend Yourself Against Alien Abduction* (New York: Three Rivers Press, 1998).
344 Mack, *Passport to the Cosmos*.
345 Roth, "Ufology as Anthropology: Race, Extraterrestrials, and the Occult."
346 See Otto Oscar Binder, *Flying Saucers Are Watching Us* (New York: Belmont Books, 1968); also Roth, "Ufology as Anthropology: Race, Extraterrestrials, and the Occult."
347 See Jim Marrs, *Alien Agenda: The Untold Story of the Extraterrestrials Living Among Us* (London: HarperCollins Publishers, 1997); also see Richard C. Hoagland and Mike Bara, *Dark Mission: The Secret History of the National Aeronautics and Space Administration* (Port Townsend, WA: Feral House, 2007); Budd Hopkins and Carol Rainey, *Sight Unseen: Science, UFO Invisibility and Transgenic Beings* (New York: Atria Books, 2003).
348 Mack, *Passport to the Cosmos*, 10.
349 Ibid., 373; also see C.D.B. Bryan, *Close Encounters of the Fourth Kind: A Reporter's Notebook on Alien Abduction, UFOs, and the Conference at M.I.T.* (New York: Arkana, 1995).
350 Bill Chalker, *Hair of the Alien: DNA and Other Forensic Evidence for Alien Abductions* (New York: Paraview Pocket Books, 2005).
351 See Jacques Vallée, *Passport to Magonia: On UFOs, Folklore, and Parallel Worlds* (Chicago, IL: Contemporary Books, 1993).
352 See David G. Robertson, "Transformation: Whitley Strieber's Paranormal Gnosis," *Nova Religio: The Journal of Alternative and Emergent Religions* 18 (1) (2014): 69.
353 For example, Steven M. Greer, *Hidden Truth: Forbidden Knowledge; It is Time for You to Know* (Crozet, VA: Crossing Point, 2006).
354 See Larry Holcombe, *The Presidents and the UFOs: A Secret History from FDR to Obama* (New York: St. Martin's Press, 2015), 134–135.

355 Ibid., 134.

356 Ibid., 138.

357 Ibid.

358 Scranton, *Learning to Die in the Anthropocene*, 21.

359 See Viktor E. Frankl, *Man's Search for Meaning* (New York: Simon & Schuster, 1984).

360 Barušs, *Authentic Knowing*.

361 See Sebastian Junger, "War Reporter Sebastian Junger on Why Peace Can Be More Traumatic for Vets than War," *The Current with Anna Maria Tremonti*, CBC Radio, http://www.cbc.ca/radio/thecurrent/the-current-for-august-1-2016-1.3703017/august-1-2016-full-episode-transcript-1.3703352#segment0.

362 Scranton, *Learning to Die in the Anthropocene*, 82.

363 See Sebastian Junger, *Tribe: On Homecoming and Belonging* (Toronto: HarperCollins, 2016).

364 See Maria Paula Rayo Gomez, "Surrendering to the Vine of the Soul: Ayahuasca Shamanism as a Logotherapy," B.A. Thesis, King's University College at Western University, http://ir.uwo.lib.ca/cgi/viewcontent.cgi?article=1040&contxt=psychK_uht.

365 Barušs, "Questions about Interacting with Invisible Intelligences."

366 See J.H. Brennan, *Whisperers: The Secret History of the Spirit World* (New York: The Overlook Press, 2013).

367 See Charles A. Lindbergh, *The Spirit of St. Louis* (New York: Charles Scribner's Sons, 1953).

368 Barušs, *Alterations of Consciousness*; Barušs and Mossbridge, *Transcendent Mind*.

369 See Jacobs, *UFOs and Abductions: Challenging the Borders of Knowledge*; also see Steven M. Greer, *Hidden Truth: Forbidden Knowledge: It is Time for You to Know*.

370 See Düdjom Lingpa, "The Foolish Dharma of an Idiot Clothed in Mud and Feathers," in Düdjom Lingpa et al., eds., *Heart of the Great Perfection: Düdjom Lingpa's Visions of the Great Perfection* (Somerville, MA: Wisdom Publications, 2016), 149, emphases in original.

371 The incidence of reported mystical experiences in the general population is about 1%. Usually much higher numbers are given, but those are typically based on responses to a single ambiguous question. See Eugene L. Thomas and Pamela E. Cooper, "Incidence and Psychological Correlates of Intense Spiritual Experiences," *The Journal of Transpersonal Psychology* 12 (1) (1980): 75–85.

372 Barušs, *Alterations of Consciousness*.

373 See Bernadette Roberts, *The Path to No-Self: Life at the Center* (Albany, NY: SUNY Press, 1991); and Roberts, *The Experience of No-Self: A Contemplative Journey* (Albany, NY: SUNY Press, 1993).

374 See Alan Wallace, *Dreaming Yourself Awake: Lucid Dreaming and Tibetan Dream Yoga for Insight and Transformation* (Boston, MA: Shambhala, 2012);

Malamud, "Becoming Lucid in Dreams and Waking Life;" also Steve Taylor, *The Leap: The Psychology of Spiritual Awakening* (Novato, CA: New World Library, 2017).

375 See Lingpa, "The Foolish Dharma of an Idiot Clothed in Mud and Feathers;" also see Walsh, *Staying Alive: The Psychology of Human Survival*.

376 Roberts, *The Path to No-Self*; and *The Experience of No-Self*.

377 See my *Authentic Knowing*; *Alterations of Consciousness*; "Franklin Wolff's Mathematical Resolution of Existential Issues," *Journal of Scientific Exploration* 21 (4) (2007): 751–756; and *Science as a Spiritual Practice*.

378 And that a double dose of mescaline accomplished what the meditation could not (see Huston Smith, *Cleansing the Doors of Perception: The Religious Significance of Entheogenic Plants and Chemicals* (New York: Jeremy P. Tarcher/Putnam, 2000)).

379 Taylor, *The Leap: The Psychology of Spiritual Awakening*.

380 Ibid., 183–210.

381 Ibid.

382 See my *Alterations of Consciousness*; and *Science as a Spiritual Practice*; also see David B. Yaden et al., "The Noetic Quality: A Multimethod Exploratory Study," *Psychology of Consciousness: Theory, Research and Practice* 4 (1) (2017): 54–62.

383 Taylor, *The Leap: The Psychology of Spiritual Awakening*, 8.

384 Ibid., 123.

385 As quoted in Taylor, *The Leap: The Psychology of Spiritual Awakening*, 115.

386 I served as an Advisor for Jeffery Martin's Transformative Technology Lab at Sofia University until October 11, 2017, when I resigned so as to avoid any conflict of interest.

387 See Jeffery A. Martin, "Clusters of Individual Experiences Form a Continuum of Persistent Non-Symbolic Experiences in Adults," http://nonsymbolic.org/PNSE-article.pdf; also see Jeffery A. Martin, *The Finders* (Charleston, SC: Integration Press, 2014).

388 Martin, "Clusters of Individual Experiences Form a Continuum of Persistent Non-Symbolic Experiences in Adults;" Martin, *The Finders*.

389 See Franklin Merrell-Wolff, *Franklin Merrell-Wolff's Experience and Philosophy: A Personal Record of Transformation and a Discussion of Transcendental Consciousness* (Albany, NY: SUNY Press, 1994), 280.

390 Ibid., 282.

391 Jeffery A. Martin, "Clusters of Individual Experiences Form a Continuum of Persistent Non-Symbolic Experiences in Adults," paper presented at the *Society for Consciousness Studies Annual Conference*, Yale University, June 3–4, 2017.

392 Jeffery Martin, personal communication with the author, June 3, 2017.

393 Martin, "Clusters of Individual Experiences Form a Continuum of Persistent Non-Symbolic Experiences in Adults," paper presented at the *Society for Consciousness Studies Annual Conference*, 2017.

394 With Cronbach's alpha of .85 ($n = 52$) and .87 ($n = 50$) respectively.

395 $r(48) = -.40, p = .007$ (two-tailed).
396 Lyons, *The Disappearance of Introspection*; Barušs, *Alterations of Consciousness*.
397 See Charles Siewert, "Consciousness and Intentionality," in Edward Zalta, ed., *The Stanford Encyclopedia of Philosophy*, https://plato.stanford.edu/archives/spr2017/entries/consciousness-intentionality/.
398 Barušs and Mossbridge, *Transcendent Mind*.
399 For example, Jonathan Farrell and Tom McClelland, "Editorial: Consciousness and Inner Awareness," *Review of Philosophy and Psychology* 8 (1) (2017): 1–22; also Flanagan, *Consciousness Reconsidered*.
400 See my "Categorical Modelling of Husserl's Intentionality," *Husserl Studies* 6 (1989): 25–41.
401 Siewert, "Consciousness and Intentionality."
402 See Mihalyi Csikszentmihalyi, "The Flow Experience and Its Significance for Human Psychology," in Mihalyi Csikszentmihalyi et al., eds., *Optimal Experience: Psychological Studies of Flow in Consciousness* (Cambridge, UK: Cambridge University Press, 1988); also Csikszentmihalyi, *Flow: The Psychology of Optimal Experience* (New York: HarperPerennial, 1990).
403 See Douglas M. Baker, *Meditation: (The Theory and Practice)* (Essendon, UK: Douglas Baker, 1975); also Barušs, *Authentic Knowing*.
404 Ferrucci, *What We May Be*; Barušs, *Authentic Knowing*.
405 Barušs, *Authentic Knowing*; and *Alterations of Consciousness*.
406 Wallace, *Dreaming Yourself Awake*.
407 See the *DSM-5: Diagnostic and Statistical Manual of Mental Disorders*, 5th ed. (Arlington, VA: American Psychiatric Association, 2013).
408 See Marie Guillot, "I Me Mine: On a Confusion Concerning the Subjective Character of Experience," *Review of Philosophy and Psychology* 8 (2017): 27.
409 Ibid., 29.
410 Ibid., 31.
411 See Martine Nida-Rümelin, "Self-Awareness," *Review of Philosophy and Psychology* 8 (2017): 62.
412 Jonathan Farrell and Tom McClelland, "Editorial: Consciousness and Inner Awareness," 8.
413 See William James, *The Principles of Psychology* (Cambridge, MA: Harvard University Press, 1983); Flanagan, *Consciousness Reconsidered*; Barušs, *The Personal Nature of Notions of Consciousness*.
414 See Thomas J. Hurley III, "Etiology of Multiple Personality: From Abuse to Alter Personalities," *Institute of Noetic Sciences: Investigations; A Research Bulletin* 1 (3/4) (1985): 11–13; also see Richard P. Kluft, "Dissociative Identity Disorder," in Larry K. Michelson et al., eds., *Handbook of Dissociation: Theoretical, Empirical, and Clinical Perspectives* (New York: Plenum, 1996), 337–366.
415 See David Carse, *Perfect Brilliant Stillness: Beyond the Individual Self* (Salisbury, UK: Non-Duality Press, 2005).
416 Lyons, *The Disappearance of Introspection*.
417 See Eric Schwitzgebel, "Introspection," in Edward Zalta, ed., *The Stanford*

Encyclopedia of Philosophy, https://plato.stanford.edu/archives/win2016/entries/introspection/.

418 See Frédérique de Vignemont, "Bodily Awareness," in Edward Zalta, ed., *The Stanford Encyclopedia of Philosophy*, https://plato.stanford.edu/archives/sum2016/entries/bodily-awareness/.

419 Ibid.

420 See Olga Louchakova-Schwartz, "Qualia of God: Phenomenological Materiality in Introspection, with a Reference to Advaita Vedanta," *Open Theology* 3 (2017): 260; https://doi.org/10.1515/opth-2017-0021.

421 Ibid., 264.

422 Ibid.

423 Ibid., 265.

424 Ibid., 266.

425 As quoted in Louchakova-Schwartz, "Qualia of God: Phenomenological Materiality in Introspection, with a Reference to Advaita Vedanta," 262.

426 Ibid., 263.

427 As quoted in Louchakova-Schwartz, "Qualia of God: Phenomenological Materiality in Introspection, with a Reference to Advaita Vedanta," 264.

428 Siewert, "Consciousness and Intentionality."

429 Ring and Cooper, "Near-Death and Out-of-Body Experiences in the Blind: A Study of Apparent Eyeless Vision."

430 For example, Anthony William, *Medical Medium: Secrets Behind Chronic and Mystery Illness and How to Finally Heal* (Carlsbad, CA: Hay House, 2015).

431 Barušs and Mossbridge, *Transcendent Mind*.

432 See James C. Carpenter, *First Sight: ESP and Parapsychology in Everyday Life* (Lanham, MD: Rowman & Littlefield, 2012), 19.

433 See Russell Targ, *The Reality of ESP: A Physicist's Proof of Psychic Abilities* (Wheaton, IL: Quest Books, 2012).

434 See Andreas Mavromatis, *Hypnagogia: The Unique State of Consciousness between Wakefulness and Sleep* (London, UK: Routledge & Kegan Paul, 1987).

435 Barušs, *Science as a Spiritual Practice*.

436 Barušs, *Alterations of Consciousness*.

437 For example, Roberto Assagioli, *Psychosynthesis: A Manual of Principles and Techniques* (New York: Penguin, 1965); Ferrucci, *What We May Be*.

438 Barušs, *Alterations of Consciousness*.

439 Barušs, *The Impossible Happens*.

440 Barušs, *The Personal Nature of Notions of Consciousness*.

441 Barušs, *Science as a Spiritual Practice*.

442 Ferrucci, *Your Inner Will*.

443 Ferrucci, *What We May Be*.

444 See Franklin Merrell-Wolff, "Recognition— An Inversion in Consciousness," *Sangha: The Franklin Merrell-Wolff Newsletter* (Spring): 1.

445 Ibid., 1.

446 Wolff, as quoted in Ron Leonard, *The Transcendental Philosophy of Franklin Merrell-Wolff* (Albany, NY: SUNY Press, 1999), 49.

447 Barušs, *Science as a Spiritual Practice*.

448 See Alan Wallace, "Introduction to Dzogchen," an online course by Wisdom Academy, http://learn.wisdompubs.org/academy/lessons/dzogchen-intro-l9/.

449 Ibid.

450 Douglas E. Harding, "The Headless Way: A Method of Self-Enquiry Pioneered by Douglas Harding," http://www.headless.org.

451 Or heart. Some people see themselves as originating from the centres of their heads, some from the centres of their chests, that is to say, their "hearts" with a possible male–female split between head and heart respectively.

452 Lingpa, "The Foolish Dharma of an Idiot Clothed in Mud and Feathers," 149.

453 Barušs, *Authentic Knowing*, 155.

454 See Richard Chambers Prescott, *Vajrasattva: The Secret of the Four Wisdoms; Trekcho, Togal and Bardo* (Bloomington, IN: AuthorHouse, 2014).

455 See Shardza T. Gyaltsen, *Heart Drops of Dharmakaya: Dzogchen Practice of the Bön Tradition*, translated by Lopon Tenzin Namdak (Boston, MA: Snow Lion, 2002), 54.

456 Somewhat related to this, participants in one study were shifted toward a "mystical-type" experience through hypnosis (see Steven Jay Lynn and James Evans, "Hypnotic Suggestion Produces Mystical-Type Experiences in the Laboratory: A Demonstration Proof," *Psychology of Consciousness: Theory, Research, and Practice* 4 (1) (2017): 32).

457 As quoted in Wallace, *Dreaming Yourself Awake*, 90.

458 Wallace, *Dreaming Yourself Awake*, 92.

459 Gyaltsen, *Heart Drops of Dharmakaya: Dzogchen Practice of the Bön Tradition*, 68.

460 Barušs, *Authentic Knowing*.

461 See Eric Klinger, *Daydreaming: Using Waking Fantasy and Imagery for Self-Knowledge and Creativity* (Los Angeles, CA: Jeremy P. Tarcher, 1990).

462 See Assagioli, *Psychosynthesis*; Ferrucci, *What We May Be*; also Ferrucci, *Your Inner Will*.

463 Barušs, *Authentic Knowing*.

464 Taylor, *The Leap: The Psychology of Spiritual Awakening*.

465 Barušs, *Authentic Knowing*; Lee Sannella, *Kundalini – Psychosis or Transcendence?* (San Francisco, CA: H.S. Dakin, 1976); also see, for example, Brenda Sanders, "What is Really Real," in Jeanne M. House, ed., *Peak Vitality: Raising the Threshold of Abundance in Our Material, Spiritual and Emotional Lives* (Santa Rosa, CA: Elite Books, 2008), 454–464.

466 The Spiritual Emergence Network website, August 2017, http://spiritualemergence.org/.

467 Gyaltsen, *Heart Drops of Dharmakaya: Dzogchen Practice of the Bön Tradition*, 67.

468 Barušs, *Science as a Spiritual Practice*.

[469] Jeffery Martin, personal communication with the author, June 3, 2017.

[470] See James H. Moor, "Why We Need Better Ethics for Emerging Technologies," *Ethics and Information Technology* 7 (2005): 119.

[471] See Umberto Eco, *Serendipities: Language and Lunacy*, translated by William Weaver (New York: Columbia UP, 1998), 5–6.

[472] See Saul Fisher, "Pierre Gassendi," in Edward Zalta, ed., *The Stanford Encyclopedia of Philosophy*, https://plato.stanford.edu/archives/spr2014/entries/gassendi/.

[473] Ibid.

[474] James H. Moor, "Why We Need Better Ethics for Emerging Technologies," 2005.

[475] Ibid., 112.

[476] Peter J. Kuznick, "The Decision to Risk the Future: Harry Truman, the Atomic Bomb and the Apocalyptic Narrative," *The Asia-Pacific Journal | Japan Focus* 5 (7) (2007): 1–23.

[477] Claudia Som et al., "The Precautionary Principle in the Information Society," *Human and Ecological Risk Assessment* 10 (2004): 790.

[478] Ibid.

[479] Michael Isikoff and David Corn, *Russian Roulette: The Inside Story of Putin's War on America and the Election of Donald Trump* (New York: Twelve, 2018).

[480] Larry Dossey, *Be Careful What You Pray For ... You Just Might Get It* (New York: HarperSanFrancisco, 1997).

Bibliography

835850 Ontario Limited, producer. *Philip: The Imaginary Ghost*. 1974; DVD, 15 min. Available from the Visual Education Centre, http://www.visualed.com.

American Psychiatric Association. 2013. *Diagnostic and Statistical Manual of Mental Disorders, Fifth Edition*. Arlington, VA: American Psychiatric Association.

Appelle, Stuart, Steven J. Lynn, Leonard Newman, and Anne Malaktaris. 2014. "Alien Abduction Experiences." In *Varieties of Anomalous Experience: Examining the Scientific Evidence*, edited by Etzel Cardeña, Stephen J. Lynn and Stanley Krippner, 213–240. Washington, DC: American Psychological Association.

Assagioli, Roberto. 1965. *Psychosynthesis: A Manual of Principles and Techniques*. New York: Penguin.

Atwater, P.M.H. 2007. *The Big Book of Near-Death Experiences: The Ultimate Guide to What Happens When We Die*. Charlottesville, VA: Hampton Roads.

Atwater, P.M.H. 2011. *Near-Death Experiences: The Rest of the Story: What They Teach Us About Living, Dying, and Our True Purpose*. Charlottesville, VA: Hampton Roads.

Baker, Douglas M. 1975. *Meditation (The Theory and Practice)*. Essendon, Hertfordshire, England: Douglas Baker.

Barbour, Julian. 2000. *The End of Time: The Next Revolution in Physics*. Oxford, England: Oxford University Press.

Barnosky, Anthony D. 2014. *Dodging Extinction: Power, Food, Money, and the Future of Life on Earth*. Berkeley, CA: University of California Press.

Barrow, John D., and John K. Webb. 2005. "Inconstant Constants: Do the Inner Workings of Nature Change with Time?" *Scientific American* 292, no. 6: 56–63.

Baruss, Imants. 1986. "Quantum Mechanics and Human Consciousness." *Physics in Canada/La Physique au Canada* 42, no. 1: 3–5.

Baruss, Imants. 1987. "Metanalysis of Definitions of Consciousness." *Imagination, Cognition and Personality* 6, no. 4: 321–329.

Baruss, Imants. 1989. "Categorical Modelling of Husserl's Intentionality." *Husserl Studies* 6: 25–41.

Baruss, Imants. 1990. *The Personal Nature of Notions of Consciousness: A Theoretical and Empirical Examination of the Role of the Personal in the Understanding of Consciousness*. Lanham, MD: University Press of America.

Baruss, Imants. 1996. *Authentic Knowing: The Convergence of Science and Spiritual Aspiration*. West Lafayette, IN: Purdue University Press.

Baruss, Imants. 2001. "Failure to Replicate Electronic Voice Phenomenon." *Journal of Scientific Exploration* 15, no. 3: 355–367.

Baruss, Imants. 2003. *Alterations of Consciousness: An Empirical Analysis for Social Scientists*. Washington, DC: American Psychological Association.

Baruss, Imants. 2007. "An Experimental Test of Instrumental Transcommunication." *Journal of Scientific Exploration* 21, no. 1: 89–98.

Baruss, Imants. 2007. "Franklin Wolff's Mathematical Resolution of Existential Issues." *Journal of Scientific Exploration* 21, no. 4: 751–756.

Baruss, Imants. 2007. *Science as a Spiritual Practice*. Exeter, England: Imprint Academic.

Baruss, Imants. 2008. "Beliefs about Consciousness and Reality: Clarification of the Confusion Concerning Consciousness." *Journal of Consciousness Studies* 15, no. 10–11: 277–292.

Baruss, Imants. 2008. "Characteristics of Consciousness in Collapse-Type Quantum Mind Theories." *Journal of Mind and Behavior* 29, no. 3: 255–265.

Baruss, Imants. 2009. "Speculations about the Direct Effects of Intention on Physical Manifestation." *Journal of Cosmology* 3: 590–599.

Barušs, Imants. 2010. "Beyond Scientific Materialism: Toward a Transcendent Theory of Consciousness." *Journal of Consciousness Studies* 17, no. 7–8: 213–231.

Barušs, Imants. 2012. "What We Can Learn about Consciousness from Altered States of Consciousness." *Journal of Consciousness Exploration and Research* 3, no. 7: 805–819.

Barušs, Imants. 2013. "Learning to Forget: Deprogramming as a Precondition for the Occurrence of Non-Dual States of Consciousness." *Journal of Consciousness Exploration and Research* 4, no. 8: 816–832.

Barušs, Imants. 2013. *The Impossible Happens: A Scientist's Personal Discovery of the Extraordinary Nature of Reality.* Alresford, Hampshire, England: Iff Books.

Barušs, Imants. 2014. "Questions about Interacting with Invisible Intelligences." *EdgeScience* 18: 18–19.

Barušs, Imants. 2018. "Meaning Fields: Meaning Beyond the Human as a Resolution of Boundary Problems Introduced by Nonlocality." *EdgeScience*, 35: 8–11.

Barušs, Imants. 2019. "Categorical Modelling of Conscious States." *Consciousness: Ideas and Research for the Twenty-First Century* 7, no. 7: 1–10.

Barušs, Imants, and Robert J. Moore. 1989. "Notions of Consciousness and Reality." In *Imagery: Current Perspectives*, edited by Joseph E. Shorr, Pennee Robin, Jack A. Connella and Milton Wolpin, 87–92. New York: Plenum.

Barušs, Imants, and Robert J. Moore. 1992. "Measurement of Beliefs about Consciousness and Reality." *Psychological Reports* 71: 59–64.

Barušs, Imants, and Robert J. Moore. 1998. "Beliefs about Consciousness and Reality of Participants at 'Tucson II'." *Journal of Consciousness Studies* 5, no. 4: 483–496.

Barušs, Imants, and Julia Mossbridge. 2017. *Transcendent Mind: Rethinking the Science of Consciousness.* Washington, DC: American Psychological Association.

Barušs, Imants, and Julia Mossbridge. 2018. "Mind-Boggling Chicks. Response to Broderick." *Journal of Scientific Exploration* 32, no. 1: 159–160.

Barušs, Imants, and Vanille Rabier. 2014. "Failure to Replicate Retrocausal Recall." *Psychology of Consciousness: Theory, Research, and Practice* 1, no. 1: 82–91.

Barušs, Imants, Carolyn van Lier, and Diana Ali. 2014. "Alterations of Consciousness at a Self-Development Seminar: A Matrix Energetics Seminar Survey." *Journal of Consciousness Exploration and Research* 5, no. 11: 1064–1086.

Barušs, Imants, and Robert Woodrow. 2013. "A Reduction Theorem for the Kripke-Joyal Semantics: Forcing Over an Arbitrary Category Can Always Be Replaced by Forcing Over a Complete Heyting Algebra." *Logica Universalis* 7, no. 3: 323–334. https://doi: 10.1007/s11787-013-0084-y.

Beischel, Julie, Mark Boccuzzi, Michael Biuso, and Adam J. Rock. 2015. "Anomalous Information Reception by Research Mediums Under Blinded Conditions II: Replication and Extension." *EXPLORE: The Journal of Science & Healing* 11, no. 2: 136–142. https://doi.org/10.1016/j.explore.2015.01.001.

Bengston, William F. 2007. "Commentary: A Method Used to Train Skeptical Volunteers to Heal in an Experimental Setting." *The Journal of Alternative and Complementary Medicine* 13, no. 3: 329–331.

Bengston, William. 2010. *The Energy Cure: Unraveling the Mystery of Hands-on Healing*. Boulder, CO: Sounds True.

Bengston, William F., and David Krinsley. 2000. "The Effect of the 'Laying On of Hands' on Transplanted Breast Cancer in Mice." *Journal of Scientific Exploration* 14, no. 3: 353–364.

Bengston, William F., and Margaret Moga. 2007. "Resonance, Placebo Effects, and Type II Errors: Some Implications from Healing Research for Experimental Methods." *The Journal of Alternative and Complementary Medicine* 13, no. 3: 317–327.

Berger, Peter L. 1970. *A Rumor of Angels: Modern Society and the Rediscovery of the Supernatural*. Garden City, NY: Anchor Books.

Beseme, Sarah, William Bengston, and Dean Radin. 2018. "Transcriptional Changes in Cancer Cells Induced by Exposure to a Healing Method." *Dose-Response* 16, no. 3: 1–8. https://doi.org/10.1177/1559325818782843.

Bierman, Dick J. 2001. "On the Nature of Anomalous Phenomena: Another Reality Between the World of Subjective Consciousness and the Objective World of Physics?" In *The Physical Nature of Consciousness*, edited by Philip Van Loocke, 269–292. Amsterdam, The Netherlands: John Benjamins.

Binder, Otto Oscar. 1968. *Flying Saucers Are Watching Us*. New York: Belmont Books.

Bohm, David. 1983. *Wholeness and the Implicate Order*. London, England: Ark.

Braude, Stephen E. 2003. *Immortal Remains: The Evidence for Life after Death*. Lanham, MD: Rowman & Littlefield.

Braude, Stephen E. 2007. *The Gold Leaf Lady and Other Parapsychological Investigations*. Chicago, IL: University of Chicago Press.

Braude, Stephen E. 2014. *Crimes of Reason: On Mind, Nature, and the Paranormal*. Lanham, MD: Rowman & Littlefield.

Braude, Stephen. 2015. "Macro-Psychokinesis." In *Parapsychology: A Handbook for the 21st Century*, edited by Etzel Cardeña, John Palmer, and David Marcusson-Clavertz, 258–265. Jefferson, NC: McFarland & Company.

Braude, Stephen E. 2016. Review of The Man Who Could Fly: St. Joseph of Copertino and the Mystery of Levitation, by Michael Grosso. *Journal of Scientific Exploration* 30, no. 2: 275–278.

Brennan, J.H. 2013. *Whisperers: The Secret History of the Spirit World*. New York: The Overlook Press.

Brown, Bridget. 2007. *They Know Us Better Than We Know Ourselves: The History and Politics of Alien Abduction*. New York: New York University Press.

Bryan, C.D.B. 1995. *Close Encounters of the Fourth Kind: A Reporter's Notebook on Alien Abduction, UFOs, and the Conference at M.I.T.* New York: Arkana.

Bunn, Matthew. 2007. "Bombs We Can Stop," review of The Atomic Bazaar, by William Langewiesche. *American Scientist* 95, no. 5: 452–454.

Bunn, Matthew. 2015. "Managing the Bomb's Supply Side," review of *Unmaking the Bomb: A Fissile Material Approach to Nuclear Disarmament and Nonproliferation*, by Harold A. Feiveson, Alexander Glaser, Zia

Mian, and Frank N. von Hippel. *Physics Today* 68, no. 5: 50. https://doi.org/10.1063/pt.3.2785.

Busch, Nathan E. 2004. *No End in Sight: The Continuing Menace of Nuclear Proliferation*. Lexington, KY: The University Press of Kentucky.

Bynum, W.F., and Roy Porter, eds. 2005. *Oxford Dictionary of Scientific Quotations*. Oxford, England: Oxford University Press.

Cardeña, Etzel. 2014. "A Call for an Open, Informed Study of All Aspects of Consciousness." *Frontiers in Human Neuroscience* 8, no. 17: 1–4. https://doi.org/10.3389/fnhum.2014.00017.

Cardeña, Etzel, Steven J. Lynn, and Stanley Krippner, eds. 2014. *Varieties of Anomalous Experience: Examining the Scientific Evidence*. 2nd ed. Washington, DC: American Psychological Association.

Carpenter, James C. 2012. *First Sight: ESP and Parapsychology in Everyday Life*. Lanham, MD: Rowman & Littlefield.

Carpentier de Gourdon, Come. 2009. "The Global Crisis and the Ultimate Secret of the Empire." *Exopolitics Journal* 3, no. 2: 65–83.

Carse, David. 2005. *Perfect Brilliant Stillness: Beyond the Individual Self*. Salisbury, England: Non-Duality Press.

Chai, Jaclyn, Rachel Gordon, and Paula A. Johnson. 2014. "Malala Yousafzai: A Young Female Activist." Harvard Global Health Institute. *Harvard T.H. Chan School of Public Health* (website). http://caseresources.hsph.harvard.edu/files/case/files/2014_malala-tcs.pdf

Chalker, Bill. 2005. *Hair of the Alien: DNA and Other Forensic Evidence for Alien Abductions*. New York: Paraview Pocket Books.

Chalmers, D.J. 1995. "Facing Up to the Problem of Consciousness." *Journal of Consciousness Studies* 2, no. 3: 200–219.

Chomsky, Noam. 2016. *Who Rules the World?* New York: Metropolitan Books.

Clancy, Susan. A. 2005. *Abducted: How People Come to Believe They Were Kidnapped by Aliens*. Cambridge, MA: Harvard University Press.

Crist, Eileen and H. Bruce Rinker. 2010. "One Grand Organic Whole." In *Gaia in Turmoil: Climate Change, Biodepletion, and Earth Ethics in an Age of Crisis*, edited by Eileen Crist & H. Bruce Rinker, 3–20. Cambridge, MA: MIT Press.

Crossley, J.N., C.J. Ash, C.J. Brickhill, J.C. Stillwell, and N.H. Williams. 1972. *What is Mathematical Logic?* Oxford, England: Oxford University Press.

Csikszentmihalyi, Mihalyi. 1988. "The Flow Experience and its Significance for Human Psychology." In *Optimal Experience: Psychological Studies of Flow in Consciousness*, edited by Mihalyi Csikszentmihalyi and Isabella Selega Csikszentmihalyi, 15–35. Cambridge, England: Cambridge University Press.

Csikszentmihalyi, Mihalyi. 1990. *Flow: The Psychology of Optimal Experience.* New York: HarperPerennial.

David-Neel, Alexandra. 1971. *Magic and Mystery in Tibet.* New York: Dover Publications. First published in 1929 in French by Plon (Paris).

Davies, Jeremy. 2016. *The Birth of the Anthropocene.* Oakland, CA: University of California Press.

de Vignemont, Frédérique. 2016. "Bodily Awareness." In *The Stanford Encyclopedia of Philosophy*, edited by Edward N. Zalta, (Summer). https://plato.stanford.edu/archives/sum2016/entries/bodily-awareness/.

Dennett, Daniel C. 1978. *Brainstorms: Philosophical Essays on Mind and Psychology.* Montgomery, VT: Bradford Books.

Dossey, Larry. 1997. *Be Careful What You Pray For … You Just Might Get It.* New York: HarperSanFrancisco.

Dossey, Larry. 2011. "Dying to Heal: A Neglected Aspect of NDEs." *Explore: The Journal of Science and Healing* 7, no. 2: 59–62.

Druffel, A. 1994. "Resistance Techniques Against UFO Abduction as Reported by Credible Witnesses." In *Alien Discussions: Proceedings of the Abduction Study Conference Held at MIT, Cambridge, MA*, edited by Andrea Pritchard, David E. Pritchard, John E. Mack, Pam Kasey, and Claudia Yapp, 508–512. Cambridge, MA: North Cambridge.

Druffel, Ann. 1998. *How to Defend Yourself Against Alien Abduction.* New York: Three Rivers Press.

Dyson, Freeman J. 1998. "Innovation in Physics." In *JingShin Theoretical Physics Symposium in Honor of Professor Ta-You Wu*, edited by Jong Ping Hsu, and Leonard Hsu, 73–90. River Edge, NJ: World Scientific.

Eco, Umberto. 1998. *Serendipities: Language and Lunacy.* Translated by William Weaver. New York: Columbia University Press.

Einstein, Albert, Boris Podolsky, and Nathan Rosen. 1983. "Can Quantum-Mechanical Description of Physical Reality Be Considered Complete?" In *Quantum Theory and Measurement,* edited by John Archibald Wheeler and Wojciech Hubert Zurek, 138–141. Princeton, NJ: Princeton University Press. First published 1935 in *Physical Review.*

Eisenhower, Dwight D. 1961. "Farewell Radio and Television Address to the American People." January 17, 1961. *Public Papers of the Presidents of the United States: Dwight D. Eisenhower: 1960–61.* Washington, DC: Office of the Federal Register, National Archives and Records Service, General Services Administration.

Ehrlich, Paul, and Anne Ehrlich. 2004. *One with Nineveh: Politics, Consumption, and the Human Future.* Washington, DC: Shearwater Books.

Elitzur, Avshalom. 2006. "What's the Mind–Body Problem with You Anyway? Prolegomena to any Scientific Discussion of Consciousness." In *Mind and Its Place in the World: Non-Reductionist Approaches to the Ontology of Consciousness,* edited by Alexander Batthyany and Avshalom Elitzur, 15–22. Frankfurt, Germany: ontos verlag.

Farrell, Jonathan, and Tom McClelland. 2017. "Editorial: Consciousness and Inner Awareness." *Review of Philosophy and Psychology* 8, no. 1: 1–22.

Ferrucci, Piero. 1982. *What We May Be: Techniques for Psychological and Spiritual Growth through Psychosynthesis.* Los Angeles, CA: Jeremy P. Tarcher.

Ferrucci, Piero. 2014. *Your Inner Will: Finding Personal Strength in Critical Times.* Translated by Vivien Reid Ferrucci. New York: Jeremy P. Tarcher/Penguin.

Feynman, Richard P. 2006. *QED: The Strange Theory of Light and Matter.* Princeton, NJ: Princeton University Press. First published 1985.

Feynman, Richard P. 2005. *Perfectly Reasonable Deviations from the Beaten Track: The Letters of Richard P. Feynman.* Edited and with an Introduction by Michelle Feynman. New York: Basic Books.

Fields, R. Douglas. 2011. *The Other Brain: The Scientific and Medical Breakthroughs That Will Heal our Brains and Revolutionize our Health.* New York: Simon & Schuster.

Fisher, Saul. 2014. "Pierre Gassendi." In *The Stanford Encyclopedia of Philosophy,* edited by Edward N. Zalta, (Spring). http://plato.stanford.edu/archives/spr2014/entries/gassendi/.

Flanagan, Owen. 1992. *Consciousness Reconsidered.* Cambridge, MA: A Bradford Book.

Fodor, Jerry. 2000. *The Mind Doesn't Work That Way: The Scope and Limits of Computational Psychology.* Cambridge, MA: A Bradford Book.

Fontana, David. 2005. *Is There an Afterlife? A Comprehensive Overview of the Evidence.* Winchester, England: O-Books.

Foy, Robin P. 2008. *Witnessing the Impossible.* Diss, Norfolk, England: Torcal Publications.

Frankl, Viktor E. 1984. *Man's Search for Meaning.* rev. ed. New York: Simon & Schuster.

Freeman, Walter J. 2000. "Brains Create Macroscopic Order from Microscopic Disorder by Neurodynamics in Perception." In *Disorder Versus Order in Brain Function: Essays in Theoretical Neurobiology,* edited by Peter Århem, Clas Blomberg, Hans Liljenström, 205–219. Singapore: World Scientific Publishing.

Gerlich, Stefan, Sandra Eibenberger, Matthias Tomandl, Stefan Nimmrichter, Klaus Hornberger, Paul J. Fagan, Jens Tüxen, Marcel Mayor, and Markus Arndt. 2011. "Quantum Interference of Large Organic Molecules." *Nature Communications* 2, no. 263: 1–5. https://doi.org/10.1038/ncomms1263.

Gleick, James. 1988. "Richard Feynman Dead at 69; Leading Theoretical Physicist." *The New York Times* online. (February 17). http://www.nytimes.com/1988/02/17/obituaries/richard-feynman-dead-at-69-leading-theoretical-physicist.html.

Greer, Steven M. 2006. *Hidden Truth: Forbidden Knowledge: It is Time for You to Know.* Crozet, VA: Crossing Point.

Grigg, Madeleine, M., Michael, A. Kelly, Gastone G. Celesia, Mona W. Ghobrial, and Emanuel R. Ross. 1987. "Electroencephalographic Activity After Brain Death." *Archives of Neurology* 44: 948–954.

Grossinger, Richard. 1989. "Giving Them a Name." *ReVision: The Journal of Consciousness and Change* 11, no. 4: 43–48.

Grosso, Michael. 2016. *The Man Who Could Fly: St. Joseph of Copertino and the Mystery of Levitation*. Lanham, MD: Rowman & Littlefield.

Guiley, Rosemary E. 1991. *Harper's Encyclopedia of Mystical and Paranormal Experience*. New York: HarperSanFrancisco.

Guillot, Marie. 2017. "*I Me Mine*: On a Confusion Concerning the Subjective Character of Experience." *Review of Philosophy and Psychology* 8: 23–53.

Gyaltsen, Shardza T. 2002. *Heart Drops of Dharmakaya: Dzogchen Practice of the Bön Tradition*. Translated by Lopon Tenzin Namdak. Boston, MA: Snow Lion.

Hanson, Stephen José, and David J. Burr. 1990. "What Connectionist Models Learn: Learning and Representation in Connectionist Networks." *Behavioral and Brain Sciences* 13: 471–518.

Haraldsson, Erlendur. 2012. *The Departed Among the Living: An Investigative Study of Afterlife Encounters*. Guildford, Surrey, England: White Crow.

Harding, Douglas E. 2017. *The Headless Way: A Method of Self-Enquiry Pioneered by Douglas Harding*. Accessed September 1, 2017. http://www.headless.org.

Harney, Robert C. 2009. "Inaccurate Prediction of Nuclear Weapons Effects and Possible Adverse Influences on Nuclear Terrorism Preparedness." *Homeland Security Affairs: The Journal of the NPS Center for Homeland Defense and Security* 5, no. 3. https://www.hsaj.org/articles/97.

Harvey, David. 2014. *Seventeen Contradictions and the End of Capitalism*. London, England: Profile Books.

Heath, Pamela Rae. 2003. *The PK Zone: A Cross-Cultural Review of Psychokinesis (PK)*. New York: iUniverse.

Heidegger, Martin. 1962. *Being and Time*. Translated by John Macquarrie and Edward Robinson. New York: Harper & Row.

Hoagland, Richard C., and Mike Bara. 2007. *Dark Mission: The Secret History of the National Aeronautics and Space Administration*. Port Townsend, WA: Feral House.

Holcombe, Larry. 2015. *The Presidents and the UFOs: A Secret History from FDR to Obama*. New York: St. Martin's Press.

Holden, Janice Miner. 2009. "Veridical Perception in Near-Death Experiences." In *The Handbook of Near-Death Experiences: Thirty Years of Investigation*, edited by Janice Miner Holden, Bruce Greyson and Debbie James, 185–211. Santa Barbara, CA: Praeger.

Holden, Katherine J., and Christopher C. French. 2002. "Alien Abduction Experiences: Some Clues from Neuropsychology and Neuropsychiatry." *Cognitive Neuropsychiatry* 7, no. 3: 163–178.

Holden, M., D.G.C. McKeon, and T.N. Sherry. 2011. "The Double Slit Experiment with Polarizers." 19 October. *arXiv*: 1110.4309v1 [quant-ph]. https://arxiv.org/pdf/1110.4309v1.pdf.

Honorton, Charles. 2015. "A Moving Experience." *Journal of Scientific Exploration* 29, no. 1: 62–74.

Hood Jr., Ralph. W., Peter C. Hill, and Bernard Spilka. 2018. *The Psychology of Religion: An Empirical Approach*. 5th ed. New York: The Guilford Press.

Hopkins, Budd, and Carol Rainey. 2003. *Sight Unseen: Science, UFO Invisibility and Transgenic Beings*. New York: Atria Books.

Huber-Dyson, Verena. 1991. *Gödel's Theorems: A Workbook on Formalization*. Stuttgart, Germany: B.G. Teubner Verlagsgesellschaft.

Hurley III, Thomas J. 1985. "Etiology of Multiple Personality: From Abuse to Alter Personalities." *Institute of Noetic Sciences: Investigations: A Research Bulletin* 1(3/4): 11–13.

Huxley, Aldous. 1977. *The Doors of Perception and Heaven and Hell*. London, England: Grafton Books.

Irwin, Harvey J. 1994. *An Introduction to Parapsychology*. 2nd ed. Jefferson, NC: McFarland & Company.

Isikoff, Michael, and David Corn. 2018. *Russian Roulette: The Inside Story of Putin's War on America and the Election of Donald Trump*. New York: Twelve.

Itano, Wayne M., Daniel J. Heinzen, J.J. Bollinger, and D.J. Wineland. 1990. "Quantum Zeno Effect." *Physical Review A* 41, no. 5: 2295–2300.

Jacobs, David Michael, ed. 2000. *UFOs and Abductions: Challenging the Borders of Knowledge*. Lawrence, KS: University Press of Kansas.

Jacobs, David M. 2015. *Walking Among Us: The Alien Plan to Control Humanity*. San Francisco, CA: Disinformation Books.

James, William. 1904. "Does 'Consciousness' Exist?" *The Journal of Philosophy, Psychology and Scientific Methods* 1, no. 18: 477–491.

James, William. 1983. *The Principles of Psychology*. Cambridge, MA: Harvard University Press. First published 1890 by Henry Holt.

Junger, Sebastian. 2016. "War Reporter Sebastian Junger on Why Peace Can Be More Traumatic for Vets Than War." *The Current with Anna Maria Tremonti*, CBC Radio. Accessed August 9, 2016. http://www.cbc.ca/radio/thecurrent/the-current-for-august-1-2016-1.3703017/august-1-2016-full-episode-transcript-1.3703352#segment0

Junger, Sebastian. 2016. *Tribe: On Homecoming and Belonging*. Toronto: HarperCollins.

Keen, Montague. 2001. "The Scole Investigation: A Study in Critical Analysis of Paranormal Physical Phenomena. *Journal of Scientific Exploration* 15, no. 2: 167–182.

Keen, Montague, Arthur Ellison, and David Fontana. 1999. "The Scole Report: An Account of an Investigation into the Genuineness of a Range of Physical Phenomena Associated with a Mediumistic Group in Norfolk, England." *Proceedings of the Society for Psychical Research* 58, (Pt. 220): 149–392.

Kelly, Emily W., Bruce Greyson, and Edward F. Kelly. 2010. "Unusual Experiences Near Death and Related Phenomena." In *Irreducible Mind: Toward a Psychology for the 21st Century*. eds. Edward F. Kelly, Emily W. Kelly, Adam Crabtree, Alan Gauld, Michael Grosso and Bruce Greyson, 367–422. Lanham, MD: Rowman & Littlefield.

Klein, Naomi. 2011. "Capitalism vs. the Climate." *Nation* 293, no. 22: 11–21.

Klein, Naomi. 2014. *This Changes Everything: Capitalism vs. the Climate*. New York: Simon & Schuster.

Klinger, Eric. 1990. *Daydreaming: Using Waking Fantasy and Imagery for Self-Knowledge and Creativity*. Los Angeles, CA: Jeremy P. Tarcher.

Kluft, Richard P. 1996. "Dissociative Identity Disorder." In *Handbook of Dissociation: Theoretical, Empirical, and Clinical Perspectives*, edited by Larry K. Michelson and William J. Ray, 337–366. New York: Plenum.

Koch, Christof. 2012. *Consciousness: Confessions of a Romantic Reductionist.* Cambridge, MA: MIT Press.

Kochen, Simon, and Ernst P. Specker. 1967. "The Problem of Hidden Variables in Quantum Mechanics." *Journal of Mathematics and Mechanics* 17, no. 1: 59–87.

Kohn, Eduardo. 2013. *How Forests Think: Toward an Anthropology Beyond the Human.* Berkeley, CA: University of California Press.

Komarovski, Yaroslav. 2015. *Tibetan Buddhism and Mystical Experience.* New York: Oxford University Press.

Koons, Robert C., and George Bealer, eds. 2010. *The Waning of Materialism.* Oxford, England: Oxford University Press.

Krauss, Lawrence M. 2012. *Quantum Man: Richard Feynman's Life in Science.* New York: W.W. Norton & Company.

Kuznick, Peter J. 2007. "The Decision to Risk the Future: Harry Truman, the Atomic Bomb and the Apocalyptic Narrative." *The Asia-Pacific Journal | Japan Focus* 5, no. 7: 1–23.

Langewiesche, William. 2007. *The Atomic Bazaar: The Rise of the Nuclear Poor.* New York: Farrar, Straus and Giroux.

Lawrence, Roderick J. 2016. "Interdisciplinary Science: A Coming of Age?" *The New York Academy of Sciences Magazine* (Spring): 18.

Leary, Mark R., and Tom Butler. 2015. "Electronic Voice Phenomena." In *Parapsychology: A Handbook for the 21st Century*, edited by Etzel Cardeña, John Palmer, and David Marcusson-Clavertz, 341–349. Jefferson, NC: McFarland & Company.

Leonard, Ron. 1999. *The Transcendental Philosophy of Franklin Merrell-Wolff.* Albany, NY: State University of New York Press.

Lichfield, Gideon. 2015. "The Science of Near-Death Experiences: Empirically Investigating Brushes with the Afterlife." *The Atlantic* online (April). http://www.theatlantic.com/magazine/archive/2015/04/the-science-of-near-death-experiences/386231/.

Lieber, Kier A., and Darryl G. Press. 2013. "Why States Won't Give Nuclear Weapons to Terrorists." *International Security* 38, no. 1: 80–104. https://doi.org/10.1162/ISEC_a_00127.

Lindbergh, Charles A. 1953. *The Spirit of St. Louis.* New York: Charles Scribner's Sons.

Lingpa, Düdjom. 2016. "The Foolish Dharma of an Idiot Clothed in Mud and Feathers." In *Heart of the Great Perfection: Düdjom Lingpa's Visions of the Great Perfection,* by Düdjom Lingpa and P. Tashi. Translated by B. Alan Wallace. Vol. 1. 139–161. Somerville, MA: Wisdom Publications.

Lingpa, Düdjom, and Pema Tashi. 2016. *Heart of the Great Perfection: Düdjom Lingpa's Visions of the Great Perfection,* Translated by B. Alan Wallace. Vol. 1. Somerville, MA: Wisdom Publications.

Louchakova-Schwartz, Olga. 2016. "Qualia of God: Phenomenological Materiality in Introspection, with a Reference to Advaita Vedanta." *Open Theology* 3: 257–273. https://doi.org/10.1515/opth-2017-0021.

Lovelock, James. 2010. "Our Sustainable Retreat." In *Gaia in Turmoil: Climate Change, Biodepletion, and Earth Ethics in an Age of Crisis,* edited by Eileen Crist and H. Bruce Rinker, 21–24. Cambridge, MA: MIT Press.

Lovelock, James. 2014. *A Rough Ride to the Future.* London, England: Allen Lane.

Lynn, Steven Jay, and James Evans. 2017. "Hypnotic Suggestion Produces Mystical-Type Experiences in the Laboratory: A Demonstration Proof." *Psychology of Consciousness: Theory, Research, and Practice* 4, no. 1: 23–37.

Lyons, William E. 1986. *The Disappearance of Introspection.* Cambridge, MA: MIT Press.

Mack, John E. 1994. "Why the Abduction Phenomenon Cannot Be Explained Psychiatrically." In *Alien Discussions: Proceedings of the Abduction Study Conference Held at MIT, Cambridge, MA,* eds. Andrea Pritchard, David E. Pritchard, John E. Mack, Pam Kasey and Claudia Yapp, 372–374. Cambridge, MA: North Cambridge.

Mack, John E. 1999. *Passport to the Cosmos: Human Transformation and Alien Encounters.* New York: Three Rivers Press.

Malamud, Judith R. 1986. "Becoming Lucid in Dreams and Waking Life." In *Handbook of States of Consciousness,* edited by B.B. Wolman and M. Ullman, 590–612. New York: Van Nostrand Reinhold.

Marrs, Jim. 1997. *Alien Agenda: The Untold Story of the Extraterrestrials Among Us.* London, England: HarperCollinsPublishers.

Martin, Jeffery A. 2014. "Clusters of Individual Experiences Form a Continuum of Persistent Non-Symbolic Experiences in Adults." Accessed September 18, 2016. http://nonsymbolic.org/ PNSE-Article.pdf

Martin, Jeffery A. 2014. *The Finders*. Charleston, SC: Integration Press.

Martin, Jeffery A. 2017. "Clusters of Individual Experiences Form a Continuum of Persistent Non-Symbolic Experience in Adults." Paper presented at the *Society for Consciousness Studies Annual Conference*, Yale University, June 3–4, 2017.

Mavromatis, Andreas. 1987. *Hypnagogia: The Unique State of Consciousness Between Wakefulness and Sleep*. London, England: Routledge & Kegan Paul.

McCulloch, Warren S., and Walter H. Pitts. 1943. "A Logical Calculus of the Ideas Immanent in Nervous Activity." *Bulletin of Mathematical Biophysics* 5: 115–133.

McNeill, J.R., and Peter Engelke. 2014. *The Great Acceleration: An Environmental History of the Anthropocene Since 1945*. Cambridge, MA: The Belknap Press of Harvard University Press.

Menary, Richard, ed. 2010. *The Extended Mind*. Cambridge, MA: A Bradford Book.

Merrell-Wolff, Franklin. 1994. *Franklin Merrell-Wolff's Experience and Philosophy: A Personal Record of Transformation and a Discussion of Transcendental Consciousness*. Albany, NY: State University of New York Press.

Merrell-Wolff, Franklin. 1995. *Transformations in Consciousness: The Metaphysics and Epistemology*. Albany, NY: State University of New York Press.

Merrell-Wolff, Franklin. 2017. "Recognition—An Inversion in Consciousness." *Sangha: The Franklin Merrell-Wolff Newsletter* (Spring). First written April 22, 1937.

Mirkin, Gabe. 2014. "Richard Feynman, Physicist and Humorist." The website for *Dr. Mirkin*. (April). http://www.drmirkin.com/weekly-ezine-page/richard-feynman-physicist-and-humorist.html.

Mishlove, Jeffrey. 2000. *The PK Man: A True Story of Mind over Matter*. Charlottesville, VA: Hampton Roads Publishing Company.

Moga, Margaret M., and William F. Bengston. 2010. "Anomalous Magnetic Field Activity During a Bioenergy Healing Experiment." *Journal of Scientific Exploration* 24, no. 3: 397–410.

Moody Jr., Raymond. 2010. *Glimpses of Eternity: Sharing a Loved One's Passage from This Life to the Next*. With Paul Perry. New York: Guideposts.

Moor, James H. 2005. "Why We Need Better Ethics for Emerging Technologies." *Ethics and Information Technology* 7: 111–119. DOI: 10.1007/s10676-006-0008-0.

Moorjani, Anita. 2012. *Dying to Be Me: My Journey from Cancer, to Near Death, to True Healing*. Carlsbad, CA: Hay House.

Nahm, Michael, and Bruce Greyson. 2009. "Terminal Lucidity in Patients with Chronic Schizophrenia and Dementia: A Survey of the Literature." *The Journal of Nervous and Mental Disease* 197, no. 12: 942–944.

National Aeronautics and Space Administration. 2016. "Mars Observer (NSSDCA/COSPAR ID: 1992-063A)." (April 27). Retrieved on May 18, 2020 from http://nssdc.gsfc.nasa.gov/nmc/spacecraftDisplay. do?id=1992-063A.

Nicol, David. 2015. *Subtle Activism: The Inner Dimension of Social and Planetary Transformation*. Albany, NY: State University of New York Press.

Nida-Rümelin, Martine. 2017. "Self-Awareness." *Review of Philosophy and Psychology* 8: 55–82.

Norgaard, Kari Marie. 2011. *Living in Denial: Climate Change, Emotions, and Everyday Life*. Cambridge, MA: MIT Press.

O'Malley-James, Jack T., Charles S. Cockell, Jane S. Greaves, and John A. Raven. 2014. "Swansong Biospheres II: The Final Signs of Life on Terrestrial Planets Near the End of Their Habitable Lifetimes." *International Journal of Astrobiology* 13, no. 3: 229–243.

Orme-Johnson, David W., Charles N. Alexander, John L. Davies, Howard M. Chandler, and Wallace E. Larimore. 1988. "International Peace Project in the Middle East: The Effects of the Maharishi Technology of the Unified Field." *Journal of Conflict Resolution* 32, no. 4: 776–812.

Overbye, Dennis. 2005. "Quantum Trickery: Testing Einstein's Strangest Theory." *The New York Times* online (December 27). https://www.

nytimes.com/2005/12/27/science/quanutm-trickery-testing-einsteins-strangest-theory.html.

Owen, Iris M. 1976. *Conjuring Up Philip: An Adventure in Psychokinesis.* With Margaret Sparrow. Toronto: Fitzhenry & Whiteside.

Özerdem, Alpaslan, and Sukyana Podder, eds. 2011. *Child Soldiers: From Recruitment to Reintegration.* New York: Palgrave Macmillan.

Padfield, Suzanne. 1980. "Mind–Matter Interaction in the Psychokinetic Experience." In *Consciousness and the Physical World: Edited Proceedings of an Interdisciplinary Symposium on Consciousness Held at the University of Cambridge in January 1978,* edited by Brian D. Josephson and Vilayanur S. Ramachandran, 165–175. Oxford, England: Pergamon Press.

Panek, Richard. 2011. *The 4 Percent Universe: Dark Matter, Dark Energy, and the Race to Discover the Rest of Reality.* Boston, MA: Houghton Mifflin Harcourt.

Parnia, Sam, Ken Spearpoint, Gabriele de Vos, Peter Fenwick, Diana Goldberg, Jie Yang, Jiawen Zhu et al. 2014. "AWARE---AWAreness During REsuscitation---A Prospective Study." *Resuscitation* 85, no. 12: 1799–1805.

Paulson, Steve. 2012. "On Reconciling Atheism and Meaning in the Universe." *The Atlantic* online. (August 29.) https://www.theatlantic.com/health/archive/2012/08/on-reconciling-atheism-and-meaning-in-the-universe/261627/.

Pearson, Patricia. 2014. *Opening Heaven's Door: What the Dying May be Trying to Tell Us About Where They're Going.* Toronto: Random House Canada.

Peng, Tao, Hui Chen, Yanhua Shih, and Marlan O. Scully. 2014. "Delayed-Choice Quantum Eraser with Thermal Light." *Physical Review Letters* 112, no. 180401. https://doi.org/10.1103/PhysRevLett.112.180401.

Piccinini, Gualtiero. 2004. "Functionalism, Computationalism, and Mental States." *Studies in History and Philosophy of Science* 35: 811–833.

Pilkington, Rosemarie. 2015. "Interview with Felicia Parise, August 6, 2013." *Journal of Scientific Exploration* 29, no. 1: 75–108.

Popper Karl R., and John C. Eccles. 1981. *The Self and Its Brain*. Berlin, Germany: Springer International.

Prescott, Richard Chambers. 2014. *Vajrasattva: The Secret of the Four Wisdoms Trekcho, Togal and Bardo*. Bloomington, IN: AuthorHouse.

Pritchard, Andrea, David E. Pritchard, John E. Mack, Pam Kasey, and Claudia Yapp, eds. 1994. *Alien Discussions: Proceedings of the Abduction Study Conference Held at MIT, Cambridge, MA*. Cambridge, MA: North Cambridge Press.

Pronin, Emily, and Kathleen Schmidt. 2013. "Claims and Denials of Bias and Their Implications for Policy." In *The Behavioral Foundations of Public Policy*, edited by Eldar Shafir, 195–216. Princeton, NJ: Princeton University Press.

Pulos, Lee, and Gary Richman. 1990. *Miracles and Other Realities*. Vancouver, British Columbia: Omega Press.

Puthoff, H.E. 1996. "CIA-Initiated Remote Viewing Program at Stanford Research Institute." *Journal of Scientific Exploration* 10, no. 1: 63–76.

Pylkkö, Pauli. 1998. *The Aconceptual Mind: Heideggerian Themes in Holistic Naturalism*. Amsterdam, The Netherlands: John Benjamins.

Pylyshyn, Zenon W. 1984. *Computation and Cognition: Toward a Foundation for Cognitive Science*. Cambridge, MA: A Bradford Book.

Radin, Dean, Leena Michel, and Arnaud Delorme. 2016. "Psychophysical Modulation of Fringe Visibility in a Distant Double-Slit Optical System." *Physics Essays* 29, no. 1: 14–22.

Radin, Dean, Leena Michel, James Johnston, and Arnaud Delorme. 2013. "Psychophysical Interactions with a Double-Slit Interference Pattern." *Physics Essays* 26, no. 4: 553–566.

Radin, Dean, Leena Michel, Alan Pierce, and Arnaud Delorme. 2015. "Psychophysical Interactions with a Single-Photon Double-Slit Optical System." *Quantum Biosystems* 6, no. 1: 82–98.

Rayo Gomez, Maria Paula. 2016. *Surrendering to the Vine of the Soul: Ayahuasca Shamanism as a Logotherapy*. B.A. thesis, King's University College at Western University. Retrieved on August 9, 2016 from http://ir.lib.uwo.ca/cgi/viewcontent.cgi?article=1040&context=psychK_uht

Rescorla, Michael. 2015. "The Computational Theory of Mind." In *The Stanford Encyclopedia of Philosophy* edited by Edward N. Zalta, (Winter). http://plato.stanford.edu/archives/win2015/entries/computational-mind/.

Ring, Kenneth, and Sharon Cooper. 1997. "Near-Death and Out-of-Body Experiences in the Blind: A Study of Apparent Eyeless Vision." *Journal of Near-Death Studies* 16, no. 2: 101–147.

Rivas, Titus, Anny Dirven, and Rudolf H. Smit. 2016. *The Self Does Not Die: Verified Paranormal Phenomena from Near-Death Experiences*. Durham, NC: International Association for Near-Death Studies.

Rivas, Titus, and Rudolf H. Smit. 2013. "A Near-Death Experience with Veridical Perception Described by a Famous Heart Surgeon and Confirmed by His Assistant Surgeon." *Journal of Near-Death Studies* 31, no. 3: 179–186.

Roberts, Bernadette. 1991. *The Path to No-Self: Life at the Center*. Albany, NY: State University of New York Press.

Roberts, Bernadette. 1993. *The Experience of No-Self: A Contemplative Journey*. rev. ed. Albany, NY: State University of New York Press.

Robertson, David G. 2014. "Transformation: Whitley Strieber's Paranormal Gnosis." *Nova Religio: The Journal of Alternative and Emergent Religions* 18, no. 1: 58–78.

Robock, Alan, Luke Oman, and Georgiy L. Stenchikov, G.L. 2007. "Nuclear Winter Revisited with a Modern Climate Model and Current Nuclear Arsenals: Still Catastrophic Consequences." *Journal of Geophysical Research* 112, no. D13107. https://doi.org/10.1029/2006JD008235.

Rogo, D. Scott, and Raymond Bayless. 1979. *Phone Calls from the Dead*. Englewood Cliffs, NJ: Prentice-Hall.

Ross, Eleanor. 2016. "The Nine Countries that Have Nuclear Weapons." *The Independent* online. (January 6). http://www.independent.co.uk/news/world/politics/the-nine-countries-that-have-nuclear-weapons-a6798756.html.

Roth, Christopher F. 2005. "Ufology as Anthropology: Race, Extraterrestrials, and the Occult." In *E.T. Culture: Anthropology in Outer-*

spaces, edited by D. Battaglia, 38–93. Durham, NC: Duke University Press.

Sabom, Michael B. 1982. *Recollections of Death: A Medical Investigation*. New York: Harper & Row.

Safar, Peter. 1988. "Resuscitation from Clinical Death: Pathophysiologic Limits and Therapeutic Potentials." *Critical Care Medicine* 16, no. 10: 923–941.

Sanders, Brenda. 2008. "What is Really Real." In *Peak Vitality: Raising the Threshold of Abundance in Our Material, Spiritual and Emotional Lives*, edited by Jeanne M. House, 454–464. Santa Rosa, CA: Elite Books.

Sannella, Lee. 1976. *Kundalini – Psychosis or Transcendence?* San Francisco, CA: H.S. Dakin.

Sartori, Penny. 2008. *The Near-Death Experiences of Hospitalized Intensive Care Patients: A Five Year Clinical Study*. Lewiston, NY: Edwin Mellen Press.

Sartori, Penny. 2014. *The Wisdom of Near-Death Experiences: How Understanding NDEs Can Help Us Live More Fully*. London, England: Watkins.

Schnabel, Jim. 1997. *Remote Viewers: The Secret History of America's Psychic Spies*. New York: Dell Publishing.

Schneider, John, C. Wayne Smith, Chris Minning, Sara Whitcher, and Jerry Hermanson. 1990. "Guided Imagery and Immune System Function in Normal Subjects: A Summary of Research Findings." In *Mental Imagery*, edited by Robert G. Kunzendorf, 179–191. New York: Plenum.

Schneider, Susan. 2011. *The Language of Thought: A New Philosophical Direction*. Cambridge, MA: MIT Press.

Schwitzgebel, Eric. 2016. "Introspection." In *The Stanford Encyclopedia of Philosophy*, edited by Edward N. Zalta, (Winter). https://plato. stanford.edu/archives/win2016/entries/introspection/.

Scranton, Roy. 2015. *Learning to Die in the Anthropocene: Reflections on the End of a Civilization*. San Francisco, CA: City Lights Books.

Searle, John. R. 1983. *Intentionality: An Essay in the Philosophy of Mind*. Cambridge, England: Cambridge University Press.

Shankar, Vijay. 2015. "Subcontinental Nuclear Instability: The Spiralling Nightmare." *International Journal of Nuclear Security* 1, no. 1: 1–11. http://dx.doi.org/10.7290/V77H1GG1.

Sheldrake, Rupert. 2012. *Science Set Free: 10 Paths to New Discovery*. New York: Deepak Chopra Books.

Sherrington, Ashleigh, and Martin Smith. 2012. "International Perspectives in the Diagnosis of Brain Death in Adults." *Trends in Anaesthesia and Critical Care* 2, no. 1: 48–52.

Shrader-Frechette, Kristin. 2011. "Fukushima, Flawed Epistemology, and Black-Swan Events." *Ethics, Policy and Environment* 14, no. 3: 267–272.

Siewert, Charles. 2017. "Consciousness and Intentionality." In *The Stanford Encyclopedia of Philosophy*, edited by Edward N. Zalta, (Spring). https://plato.stanford.edu/archives/spr2017/entries/consciousness-intentionality/.

Skrbina, David. 2005. *Panpsychism in the West*. Cambridge, MA: MIT Press.

Skrbina, David. 2009. "Introduction." In *Mind that Abides: Panpsychism in the New Millennium*, edited by David Skrbina, xi–xiv. Amsterdam, The Netherlands: John Benjamins.

Smith, Huston. 2000. *Cleansing the Doors of Perception: The Religious Significance of Entheogenic Plants and Chemicals*. New York: Jeremy P. Tarcher/Putnam.

Smolensky, Paul. 1988. "On the Proper Treatment of Connectionism." *Behavioral and Brain Sciences* 11: 1–23.

Smolin, Lee. 2013. *Time Reborn: From the Crisis in Physics to the Future of the Universe*. Toronto: Alfred A. Knopf Canada.

Som, Claudia, Lorenz M. Hilty, and Thomas F. Ruddy. 2004. "The Precautionary Principle in the Information Society." *Human and Ecological Risk Assessment* 10: 787–799.

Spiritual Emergence Network. 2017. Accessed on August 11, 2017. http://spiritualemergence.org/.

Srednicki, Mark. 2007. *Quantum Field Theory*. Cambridge, England: Cambridge University Press.

Storm, Lance. 2013. "Foreword." In *The Survival Hypothesis: Essays on Mediumship*, by A.J. Rock, 1–4. Jefferson, NC: McFarland & Company.

Strauss, Valerie. 2012. "Texas GOP Rejects 'Critical Thinking' Skills. Really." *The Washington Post* online. (July 9). https://www. washingtonpost.com/blogs/answer-sheet/post/texas-gop-rejects-critical-thinking-skills-really/2012/07/08/gJQAHNpFXW_blog.html.

Sudbery, Anthony. 1986. *Quantum Mechanics and the Particles of Nature: An Outline for Mathematicians*. Cambridge, England: Cambridge University Press.

Targ, Russell. 2012. *The Reality of ESP: A Physicist's Proof of Psychic Abilities*. Wheaton, IL: Quest Books.

Tart, Charles. T. 2009. *The End of Materialism: How Evidence of the Paranormal is Bringing Science and Spirit Together*. Oakland, CA: New Harbinger Publications.

Taylor, Steve. 2017. *The Leap: The Psychology of Spiritual Awakening*. Novato, CA: New World Library.

Tegmark, Max. 2015. "Nuclear War from a Cosmic Perspective." *arXiv*: 1505.00246v2 [physics.soc-ph] 21 May. https://arxiv.org/pdf/1505.00246v2.pdf.

Thomas, L. Eugene, and Pamela E. Cooper. 1980. "Incidence and Psychological Correlates of Intense Spiritual Experiences." *The Journal of Transpersonal Psychology* 12, no. 1: 75–85.

Toon, Owen B., Alan Robock, Richard P. Turco, Charles Bardeen, Luke Oman, and Georgiy L. Stenchikov. 2007. "Consequences of Regional-Scale Nuclear Conflicts." *Science* 315: 1224–1225.

The Afterlife Investigations. 2011. Venice, CA: UFO TV. 2 DVD Discs, 200 min.

Vaillant, George E., Michael Bond, Caroline O. Vaillant. 1986. "An Empirically Validated Hierarchy of Defense Mechanisms." *Archives of General Psychiatry* 43, no. 8: 786–794.

Vallée, Jacques. 1991. *Revelations: Alien Contact and Human Deception*. New York: Ballantine.

Vallée, Jacques. 1993. *Passport to Magonia: On UFOs, Folklore, and Parallel Worlds*. Chicago, IL: Contemporary Books.

Volders, Brecht, and Tom Sauer. 2016. "Introduction." In *Nuclear Terrorism: Countering the Threat*, edited by Brecht Volders and Tom Sauer, 3–11. London, England: Routledge.

Waggoner, Robert. 2009. *Lucid Dreaming: Gateway to the Inner Self.* Needham, MA: Moment Point.

Walborn, S.P., M.O. Terra Cunha, S. Pádua, C.H. Monken. 2002. "Double-Slit Quantum Eraser." *Physical Review A* 65, no. 033818. https://doi.org/10.1103/PhysRevA.65.033818.

Walker, Evan Harris 2000. *The Physics of Consciousness: Quantum Minds and the Meaning of Life.* Cambridge, MA: Perseus.

Wallace, B. Alan. 2012. *Dreaming Yourself Awake: Lucid Dreaming and Tibetan Dream Yoga for Insight and Transformation.* Boston, MA: Shambhala.

Wallace, B. Alan. 2016. "Introduction to Dzogchen." Online course by *Wisdom Academy.* http://learn.wisdompubs.org/academy/lessons/dzogchen-intro-l9/.

Walsh, Roger. 1984. "Journey Beyond Belief." *Journal of Humanistic Psychology* 24, no. 2: 30–65.

Walsh, Roger N. 1984. *Staying Alive: The Psychology of Human Survival.* Boulder, CO: New Science Library.

Ward, Peter. 2009. *The Medea Hypothesis: Is Life On Earth Ultimately Self-Destructive?* Princeton, NJ: Princeton University Press.

Watson, Donald E., and Bernard O. Williams. 2003. "Eccles' Model of the Self Controlling Its Brain: The Irrelevance of Dualist-Interactionism." *NeuroQuantology* 1: 119–128.

Watts, Alan W. 1965. *The Joyous Cosmology: Adventures in the Chemistry of Consciousness.* New York: Vintage Books.

William, Anthony. 2015. *Medical Medium: Secrets Behind Chronic and Mystery Illness and How to Finally Heal.* Carlsbad, CA: Hay House.

Wood, Thomas W., Bruce D. Reid, Christopher M. Toomey, Kannan Krishnaswami, Kimberly A. Burns, Larry O. Casazza, Don S. Daly, and Leesa L. Duckworth. 2014. "The Future of Nuclear Archaeology: Reducing Legacy Risks of Weapons Fissile Material." *Science & Global Security* 22: 4–26.

Wren-Lewis, John. 1988. "The Darkness of God: A Personal Report on Consciousness Transformation Through an Encounter with Death." *Journal of Humanistic Psychology* 28, no. 2: 105–122.

Wren-Lewis, John. 1994. "Aftereffects of Near-Death Experiences: A Survival Mechanism Hypothesis." *Journal of Transpersonal Psychology* 26, no. 2: 107–115.

Yaden, David B., Khoa D. Le Nguyen, Margaret L. Kern, Nancy A. Wintering, Johannes C. Eichstaedt, H. Andrew Schwartz, Anneke E. K. Buffone, Laura K. Smith, Mark R. Waldman, Ralph W. Hood Jr., and Andrew B. Newberg. 2017. "The Noetic Quality: A Multimethod Exploratory Study." *Psychology of Consciousness: Theory, Research, and Practice* 4, no. 1: 54–62.

Young, Roger. 2001. *How Computers Work: Processor and Main Memory.* Accessed August 12, 2016, http://www.fastchip.net/howcomputerswork/bookbpdf.pdf

Index